US National Cybersecurity

This volume explores the contemporary challenges to US national cybersecurity.

Taking stock of the field, it features contributions by leading experts working at the intersection between academia and government and offers a unique overview of some of the latest debates about national cybersecurity. These contributions showcase the diversity of approaches and issues shaping contemporary understandings of cybersecurity in the West, such as deterrence and governance, cyber intelligence and big data, international cooperation, and public–private collaboration. The volume's main contribution lies in its effort to settle the field around three main themes exploring the international politics, concepts, and organization of contemporary cybersecurity from a US perspective. Related to these themes, this volume pinpoints three pressing challenges US decision makers and their allies currently face as they attempt to govern cyberspace: maintaining international order, solving conceptual puzzles to harness the modern information environment, and coordinating the efforts of diverse partners.

The volume will be of much interest to students of cybersecurity, defense studies, strategic studies, security studies, and IR in general.

Damien Van Puyvelde is Assistant Professor of Security Studies at The National Security Studies Institute, The University of Texas at El Paso.

Aaron F. Brantly is Assistant Professor in the Department of Social Sciences and the Army Cyber Institute, West Point, USA. He is author of *The Decision to Attack: Military and Intelligence Cyber Decision-Making* (2016).

Routledge Studies in Conflict, Security and Technology

Series Editors: Mark Lacy, Dan Prince
Lancaster University
Sean Lawson
University of Utah
and Brandon Valeriano
Cardiff University

The *Routledge Studies in Conflict, Technology and Security* series aims to publish challenging studies that map the terrain of technology and security from a range of disciplinary perspectives, offering critical perspectives on the issues that concern publics, business and policymakers in a time of rapid and disruptive technological change.

Nonlinear Science and Warfare
Chaos, complexity and the U.S. military in the information age
Sean T. Lawson

Terrorism Online
Politics, law, technology
Edited by Lee Jarvis, Stuart Macdonald and Thomas M. Chen

Cyber Warfare
A multidisciplinary analysis
Edited by James A. Green

The Politics of Humanitarian Technology
Good intentions, unintended consequences and insecurity
Katja Lindskov Jacobsen

International Conflict and Cyberspace Superiority
Theory and practice
William D. Bryant

Conflict in Cyber Space
Theoretical, strategic and legal perspectives
Edited by Karsten Friis and Jens Ringsmose

US National Cybersecurity
International Politics, Concepts and Organization
Edited by Damien Van Puyvelde and Aaron F. Brantly

US National Cybersecurity

International Politics, Concepts and
Organization

**Edited by Damien Van Puyvelde and
Aaron F. Brantly**

LONDON AND NEW YORK

First published 2017
by Routledge

2 Park Square, Milton Park, Abingdon, Oxfordshire OX14 4RN
52 Vanderbilt Avenue, New York, NY 10017

Routledge is an imprint of the Taylor & Francis Group, an informa business

First issued in paperback 2018

British Library Cataloguing in Publication Data
A catalogue record for this book is available from the British Library

Library of Congress Cataloging in Publication Data
Names: Van Puyvelde, Damien, editor. | Brantly, Aaron F., editor.
Title: US national cybersecurity : international politics, concepts and
organization / edited by Damien Van Puyvelde and Aaron F. Brantly.
Other titles: U.S. national cybersecurity | United States national
cybersecurity
Description: Abingdon, Oxon ; New York, NY : Routledge, 2017. |
Series: Routledge studies in conflict, security and technology | Includes
bibliographical references and index.
Identifiers: LCCN 2017010761| ISBN 9780415787994 (hardback) |
ISBN 9781315225623 (ebook)
Subjects: LCSH: Computer networks–Security measures–United States. |
Cyberspace–Security measures–United States. | Cyber intelligence
(Computer security)–United States. | Computer security–Government
policy–United States. | National security–United States.
Classification: LCC TK5105.59 .U68 2017 | DDC 363.325–dc23
LC record available at https://lccn.loc.gov/2017010761

ISBN: 978-0-415-78799-4 (hbk)
ISBN: 978-0-367-15067-9 (pbk)

Typeset in Times New Roman
by Wearset Ltd, Boldon, Tyne and Wear

Contents

Illustrations

Figures

Tables

Contributors

Scott Bethel (MSc Strategic Intelligence, Joint Military Intelligence College, Washington, DC; National Defense Fellow, Boston University) is a retired US Air Force Brigadier General. He is CEO of Integrity ISR LLC, and Senior Vice President for Intelligence and International Training, JMark Services, Inc.

Randy Borum is a Professor and Coordinator of Strategy and Intelligence Studies in the School of Information at the University of South Florida. He is author/co-author of approximately 160 professional publications, has worked with three Directors of National Intelligence (DNI) on the Intelligence Science Board, served on the Defense Science Board Task Force on Understanding Human Dynamics, and is an instructor with the Bureau of Justice Assistance State and Local Anti-Terrorism Training Programs for Investigations and Intelligence.

Aaron F. Brantly is Assistant Professor of Cyber and International Relations in the Departments of Social Sciences and Electrical Engineering & Computer Science, Cyber Fellow at the Army Cyber Institute and Cyber Fellow at the Combating Terrorism Center at the United States Military Academy. He has a Ph.D. from the University of Georgia and a Masters of Public Policy from The American University. He served as United States Peace Corps Volunteer in Ukraine. He worked for 10 years in democracy development, most recently as a Senior Program Officer for ICT Innovation at the National Democratic Institute for International Affairs and previously at the International Republican Institute for Advancing Democracy World-wide. His latest book, The Decision to Attack. Military and Intelligence Cyber Decision-Making, was published by University of Georgia Press.

Nerea M. Cal is an Army Aviation officer currently serving as an International Relations instructor at the United States Military Academy. She received her BSc in Comparative Politics from West Point and her MA in Global Affairs in 2016 from Yale University. She has presented and published research she conducted for the Georgetown Institute for Women, Peace and Security on the role of women in Kosovo's post-conflict reconstruction. Her research interests include state-building, international law, and the role of cyber operations in international relations.

Ryan F. Gagnon is a Signal Corps Officer serving in the New York Army National Guard. He is a graduate of Rensselaer Polytechnic Institute where he received his Bachelor of Science in Computer and Systems Engineering. Second Lieutenant Gagnon has contributed to the efforts of the Army Cyber Institute as a research volunteer and was a co-author for the article "Why Government Organizations Don't Care: Perverse Incentives and an Analysis of the OPM Hack" published in *Heinz Journal* at Carnegie Mellon University. His interests include cyber defense policy and military involvement within the cyber domain.

Erik Gartzke is a professor in the Department of Political Sciences at the University of California, San Diego, where he studies the impact of information on war, peace, and international institutions. Professor Gartzke's research has appeared in *American Journal of Political Science, International Organization, International Studies Quarterly*, the *Journal of Conflict Resolution, The Journal of Politics*, and elsewhere.

Steve "Scuba" Gary is Assistant Professor of Practice in the School of Information, College of Arts and Sciences, at the University of South Florida (USF). Before he joined USF, Scuba served as Chief of the Cyber Intelligence Support Element and Chief of the Information Operations Intelligence Integration branch at US Special Operations Command. He earned a BSc degree from Regents College, an MSc in Cyber Operations from the Air Force Institute of Technology, and is currently pursuing a PhD in Career and Workforce Education at USF. He currently holds a Security+ certification and is a Certified Information Systems Security Professional.

Katherine R. Hutton was formerly a Special Advisor at the United States Secret Service and is currently serving as a Research Scientist intern at the Army Cyber Institute at West Point. She graduated from Duke University with a BSc in Biology and minor in Chemistry and holds an MBA from the Duke University Fuqua School of Business Cross Continent Program. She is currently pursuing a Master of Professional Studies in Cybersecurity Strategy and Information Management at George Washington University.

Jan Kallberg is an assistant professor at United States Military Academy (West Point) and a Research Fellow at Army Cyber Institute at West Point. His works have been published in *Joint Forces Quarterly, Strategic Studies Quarterly, Military Review, IEEE Access, IEEE Professional, IEEE Technology & Society*, and *IEEE Security & Privacy*. His personal website is www.cyberdefense.com—a domain name registered in 1996.

Jon Lindsay is Assistant Professor of Digital Media and Global Affairs at the University of Toronto Munk School of Global Affairs. Formerly, Lindsay was an assistant research scientist with the University of California Institute on Global Conflict and Cooperation and assistant adjunct professor at the School of International Relations and Pacific Studies at UC San Diego. He studies the impact of technology on international security, focusing on military innovation, cybersecurity, and grand strategy. He is a co-editor and contributor to *China and Cybersecurity* (2015), and his work has appeared in journals such as *International Security, Security Studies*, and *Journal of Strategic Studies*.

Brian M. Mazanec is an Assistant Director for Defense Capabilities and Management with the US government and an adjunct professor in the School of Policy, Government, and International Affairs in the Department of Public and International Affairs at George Mason University. He has written on cyber and national security issues, is the author of the book *The Evolution of Cyber War: International Norms for Emerging Technology Weapons* and co-author of the book *Deterring Cyber Warfare: Bolstering Strategic Stability in Cyberspace*.

Tim Ridout is a Fellow at the German Marshall Fund, where he focuses on political and economic issues in Brazil, in addition to global security challenges such as cybersecurity. Ridout regularly contributes to the Huffington Post and has published pieces in the *Boston Herald, Christian Science Monitor, Hartford Courant*, and *Providence Journal*. He received his master's degree from the Fletcher School of Law and Diplomacy in 2011. A version of his Master's thesis on peace building in Somaliland was published in the *Journal of the Middle East and Africa*. Ridout sits on the advisory board of The Fletcher Forum of World Affairs.

Kristan Stoddart is a Reader at the Department of International Politics at Aberystwyth University. He is the author and co-author of four books and many articles. He currently works on a project examining cyber security life cycles funded by Airbus Group and the Welsh Government. He is the Deputy Director of the Centre for Intelligence and International Security Studies, a member of the Independent Digital Ethics in Policing Panel, a member of the Project on Nuclear Issues, a Fellow of the Higher Education Academy, and a Fellow of the Royal Historical Society.

Damien Van Puyvelde is Assistant Professor of Security Studies at the National Security Studies Institute—An Intelligence Community Center for Academic Excellence at the University of Texas at El Paso. His main research and teaching interests are in the fields of intelligence, strategic and security studies, with a focus on issues of democratic governance, interagency coordination, and new technologies.

John Whisenhunt (MSc IT-Cybersecurity, Univ. of Maryland) is a retired US Air Force Lieutenant Colonel and independent consultant.

Ernest Y. Wong is a Military Intelligence Officer in the US Army who is currently serving as the Chief of Staff at the Army Cyber Institute and an assistant professor with the Department of Systems Engineering at West Point. He graduated from the United States Military Academy with a BSc in Economics, and holds a MSc in Management Science and Engineering from Stanford University, a MA in Education from Stanford University, and a Master of Military Science from the Mubarak al-Abdullah Joint Command and Staff College in Kuwait. His research interests include disruptive innovations, cyber resiliency, and the application of systems engineering tools for resolving complex problems.

Acknowledgments

This book project was inspired by a colloquium on "Cyber threats to the United States and private sectors" organized by the National Security Studies Institute at the University of Texas at El Paso in March 2015. This colloquium was funded thanks to an Intelligence Community Center for Academic Excellence grant from the Defense Intelligence Agency. We would like to thank all those who participated and made this event a success.

At the National Security Studies Institute, thanks to Dr. Larry Valero for planting the seeds of this project and encouraging us to publish an edited volume on national cybersecurity. Thanks also to our former graduate students Sean Curtis, Justin Magee, and Gus Sias for their help. Last, but not least, thanks to Roberto Noriega, who spent countless hours helping us edit parts of this volume.

Tim Ridout, who authors a chapter on cyberspace governance in this volume, was always generous with his time and did not hesitate to comment on some of the chapters we shared with him. All the other authors were very patient and stood by us on the long road toward publication. We are grateful for their help and understanding.

At Routledge, we wish to thank Andrew Humphrys for believing in this project, and Hannah Ferguson for her help and patience. Thanks also to Mark Lacy, Dan Prince, Sean Lawson, and Brandon Valeriano, the editors of the book series *Routledge Studies in Conflict, Security and Technology*.

Abbreviations

A2/AD	Anti-Access, Area-Denial
ABM	Anti-Ballistic Missile
ACI	Army Cyber Institute
APT	Advanced Persistent Threat
ASAT	Anti-Satellite Weapons
ASD-GSA	Assistant Secretary of Defense for Global Strategic Affairs
BMEWS	Ballistic Missile Early Warning System
C2	Command and Control
CCDCoE	NATO Cooperative Cyber Defence Centre of Excellence
CDD	Cross-Domain Deterrence
CDDI	Cross-Domain Deterrence Initiative
CERT	Computer Emergency Response Team
CESG	Communications-Electronics Security Group
CGC	Cyber Grand Challenge
CIA	Central Intelligence Agency
CIO	Chief Information Officer
CISA	Cybersecurity Information Sharing Act
CISSP	Certified Information Systems Security Professional
CM	Collection Management
CNA	Computer Network Attack
CND	Computer Network Defense
CNE	Computer Network Exploitation
COIN	Counterinsurgency
COPUOS	UN Committee on the Peaceful Uses of Outer Space
CSEC	Communications Security Establishment Canada
CSOC	Cyber Security Operations Centre
CTA	Cyber Threat Actor
CTIIC	Cyber Threat Intelligence Integration Center
CYBERCOM	United States Cyber Command
CYBERINT	Cyber Intelligence
DDoS	Distributed Denial of Service
DHS	Department of Homeland Security
DIA	Defense Intelligence Agency

DIKW	Data, Information, Knowledge, and Wisdom
DNI	Director of National Intelligence
DNC	Democratic National Committee
DoD	Department of Defense
DoS	Denial of Service
EO	Executive Order
EPI	Epidemiological
EU	European Union
FBI	Federal Bureau of Investigation
FOSS	Free and Open Source Software
G-7	Group of Seven
G-20	Group of Twenty
GCHQ	Government Communications Headquarters
GCIG	Global Commission on Internet Governance
GEOINT	Geospatial Intelligence
GGE	Group of Governmental Experts on the Developments in the Field of Information and Telecommunications in the Context of International Security
HSDL	Hardware Security Development Lifecycle
HUMINT	Human Intelligence
IC	Intelligence Community
ICANN	Internet Corporation for Assigned Names and Numbers
ICBM	Intercontinental Ballistic Missile
ICOC	International Code of Conduct against Ballistic Missile Proliferation
ICT	Information and Communications Technologies
IDS	Intrusion Detection System
IMINT	Imagery Intelligence
IoT	Internet of Things
IP	Internet Protocol
ISAC	Information Sharing and Analysis Center
ISAO	Information Sharing and Analysis Organizations
ISC	Intelligence and Security Committee
IT	Information Technology
ITU	International Telecommunications Union
MASINT	Measurement and Signature Intelligence
MIRV	Multiple Independent Targetable Re-entry Vehicle
MNF-I	Multi-National Force – Iraq
MTCR	Missile Technology Control Regime
NASA	National Aeronautics and Space Administration
NATO	North Atlantic Treaty Organization
NCCIC	National Cybersecurity and Communications Integration Center
NCSC	National Cyber Security Centre
NGA	National Geospatial Intelligence Agency
NIST	National Institute of Standards and Technology

NORAD	North American Aerospace Defense Command
NSA	National Security Agency
OCO	Offensive Cyber Operations
OCSIA	Office of Cyber Security and Information Assurance
OIF	Operation Iraqi Freedom
OODA	Observe, Orient, Decide, Act
OPM	Office of Personnel Management
OSINT	Open Source Intelligence
OST	Outer Space Treaty
PAROS	Prevention of an Arms Race in Outer Space
PERSEREC	Defense Personnel and Security Research Center
PPD	Presidential Policy Directive
PRISM	Planning Tool for Resource Integration, Synchronization, and Management
RAT	Remote Access Tool
SDSR	Strategic Defence and Security Review
SEIR	Susceptible, Exposed, Infectious, and Recovered
SIGINT	Signals Intelligence
SIS	Secret Intelligence Service
SLBM	Submarine-Launched Ballistic Missile
SOC	Security Operations Center
SOCMINT	Social Media Intelligence
SSDLC	Secure Software Development Life Cycle Process
STRATCOM	United States Strategic Command
TSA	Transportation Security Administration
TTP	Tactics, Techniques, and Procedures
UK	United Kingdom
UN	United Nations
US	United States
US-CERT	United States Computer Emergency Response Team
USB	Universal Serial Bus
WAPS	Wide Area Persistent Surveillance
WHO	World Health Organization

1 Introduction

Damien Van Puyvelde and Aaron F. Brantly

In recent decades, cyber threats have posed a growing challenge to national and international security and, as such, they have been the subject of much policy and academic attention. The Center for Strategic and International Studies, a think tank based in Washington, DC, lists over 220 significant cyber incidents since 2006.[1] These incidents have spread across the continents of Africa, North and South America, Asia, Europe, and Oceania. They have targeted all sorts of victims across the public–private divide and had impacts on all the elements of power: diplomacy, information, military, and the economy.

Among the hundreds of cyber threats that have made the headlines of Western newspapers in the last decade, three stand out in particular. In July 2016, thousands of emails taken from the Democratic National Committee during a cyberattack were leaked online in what the intelligence community's consensus believes to be a Russian effort to meddle in the US presidential elections. This hacking illustrates how cyberattacks can achieve political effects and threaten the core of the US democracy.[2] As we put the final touches to this edited volume, the administration of Barack Obama decided to implement a series of economic and diplomatic sanctions to punish Russia for its interference in the US presidential elections of 2016, thus showing how cyber threats can yield responses in other domains.

Cyberattacks also pose significant threats to critical infrastructure.[3] On December 23, 2015, a coordinated cyberattack on Ukrainian power companies led to power outages impacting some 225,000 customers.[4] The primary suspect behind this attack is Russia, which continues to challenge Ukrainian sovereignty following the annexation of Crimea and invasion of Eastern portions of Ukraine. However, Russia is not the only potent power in cyberspace. In 2010, the media reported that a malicious software, or malware, had infected the computer systems used to control and monitor the centrifuges used by the Iranian government to enrich uranium. This malware, named Stuxnet, incapacitated hundreds of centrifuges and significantly delayed the Iranian nuclear program. Experts believe that Stuxnet was the product of a joint operation between the United States and Israel. Stuxnet is widely considered the first successful use of a cyber weapon to sabotage an adversary's capabilities. The malware demonstrated how such weapons can be used with real effect to weaken an adversary.[5] These events demonstrate that cyberspace has become an important playing field in contemporary international relations. Today's cyber powers, the United States, Russia, and China, but also Israel, the United Kingdom, Iran, and France, as well as a plethora of non-state actors, have invested significant resources to develop and acquire the capabilities necessary to fulfill their objectives in the digital domain.

The study of security in cyberspace remains a disparate field characterized by the multiplicity of approaches taken to its study as well as strong policy relevance. The field has expanded well beyond computer science and engineering to include humanities and the social sciences.[6] Historians, for instance, have sought to trace the roots of cybersecurity as a policy issue, and political scientists and international relations scholars have started testing well-established concepts and models of state behavior in cyberspace.[7] A large portion of these social scientific debates have focused on the core concerns of strategic studies: war, strategy, and intelligence. This edited volume follows a similar approach and explores some, but certainly not all, of the questions that have captured the attention of policymakers, strategists, and practitioners.

National cybersecurity in the United States

The chapters of this book are articulated around the concept of "national cybersecurity," a term chosen to emphasize the continuing relevance of state actors in cyberspace. To be sure, non-state actors, including hacktivists and hackers, companies, and transnational criminal organizations, play an important role in cyberspace. Hackers, disgruntled insiders, criminal organizations, and terrorists are significant sources of cyber insecurity. Among the multiple actors that populate cyberspace, state actors are particularly worthy of attention because they have unparalleled access to resources and expertise, granting them significant power in cyberspace. This power, and the legitimacy and authority modern states benefit from, put them in an ideal position to shape current and future standards of conduct in cyberspace.

This volume is primarily concerned with national security in cyberspace. National security is concerned with the protection of the state and its citizens and the values they cherish, all of which can be considered as referent objects. National security is objective when providing for the physical safety of societal institutions and citizens, and subjective when protecting national values.[8] In a democracy like the United States, these values are enshrined in the constitution and include civil liberties, the rule of law, and government transparency, and are apparent in the evolving American way of life. To maintain national security, governments can wield multiple instruments of power to include diplomacy, intelligence, the military, and the economy. When doing so, governments often seek to collaborate with actors in the private sector and with international partners.

National security takes specific forms in the social-technical-economic environment that is cyberspace. Cyberspace consists of many different and often overlapping networks, as well as the nodes (any device or logical location with an Internet Protocol address or other analogous identifier) on those networks, and the system data (such as routing tables) that support them. Cyberspace is best understood as three overlapping layers: physical networks, logical or digital networks, and cyber-personas (the human dimension).[9] Cyber threats, like viruses and worms, seek to disrupt or destroy entities operating one or more of these layers.

Focusing on the national level can seem at odds with the reality of cyberspace, a realm that is often considered to be boundless. Whilst we acknowledge the boundless character of the logical network of cyberspace, cyber actors and networks remain physically grounded and, as such, they are tied to the pre-existing system of nation states that continues to characterize the international order. Non-state actors and international organizations play an important part in this system, and various contributions to this volume consider their role, however, the main focus of this volume is the nation state and specifically the US government's ability to exert power, or influence, in cyberspace.

We decided to focus on the United States for three reasons. First, the United States is the greatest power in the international order, and a leading cyber power. As a result, US approaches and decisions are worthy of interest because they influence the rest of the world. Second, many of the architectures and systems used to develop the networks at the core of cyberspace originated in the United States.[10] The United States has more experience developing and discussing cyber tools than any other nation on earth. Third, though many cybersecurity tactics, techniques, and procedures (TTP) remain classified, the United States has been more open than most other countries. Consequently, much information is available on US cyber policies, strategies, operations, and tactics. Relying on the US case is convenient, but it also limits the scope of this volume and the understanding we can offer to our readers. US approaches and debates on cybersecurity differ greatly from Chinese, Israeli, or Russian approaches, for instance.[11]

International politics, concepts, and organization

The contributions to this volume showcase the diversity of approaches and issues shaping contemporary understandings of national cybersecurity in the United States. Discussions in the field have focused on war, strategy, deterrence, espionage, terrorism, propaganda and influence operations, crime, critical infrastructure protection, Internet governance, international law, etc. One of the main challenges confronting students of cybersecurity is to make sense of an increasingly diverse set of debates and approaches. To address this problem, we organized the volume around three main themes exploring the international politics, concepts, and organization of US national cybersecurity. Related to these themes are what we perceive to be three pressing challenges US decision makers and US allies face as they attempt to govern cyberspace: maintaining international order; solving conceptual puzzles to effectively harness the resources available in the information environment; and coordinating the efforts of diverse partners.

Part I examines the international politics of cybersecurity and emphasizes efforts to bring order to the anarchic cyber realm. In Chapter 2, Jon Lindsay and Erik Gartzke explore the historical and conceptual overlap between cross-domain deterrence (CDD) and cybersecurity. They explain how the projection of national power across different domains, through CDD, both constrains and enables threats in cyberspace. The analysis exposes the complexity and uncertainty of deterrence, and by extension of international relations, in the cyber age.

The following chapters are concerned with the emergence of international norms to govern cyberspace. Neither current international law nor US defense policy has resolved the question of what classifies an armed attack in cyberspace nor how to adjudicate attacks perpetrated by non-state actors. In Chapter 3, Nerea Cal examines what constitutes an "armed attack" in cyberspace, and how—once it has attributed responsibility—the United States should respond to this type of warfare. Written with the presumption that the United States should lead efforts to shape international law in this field, Cal's chapter briefly outlines the set of international laws governing war, the challenges in applying them to cyberwarfare, and provides recommendations for how to apply the law of armed conflict in cyberspace. Cal advocates for an effects-based definition of an armed attack that will provide a legal avenue for the United States to respond to cyber-attacks perpetrated by non-state actors.

In Chapter 4, Brian Mazanec assesses the outlook for constraining international norms for offensive cyber operations, or cyberwarfare. Mazanec's analysis relies on the concept of emerging-technology weapons and norm evolution theory. He uses these conceptual building blocks to review the current state of international norms for cyberwarfare, with a focus on China, Russia, and the United States. The chapter concludes that constraining norms are unlikely to develop into a regime that could successfully manage and contain the threat.

In the following chapter, Tim Ridout examines the broader debate on the governance of cyberspace based on the premises that new capabilities in cyberspace require legal and normative frameworks to restrain abuses and reckless behavior. His chapter draws lessons for cyberspace from efforts to conceptualize and develop global security frameworks for the outer space domain. Ridout finds that work to develop a governance framework for cyberspace is less robust than it was for outer space, and this slows preference formation and fragments dialogue. He outlines the contours of a possible framework, but notes that more time and resources will be necessary for the international community to develop and agree on such a framework.

Part II explores some of the concepts behind national cybersecurity. When doing so, the chapters of this section help explain how governments can exert power in cyberspace. The first two chapters in this section adopt a general approach. In Chapter 6, Jan Kallberg explores how the specificity of cyberspace challenges traditional military thinking. First, the lack of object permanence in cyberspace undermines the concept of maneuver. Second, the difficulty of measuring effectiveness in offensive cyber operations complicates the application of strategies. Third, conflicts that are executed at computational speed remove the time window for meaningful strategic leadership. Fourth, anonymity makes the parties to cyber conflict unknown. In these conditions, Kallberg argues that the application of traditional military thinking in cyberwarfare could lead to incorrect conclusions regarding strategic achievements and abilities in the pre-conflict stage. In turn, using inappropriate models increases the risk of strategic failure in conflict.

In Chapter 7, Aaron Brantly develops an alternative conceptual approach to national cybersecurity, based on epidemiology. Medicine provides cyber researchers with a rich history of data collection, analysis, and application. Brantly examines the history of progress in public health with a focus on the spread of pathogens and draws out parallels useful for network administrators and policymakers to combat the increasingly dynamic problem set they confront in cyberspace. By engaging in cross-disciplinary analysis, cybersecurity researchers can learn new analytic techniques and build new sets of "best practices" to solve the complex problems nation states confront in cyberspace. Brantly advocates the development of a national cyber health system based on the automated analysis of large amounts of cybersecurity data and information.

The need to define new ways of operating in cyberspace is at the core of Chapter 8. Ernest Wong, Katherine Hutton, and Ryan Gagnon explore the concept of innovation and its application in cyber operations. They distinguish between four types of innovation: disruptive, breakthrough, sustaining, and incremental. Despite all the innovation that has taken place in the domain of cyber defense, new types of innovation will be necessary to effectively counter cyber offenses. Innovations, the authors argue, should focus on disruptive cyber defense, and be deployed as a part of a broader cyber strategy. In this context, the recent counterinsurgency campaigns in Afghanistan and Iraq offer useful lessons to set up a strategy to fight the asymmetric threats posed by malicious cyber actors.

Chapters 9 and 10 focus on the currencies of cyberspace: data, information, and intelligence. Gary and Borum examine the evolving meanings attached to the term "cyber intelligence." The distinction between data, information, and intelligence is at the core of their chapter. They argue that the development of cyber intelligence as a discipline of practice has followed three key phases: the data age, the information age, and the age of actionable intelligence. Each of these phases is characterized by different cybersecurity postures, and a specific approach to the intelligence cycle and related practices. The main challenge defining the current cyber era, the age of cyber intelligence, is the need to achieve integration.

The following chapter, by Aaron Brantly, focuses on another buzzword in the contemporary public debate on national security: "big data." Big data are growing in importance as more and more sensors and systems join cyberspace. As cyberspace becomes ubiquitous, it is incumbent on intelligence agencies to leverage and incorporate data to provide strategic and tactical insights for decision makers. Brantly identifies six types of large-scale data collection, generating multiple big data problems that filter into the intelligence community (IC). In the age of big data, improvements should focus on the development of more efficient and rigorous analytical products in support of national security. Understanding the IC as a big data computational system can help improve system design and function to better serve senior officials. Understanding concepts like cyber intelligence and big data can help define new policies, procedures, and processes to organize national cybersecurity.

Part III explores the organization of national cybersecurity efforts. Whilst the perspective is centered on the US government, the three chapters in this third section of the volume pay significant attention to US allies and partners in the private sector. As we noted above, whilst government have a key role to play in maintaining national cybersecurity, the multiplicity of actors involved in cyberspace creates a need for collaboration that transcends state boundaries. In Chapter 11, Kristan Stoddart compares US and UK efforts to provide for national cybersecurity. Stoddart first considers the common threats these two countries face in the field of cybersecurity. He then explains how the US and UK governments organized their respective efforts to combat cyber threats, and considers how these efforts have been received by civil society. Stoddart demonstrates the limitations of current efforts and argues that cyber deterrence needs to be built on agreed red lines between nation states. Upholding the rule of law within and between states in areas of cybercrime and cyber espionage is essential to determine these red lines. To be successful, this process should involve government agencies as well as civil society and private industry.

The next chapter, authored by Damien Van Puyvelde, focuses on the need for coordination between the public and private sectors. Van Puyvelde assesses the extent to which intelligence contractors pose a risk to government information security. He first examines historical espionage cases to show that intelligence contractors have been a relatively frequent target of hostile infiltration, although certainly not a more frequent target than government employees. The advent of cyberspace has not fundamentally changed the field of information security, as vulnerabilities continue to originate at the human and technical levels and across the public–private divide. On the whole, threats to information security in the cyber era require the US government and the private sector to collaborate more effectively. Effective collaboration requires adequate processes to coordinate cyber defense, but also adequate incentives for public and private cyber actors to work together.

In Chapter 13, Scott Bethel and John Whisenhunt explore the requirements for developing and enhancing military cooperation in cyberspace. They present some of the main obstacles faced on this pathway and recommend specific approaches for building expertise and teamwork in cyber operations. To successfully develop combined cyber consortiums, the United States must become a successful partner as well as leader, through sharing of information, best practices, and side-by-side experience with its allies. The chapters in this third part of the volume underline the fact that the US government cannot achieve national cybersecurity on its own. Public officials need to find effective ways of reaching out to partners whose behavior is driven by different cultures and incentives.

Notes

1 Center for Strategic and International Studies, "Significant Cyber Incidents since 2006," at https://csis-prod.s3.amazonaws.com/s3fs-public/160824_Significant_ Cyber_Events_List.pdf.
2 Aaron F. Brantly, "The Decision to Attack the DNC and its Implications," August 9, 2016, at https://ugapress.wordpress.com/2016/08/09/the-decision-to-attack-the-dnc-and-its-implications/; Thomas Rid, "How Russia Pulled Off the Biggest Election Hack in US History," *Esquire*, October 20, 2016, at www.esquire.com/news-politics/ a49791/russian-dnc-emails-hacked/.
3 See, for example: Kristan Stoddart, "UK cyber security and critical national infrastructure protection," *International Affairs* 92/5 (2016): 1079–1105.
4 ICS-CERT, "CyberAttack Against Ukrainian Critical Infrastructure," February 25, 2016, at https://ics-cert.us-cert.gov/alerts/IR-ALERT-H-16-056-01.
5 James P. Farwell and Rafal Rohozinski, "Stuxnet and the Future of Cyber War," *Survival* 53/1 (2011): 23–40; Kim Zetter, "An Unprecedented Look at Stuxnet, the World's First Digital Weapon," *Wired*, March 11, 2014, at www.wired.com/2014/11/ countdown-to-zero-day-stuxnet/.
6 See, for example: Franklin D. Kramer, Stuart H. Starr, and Larry K. Wentz, *Cyberpower and National* Security (Washington, DC: National Defense University Press, 2010); Derek Reveron, *Cyberspace and National Security. Threats, Opportunities, and Power in a Virtual World* (Washington, DC: Georgetown University Press, 2012); Jan-Frederik Kremer and Benedikt Müller (eds) *Cyberspace in International Relations. Theory, Prospects and Challenges* (New York: Springer, 2014); Brandon Valeriano and Ryan C. Maness, *Cyber War versus Cyber Realities* (New York: Oxford University Press, 2015); Aaron F. Brantly, *The Decision to Attack* (Athens, GA: Georgia University Press, 2016).
7 Michael Warner, "Cybersecurity: A pre-history," *Intelligence and National Security* 27/5 (2012): 781–799; Jon R. Lindsay, "Stuxnet and the limits of cyber warfare," *Security Studies* 22/3 (2013): 365–404.
8 Paul D. Williams (ed.), *Security Studies. An Introduction* (London: Routledge: 2013), 6; Arnold Wolfers, "'National security' as an ambiguous symbol," *Political Science Quarterly* 67/4 (1952): 481–502.
9 For a similar definition, see: Martin C. Libicki, *Conquest in Cyberspace: National Security and Information Warfare* (Cambridge: Cambridge University Press, 2007), 8–9.
10 Barry M. Leiner et al., "A brief history of the Internet," *ACM SIGCOMM Computer Communication Review* 39/5 (2009): 22–31.
11 See: W. Alexander Vacca, "Military culture and cyber security," *Survival* 53/6 (2011): 160–161; Giles Keir, "'Information Troops'—A Russian Cyber Command?" 3rd International Conference on Cyber Conflict (ICCC), 2011, 1–16; Lior Tabansky, "Cyberdefense Policy of Israel: Evolving Threats and Responses," January 2013, at www.chaire-cyber.fr/IMG/pdf/article_3_12_-_chaire_cyberdefense.pdf; Jon R. Lindsay, Tai Ming Cheung, and Derek Reveron, *China and Cyber Security. Espionage, Strategy, and Politics in the Digital Domain* (Oxford: Oxford University Press, 2015).

Part I
The international politics of cybersecurity

2 Cybersecurity and cross-domain deterrence

The consequences of complexity

*Jon Lindsay and Erik Gartzke**

Increasing societal dependence on computing infrastructure, together with confusion about how to respond to serious cyberattacks, have prompted policymakers to look beyond cyberspace for tools to disarm or deter attackers. The May 2011 White House *International Strategy for Cyberspace* thus declared, "We reserve the right to use all necessary means—diplomatic, informational, military, and economic—as appropriate and consistent with applicable international law, in order to defend our Nation, our allies, our partners, and our interests." At the same time, cyberspace has expanded the palette of options that actors can use to work around the deterrence policies of their adversaries. The United States used Stuxnet to attempt to disrupt Iran's nuclear program without starting a war, and Russia sought to influence the course of the 2016 US presidential election without provoking an explicit confrontation. Computing networks, moreover, are increasingly essential for the command and control of military capabilities used for deterrence or defense on land, at sea, in the air, or in outer space; the security of the cyber domain thus affects all other domains.

Yet, deterrence is only one aspect of cybersecurity. Indeed, many experts are skeptical of cyber deterrence and thus favor reliance on denial and resilience for network defense.[1] Similarly, not every use of deterrence relies on different means. Modern deterrence theory itself was built around the within-domain challenge of using nuclear weapons to prevent nuclear war.[2] Cross-domain deterrence (CDD) goes beyond this initial framework to use threats of one type to discourage behavior of another type, for example promising economic sanctions or a military strike in response to a cyberattack. Offensive and defensive cyber operations may play out completely within cyberspace, whilst CDD can deal with threats and responses beyond the cyber domain, exhibiting little operational interaction with the virtual world. Whereas cybersecurity is a relatively recent problem resulting from decades of economic and technological innovation, CDD has been practiced for millennia wherever actors have leveraged a diverse set of available strategic options, for instance relying on command of the sea to deter land invasion. Thus, CDD occupies a niche in the broader cybersecurity policy debate, and cyberspace is one domain among many in a broader deterrence calculus.

Nevertheless, cybersecurity and CDD are closely entwined as defense policy issues. Cyberspace, a human-built information and control infrastructure, is not valuable just for its own sake but rather because it enables firms and governments to expand their control over commercial and political activities. The cyber domain is inherently cross-domain. Some aspects of cyberspace relative to traditional military operating environments, such as low barriers to entry, the secrecy of capabilities, and the attribution problem, appear to pose serious challenges for deterrence policy. Although the practice of CDD is nothing new, and may be as old as deterrence itself, cybersecurity catalyzed the concept of CDD as an explicit concern in the US national security community. The vulnerability of industrial control systems and military command and control networks and their dependence on technology largely invented, owned, and operated by the private sector posed serious challenges to traditional notions of deterrence that assumed attacks would be easily attributed to nation states.

More fundamentally, CDD and cybersecurity are closely entwined theoretically. Both are symptomatic of increasing sociotechnical complexity in the modern world and the information problems created by greater diversity of actors, capabilities, and linkages between them. Cyberspace is literally built out of information technology, and cyberattacks rely on stealth and deception. Cybersecurity thus becomes a race between attackers exploiting pervasive information asymmetries and defenders patching the informational inefficiencies in cyberspace.[3] Deterrence is also an information problem as defenders seek to generate credible signals of resolve and intent for challengers. The evolution of CDD is, likewise, a race between an expanding portfolio of means available to inflict harm on others, which tends to increase dangerous uncertainty, and the adaptation of policy to restore some clarity and credibility in coercive communication. Cybersecurity and CDD, conceptually separable though they may be, both directly confront with the information problems inherent in conflict, and in practice they both generate additional information problems that exacerbate conflict.

Modern computing systems, too complex to understand in formal detail, are rife with uncertainty. Policymakers also confront great uncertainty in trying to deter ambiguous threats posed by new technologies and actors. The rationalist bargaining theory of war, a workhorse in the field of security studies, highlights uncertainty and commitment problems as major causes of conflict.[4] Uncertainty emerges from objective complexity in the world, imperfections in subjective assessments, and deliberate secrecy and misrepresentation. The bargaining model of war can help to understand how the uncertainty inherent in cybersecurity and CDD affects conflict, but the implications are neither straightforward nor determined by technology alone. Explicit focus on the bargaining implications of increasing complexity, moreover, holds promise for both the development of deterrence theory and an improved understanding of cybersecurity.

The coevolution of cybersecurity and CDD

Deterrence is an ancient phenomenon. Many animals produce dramatic threat displays to warn away competitors, and some prey animals mimic the patterning of poisonous species to fool predators. Threats to invade and conquer are commonplace in human history, but so is war itself because threats are often miscommunicated or doubted. The nuclear revolution brought deterrence to the forefront of strategy because, as Bernard Brodie stressed, the horrendous cost of nuclear war for the first time exceeded any conceivable benefit of victory.[5] As defense against large numbers of ballistic missiles from hidden or inaccessible launch points appeared futile or prohibitively expensive, deterrence appeared to be the only option for preventing Armageddon. The strategy of deterrence had always been available, but now it had to be explicitly conceptualized to guide defense policy. The point is worth stressing: innovation in a particular technological means forced a conceptual reconsideration of the strategic difference between deterrence and defense, or in Thomas Schelling's terms, between contests of resolve and contests of strength.[6] Both strategies have always existed and have usually intermingled, but nuclear weapons led strategists to bring to the forefront the logic of deterrence in an effort to ensure that they were never used.[7]

Cross-domain deterrence follows a similar evolution. Policymakers and commanders have always employed a diversity of means to pursue their ends and to work around the strategies of their opponents, but they didn't need a special term to describe what they were doing. Sparta tried to deter Athens with its formidable army whilst Athens tried to deter Sparta with its unequaled navy; deterrence failed to prevent a war but, ironically, succeeded in prolonging it.[8] The British Royal Navy has long posed a powerful deterrent to invasion by superior continental armies. In 1940, Germany responded with an air campaign intended to defeat the Royal Air Force in order to expose the Royal Navy, but superior defense in the Battle of Britain convinced Germany to abandon its invasion plans.[9] Germany later turned to the undersea domain to design around the Royal Navy and enjoyed some success until the Allies managed to cobble together a viable system of intelligence collection and anti-submarine warfare. Each side played a form of "rock, paper, scissors" to coerce in one domain or work around coercion in another. Likewise, during the Cold War, the North Atlantic Treaty Organization and the Soviet Union fielded sophisticated nuclear and conventional capabilities on land, in the skies, on and under the sea, and in orbit around the Earth, as well as irregular proxy forces. The complicated set of options in the Cold War strategic portfolio enabled states to think the unthinkable, to continue to compete over practical geopolitical objectives in the shadow of nuclear conflagration. Historically, states have also used nonmilitary means, such as economic sanctions and immigration policy, to attempt to shape the target's behavior in the security realm. Where even conventional military conflict was deemed prohibitively costly or risky—and thus mutual deterrence existed—adversaries shifted their threats or actions to domains where aggression could more safely be contemplated. There seems to be no upper bound on the evolving heterogeneity of coercive tools and methods.

Whereas innovation in a single technology—nuclear weapons—raised the problem of deterrence to the fore, innovation across a range of technologies makes CDD an explicitly pressing problem. There has always been diversity in the methods for inflicting harm, but the entire portfolio has never been so exten-sive and, thus, complex. The proliferation of dual-use threat technologies (e.g., large-scale data networks, automated robotics, additive manufacturing, synthetic biology, and the list goes on), their interaction in the global economy, and their use across bureaucratic jurisdictions pose a series of challenges for deterrence. Who is the target if attribution is uncertain? What is the cost of punishment if a capability is untested? What is a credible signal if the means of punishment must be kept secret? Yet, one technology looms above others for contemporary CDD, precisely because it increasingly connects and controls all other technologies. Information technology is vital for nearly all engineering and administrative functions in the twenty-first century globalized environment and thus offers a vector for potential influence over any other type of capability or activity. The ambiguity and accessibility of cyber weapons thus appears, some would argue, to undermine deterrence as surely as nuclear weapons undermined defense.

Throughout the 2000s, the US government became increasingly worried about the threats (and opportunities) of ubiquitous cyberspace. The Internet cata-lyzed economic growth but also connected systems that had never been designed with network security in mind. Russia's service denial attacks in Estonia in 2007 and Georgia in 2008 demonstrated that governments or "patriotic hackers" might use the Internet to inflict costs on the civilian economy or support a military invasion.[10] The Stuxnet attack on Iranian nuclear enrichment infrastructure, inad-vertently revealed in late 2010, demonstrated that cyber-physical disruption was not just science fiction.[11] Chinese military modernization throughout the decade stressed the pursuit of "informatization," loosely modeled on US network-centric warfare with particular emphasis on the use of cyberattack as a rapid, long-range, low-cost, high-impact countermeasure against American power projec-tion.[12] Wide-ranging Chinese espionage against government, commercial, and civil society targets during the same period underlined the scope and severity of the emerging cyber threat. A number of reorganizations of cyber authorities within the US Department of Defense culminated in the May 2010 launch of US Cyber Command (CYBERCOM), collocated with the National Security Agency and commanded by its director, as a sub-unified command under US Strategic Command (STRATCOM). After years of terminological debate, the DoD for-mally recognized cyberspace as a man-made "domain" of military operations alongside the traditional physical domains of land, sea, air, and outer space.[13]

Space assets and cyber networks together form a global information infra-structure that is vital for US economic and military performance. Notably, almost all of the important services provided by satellites in orbit are informa-tional in nature (i.e., intelligence collection, communications, early warning, timing, and navigation, etc.), and control of satellites is utterly dependent on electronic datalinks. Loss or degradation of critical space-based capabilities could imperil American ability to project power or even to secure domestic facil-ities and infrastructure. Whilst China was by no means the first to develop space weapons (both superpowers experimented with them in the Cold War), the vulnerability of space infrastructure was dramatically demonstrated in 2007 by the Chinese test of a direct ascent anti-satellite weapon that created a large debris cloud in low earth orbit.[14] The space and cyberwarfare ambitions (if not yet capabilities) of China in particular were perceived by US officials as key pillars in an "anti-access, area-denial" (A2/AD) strategy, which also included an emerging arsenal of capabilities in other domains, including land-based ballistic missiles, fast naval patrol craft, and advanced fighters, all aimed at contesting American "command of the commons."[15]

Upon taking office, the Obama administration reorganized the Office of the Secretary of Defense, establishing the Assistant Secretary of Defense for Global Strategic Affairs (ASD-GSA) to consolidate policy for nuclear forces, ballistic missile defense, space, and cyberspace. The combination of these diverse activities under one tent suggested that space and cyber threats were seen to pose strategic problems on par with nuclear weapons. Unsurprisingly, the term CDD appears to have emerged around this same time within STRATCOM, an agency historically focused on existential threats. Yet the impetus for change was not only functional but also regional. The ability of the United States to deter Chinese aggression in the East or South China Seas appeared to be systematically eroding as A2/AD capabilities improved and China engaged in provocative actions well below the threshold of US military retaliation (e.g., aggressive merchant vessel maneuvers, island reclamation, and cyber campaigns). Space and cyberwarfare thus seemed to pose immediate threats to the freedom of US military operations, whilst relentless human and cyber espionage posed a long-term competitive threat. Whilst China continues to exhibit difficulties in the absorption of certain types of military innovation, the illicit transfer of sensitive technology promises to enhance their capabilities in every domain. Russia and Iran posed different but related difficulties as they mobilized tailored capabilities in different domains to undermine various aspects of the US deterrent posture. The proliferation of novel capabilities to terrorist and other seemingly non-deterrable non-state actors was another variation on the theme.[16]

ASD-GSA convened a "Cross-Domain Deterrence Initiative" (CDDI) working group in 2010 to discuss these issues. The CDDI invited senior academic scholars and industry experts specializing in deterrence strategy and particular regional and technological threats to the Pentagon and provided them with classified briefings on alarming developments in each area. Ensuing discussion in the CDDI highlighted a number of serious challenges to implementing effective deterrence policy. Foremost was the uncertainty inherent in the use of complex technologies, let alone subtle combinations of them, in a signaling role across domains and across cultures. Without an observable history of use or common norms regarding the intent, appropriateness, and proportionality of moves with novel capabilities, the attempt of one side to de-escalate could trigger preemption from an adversary. Cyberspace (including its space-based infrastructure) loomed large in the discussion because of its global reach, low barriers to entry, and pervasive ambiguity about the extent and intention of an intrusion (the same methods support intelligence collection and infrastructure disruption) and the identity of the responsible actor (who might even be a non-state entity). How is it possible to deter attacks that have no return address? Conversely, how is it possible to credibly threaten military retaliation for cyber-attacks that turn out to be mere nuisances? How should government declaratory policy protect civilian technology it does not control without distorting competition and responsible risk taking in markets that brought that technology into being? Does complexity itself doom deterrence?[17]

Deterrence by other means

The answer is no, or at least, not always. The same complexity that creates the impetus to pursue deterrence across domains also provides an opportunity to revisit the assumptions of deterrence theory. Success in policy and conflict is not about an ideal of perfection, but of relative capabilities, foresight, or acumen. Complexity, faced by adversaries on both sides, can be an advantage to the faction that is most skilled in addressing and exploiting its challenges. In an increasingly complex world, victory goes not to the bold per se, but to the better informed.

Moreover, complexity in strategic affairs is, counterintuitively, a reaction to the efficacy of deterrence. When deterrence works in one respect, a challenger has incentives to "design around" the barrier in another.[18] As a nation, American security problems seem terribly difficult today because we have the luxury of attending to them, confident that the bigger problems of yesterday are under control. Urban terrorism and ubiquitous surveillance are "First World problems" that become salient when a society's existential concerns are attenuated, the risk of major power war receding in probability. In some situations, however, the risk of serious war may increase when technology creates new "moves" that are not countenanced under an existing declaratory policy, forcing policymakers to improvise and, potentially, to miscalculate. Consternation about the potential for deterrence failure as a result of complexity usually reflects a desire to extend the success of deterrence to cover new provocations in the "gray zone," not the categorical failure of deterrence.

With apologies to Raymond Carver, we must ask, what do we talk about when we talk about deterrence? Several things, it turns out. Intuitively, deterrence uses the threat of some future penalty to dissuade an opponent from acting to realize a benefit: "don't come any closer or I'll shoot." Deterrence is often contrasted with compellence, which uses threats to persuade an opponent to act in ways it otherwise would not: "give me your wallet or I'll shoot." The distinction is often muddied in practice, as when an offensive action to compel change includes measures to deter preemption: "stay back and toss over your wallet or I'll shoot." China may view A2/AD as a means of deterring US intervention in its local or even internal affairs (i.e., Taiwan), whilst the United States may view the same action as a means of compelling America to accept a Chinese fait accompli intended to revise the status quo. For tactical, normative, or psychological reasons, actors tend to represent their intentions as defensive even when they are acting aggressively. The difference between deterrence and compellence may thus be in the eye of the beholder. Both forms of coercion, in Schelling's formulation, rely on credible communication about "the power to hurt" in the future rather than "brute force" in the present.[19] One of the key challenges of CDD turns on ambiguity about the credibility of such threats—the magnitude of potential harm, the meaning of force—and on a blurring of the distinction between threatening in the future and using force in the present. A second challenge has to do with the complexity of threats or actions in a world posing an increasing number of options. The actors themselves may not know what they plan to do in response to aggressive measures by an adversary. Actors cannot threaten credibly if they do not yet understand their own options or intentions. Nevertheless, we can make some analytical progress by disaggregating the capabilities that affect disparate dimensions of deterrence.

The US military defines deterrence as "The prevention of action by the existence of a credible threat of unacceptable counteraction and/or belief that the cost of action outweighs the perceived benefits."[20] There are several different ideas at work in this definition. Deterrence is about "prevention of action" or preserving one's favored distribution of benefits, the status quo. The parts about "credible threat" and "belief" point to the mind of the target, who must decide if a given threat (a signal implied or articulated) is really expositive of the defender's intent, or just a bluff. Finally, the target must decide that "the cost of action outweighs the perceived benefits." The definition is ambiguous about whether costs result from "unacceptable counteraction" or some other source, such as the target's private concerns about blowback, collateral damage, or mission failure that might produce "self-deterrence." The other side of the cost equation—the defender's costs for carrying through on the threat—is not explicit in the Pentagon definition, but the usual assumption is that successful deterrence without a fight is preferable to failed deterrence with a fight. Threatening to fight is usually cheaper than fighting, which is of course why deterrence poses a credibility problem; anyone can make "cheap talk." It is, however, possible that an actor might, in some cases, prefer to fight rather than make a threat at all, especially if the costs of "prevention of action" by other means are somehow less than making a truly "credible threat."[21]

Deterrence is thus not a single integrated activity but a bundle of different objectives and policy options, each of which pose military and/or policy trade-offs in terms of one another. At its most basic, deterrence is the attempt to get your way, without a fight, at low cost. There may be many other objectives as well in any particular case—ensuring the legitimacy of one's behavior, satisfying a domestic interest group, cultivating a reputation for resolve, redirecting investment toward butter over guns, maintaining open trade in the midst of rising international tensions, etc. We will use the terms *winning* and *warning* to capture two of the most fundamental goals in any coercive interaction (these two alone generate complex trade-offs and are thus useful for making headway to an understanding of CDD). Getting one's way ("winning") requires challenging or defending the status quo. If the disposition of politics or policy as an objective is particularly important, then capabilities and the resolve to fight will be needed to prevail if deterrence fails. Avoiding a fight ("warning"), in contrast, means ensuring that both sides clarify their interests, capabilities, and intentions to one another so that mutually acceptable diplomatic bargains can be worked out, obviating the need for war. Warnings must be made as clear and credible as possible, so that the target understands just where red lines are drawn and where the risk of escalation becomes unacceptable. This will often mean making some compromises, either in negotiations or in the nature and expectations of threats. Deterrence fails when the target of a deterrent threat is asked to concede too much, or when demands appear unlikely to be acted on; everyday examples abound: "if you make me go to bed, I will hold my breath until I turn blue." Military capabilities have this dual role of changing the balance of power (winning in war) and communicating interests (warning in politics).

We focus on these two distinct goals because they follow readily from the basic bargaining model of war. Adversaries can either make a deal to keep or revise some division of the disputed good, or they can participate in a costly lottery (war), which destroys some of the surplus they could have divided. A deal enables both sides to avoid the costs of conflict even if one or the other has to give way on their preferred distribution of benefits. Yet, each side has incentives to misrepresent costs and power, either by bluffing to get a better deal in the *ex ante* bargaining or by concealing capabilities to improve performance in the *ex post* fighting. Capabilities that improve military (or intelligence) performance alter the relative balance of power, and thus the probability of doing well in a contest of strength if bargaining fails. By contrast, capabilities that send credible signals help to reduce uncertainty about the true balance of power and the costs of conflict.

CDD emerges when different types of capabilities differentially affect winning or warning. Airpower is very useful for attacking land forces maneuvering in the open because of its great mobility and firepower. Yet this same maneuverability means that air forces can be quickly withdrawn or revectored, raising questions about whether this kind of military capability will actually be engaged when needed. Ground forces, by contrast, might suffer higher costs in attempting to repel an invasion should it occur, but since it is hard to move them out of the way of an attack, with limited mobility and logistic impedimenta, they provide a more credible signal of intent to become involved, should active combat occur. By this logic, the US deployment of ground forces in Europe during the Cold War and in Korea to this day acted as commitment mechanisms to ensure the United States would go to war if this tripwire was tripped. Naval forces face similar trade-offs, providing power projection and influence to keep disputes further from the home power's shores, but their very mobility across the seas makes their deployment in the event of a distant crisis much more uncertain. At the same time, the costs of losing a warship, measured in hundreds if not thousands of souls, can be used to signal commitment if the signaler can somehow avoid redeploying warships out of the danger zone. Many variations are possible. Forward basing of aircraft with investment in supply and facilities may improve the credible threat to use them when needed. An adversary that equips ground forces with advanced air defenses may deter the use of aircraft altogether. Ground forces that rely on special operations and proxies sacrifice their signaling role by relying on secrecy and stratagem.

In many arenas, it is possible to use different capabilities to reinforce one another. In combined arms warfare, for example, the firepower of artillery, the mobility of armor, and the ability of infantry to identify and report on threats work as complements; the strengths of one capability cover weaknesses of the other, together enhancing the combat power of the group. Coordination of different specialized military capabilities increase the probability of winning in battle.[22] Combined arms teams can also pose a formidable deterrent, provided that elements operate together effectively (no easy task) and assuming that potential adversaries know of their effectiveness, either from the outcomes of previous contests or because they have been observed in exercises. For all the shortfalls and controversy regarding the ideology of the "network-centric" revolution in military affairs, US mastery of this mode of fighting provides a powerful deterrent against risking conventional military combat against the United States.[23]

However, winning and warning are sometimes incompatible. Nowhere is this more apparent than in the combination of cyber operations and nuclear weapons. These two capabilities are nearly perfect complements, with opposite bargaining characteristics. The fundamental utility of nuclear forces is in signaling vital national interests, not in winning a war. The nuclear domain is stable for actors armed with a secure second strike (or maybe even something less) because mutual warnings are clear and credible for all parties. By contrast, the fundamental utility of cyber operations is for changing the distribution of power by enhancing intelligence advantage or supporting the application of military force, not for signaling.[24] The revelation of a cyber exploit or an active intrusion facilitates effective defense against it through system reconfiguration or patching, whilst vague threats of hacking are far less credible.[25] The cyber domain is notoriously unstable as actors are constantly probing, exploiting, defending, and adapting their networks in the face of great uncertainty about the concurrent activities of the other side. What happens when these complements combine? On one hand, the stability of the nuclear domain provides an upper bound on cyber aggression, strongly discouraging any catastrophic infrastructure attack for fear that this might trigger unacceptable retaliation. On the other hand, the instability of the cyber domain can be a worrisome destabilizer of nuclear relationships, since one side can compromise the reliability of the other side's nuclear forces but cannot reveal this coup without undermining success. This inadvertently leads the other side to run risks in false confidence that its deterrent remains credible. Cyberattacks against a nation's nuclear deterrent can take many forms, interdicting the complex chain of events involved in nuclear deterrent capabilities anywhere from satellite sensing of enemy ballistic missile launch, to command and control systems, to the actual missile launch, guidance, and warhead detonation. In each case, the critical factor is an attacker's incentives to conceal successes from the target of attack, to exercise advantages in future (nuclear) battles, rather than to exercise military successes in cyberspace in the form of diplomatic leverage. If the prospect of inadvertent escalation in the nuclear domain seems undesirable and effective warning thus desirable, then it becomes important to sacrifice some capability for winning in the cyber domain (or at least that corner of it that innervates nuclear command and control).[26]

Deterrence has always included multiple objectives. What has changed are the many means now available to pursue them. Since different means may differentially affect the pursuit of different ends, a full theory of deterrence must account for how choices among means influence the quality of deterrence produced with them. CDD is not a different kind of deterrence, but rather a more general account of how deterrence works. Deterrence within a domain, matching threats of one type to capabilities of the same type (i.e., apples versus apples), is simply the special case of a much more general phenomenon. Classical deterrence theory focused on using nuclear weapons to prevent nuclear war and did not emphasize choice among means as a decisive act. Now that there are more means that are far less hurtful or provocative than nuclear war—some of which do not even rise to the level of force—the question for policymakers and careful observers is why and how choices are made to threaten or exercise one implement of power as opposed to others. Indeed, the increase in the diversity of means tends to fill out the lower end of the conflict spectrum, where policies for credible warning do not yet exist. Deterrence becomes more complex where uncertainty about the effects of threats and provocations is greater and the resolve to employ or counter them is more in doubt. Thus, not only does deterrence in the cyber domain suffer from an ambiguity of novelty (policymakers and practitioners are uncertain about the effects of cyber conflict), but it also struggles with an ambiguity of interaction (policymakers and practitioners do not know how conflict in the cyber domain substitutes for or complements the potential to hurt in other dimensions).

Information and complexity

In our sketch of the logic of CDD, we have discussed cyberspace as merely one domain among many. Cyber means become particularly attractive as a non-kinetic or non-intrusive way of tweaking the balance of power, even as their signaling utility is low. Yet there is a deeper relationship between cyberspace and CDD stemming from the essential role of information in economics and politics. Information becomes more salient as systems become more complex.

"Information" has a number of contradictory colloquial connotations: meaningless bits of data or the meaningful content of data; something that provides knowledge or something distinct from it; something universal or something peculiarly human.[27] Formal "information theory," developed simultaneously by Claude Shannon and Norbert Weiner with some influence by John Von Neumann, provides a better-defined set of concepts; these ideas underlie modern communications and electronics engineering, robotic and vehicle control, cryptology and cryptography, and game theory.[28] Information here is a measure of the probability of receiving a particular message given the variety of values a message can take. The larger the variety of possible states, the lower the probability of receiving any particular message and thus the more informative it is to receive it. Generally, a particular message is informative about something when the state of the message is correlated with the true state of that thing and is distinguishable from what would have appeared by chance in the message. In engineering a reliable communication circuit, the task is to devise encodings and error-correction schemes that faithfully transmit signals from a source to a receiver in the presence of noise in the channel. Bandwidth and storage capacity measured in bits describe the overall entropy of the system, so more bits enable transmission and storage of more information. In cryptography, the task is to devise encodings that appear like random noise for an interloper but can readily be identified as a deliberate signal by the intended receiver through the use of one or more decoding keys. Increasing the entropy of the encoded message (the number of possible states) makes it harder to guess the true state without the key. These and other applications of information theory are foundational in computer science.

The same information theory underlies the modern bargaining theory of war and the capacity for deterrent signaling. In non-cooperative game theory, the task is for one player to discriminate the true preferences or type of the other on the basis of observable behavior. A signal is informative when it reduces uncertainty *for the receiver* about the true state of the source, not simply when the source assumes some given state. So-called cheap talk is not informative because a reliable person and a liar would say the same thing: the signal is effectively random. By contrast, costly signaling (i.e., tying hands or burning bridges) is informative because only the true type would be willing to display such behavior: the signal is anything but random. Politicians sometimes describe their desire to "send a signal," but the receiver's ability to discriminate likely from unlikely signals ultimately determines whether any meaningful signal is received. Deterrence depends on credible signaling that enables the challenger to infer that the defender is willing and able to punish any transgression.

A system with a greater variety of possible outcomes can be described as more complex. Such a system requires more information to describe its state. A system in a highly improbable state can be said to be more organized or less random. Economic development increases the complexity of society by rearranging the material world into less probable states. The same minerals that have always been in the Earth have been rearranged, over a long span of evolutionary and historical development, into quite improbable groupings of cities, airplanes, rockets, and the Internet. It thus takes more information to describe the present state of the Earth because there are more types of things on, under, over, and around it than ever before, and there are more ways to combine them in productive and destructive activities. To coordinate and control things in the practice of government or commerce, actors need information about what state those things are in. Any measurement process that encodes and transmits information about the state of a system (usually through some combination of information technologies, administrative organization, and human interpretation) has the potential to reduce uncertainty for an observer of that system, in effect making the system more predictable. Better information then enables an observer to select from a variety of actions those that are appropriate to the state of the system and more likely to bring about an intentional goal, or maximize utility. For example, an electronic representation of a train schedule enables a passenger to leave her house on time to catch a train and visit her friend. Information about the world and decisions to act make intended states of the world more likely and less random. More complex action that moves the world into an even less probable state (many friends visiting at the same time) requires even more information.

The evolution of information technologies makes more complex control possible. All information technology from the Rosetta Stone to the World Wide Web has coevolved historically along with other human institutions to improve measurement, coordination, and enforcement in collective action. Bureaucracies rely on standardized files and statistical techniques to extend the scope of its control because their agents have limited cognitive capacities and may leave for new jobs.[29] Telecommunications and timetables can make transportation more predictable. Intelligence and surveillance systems may allow a military to know more about the state of the enemy and to strike with greater precision. The evolution of a system toward greater complexity also requires an evolution in the information technology that improves predictability and controllability in that system. The illustration of this truth is in the exceptions, when information technology does not improve quickly enough to maintain control over complexity. The Battle of Jutland provides a classic example. Innovations in government finance, propulsion, explosives, high-grade steel, and fuses out-paced communications technology as signal flags were hard to see and radio was in its infancy; battleships could thus destroy each other quickly at great distance, requiring the battlespace to expand dramatically, but Admiral Jellicoe lost track of his fleet and could not communicate effectively with his ship captains.

The increase in sociotechnical complexity is a long-term historical and coevolutionary process. Economic competition fosters a division of labor that improves the efficiency of production but also expands the scope of competition, since there are more actors and resources brought into the market. Control improvements for one competitor become a threat to the other, who will seek to disrupt enemy control systems and/or improve their own control. Military competition on a historical scale deepens the division of labor within forces and weapons systems by a similar logic. Competition becomes more nuanced as the systems that regulate it become more sophisticated. Conflict within cyberspace is exemplary in this regard because it exploits imperfections in the most complex systems human beings have ever built, relying on deception and guile rather than brute force. "Cyber" comes from a Greek word meaning control, a root shared by "government." Thus "cyberspace" as such is symptomatic of the expanding complexity and scope of control in every sector of human activity—science, commerce, entertainment, administration, and warfare—which all depend on ever more sophisticated means for representing and communicating the dynamic state of the world.[30] There is more information in the world because govern-ments, firms, and individuals enjoy more control over their affairs, and vice versa. This also creates control contests where their increased potential for control comes into conflict. Information technology improves human control over flows of labor and capital, as well as control over the controls (bureaucracy and information technology).[31]

Herein lies the basic irony of both cybersecurity and CDD: there appears to be more uncertainty and conflict variety in the world precisely because there is more information and control in the modern globalized world. Because there are more types of capabilities, linkages, and actors, more information is required to describe the state of the world, and thus there is a lot more uncertainty in detail. With more uncertainty, there is more scope for confusion and deception, and these information imperfections make conflict more likely. Yet the condition for the possibility of this complexity is a system that has moved, through a long evo-lutionary process, into a highly organized and historically improbable state. Perfect information is not available, but pretty good information often is avail-able. Thus, many states have no reason to resort to violence to renegotiate their bargains because they understand the likely costly consequences. The bargains that are uncertain and thus liable for renegotiation are for smaller stakes. Greater complexity creates more things to argue about by settling the big arguments. Put another way, disruptions are more frequent but less intense.[32]

Cybersecurity and CDD are both symptomatic of increasing sociotechnical complexity, and they both deal with threats that exploit the additional informa-tion required to fully describe the state of the complex world. Threats to the security of cyberspace and the stability of deterrence are quite literally working at the margins of the system, exploiting and predicated upon the existence of predictable exchange relationships. Because people place more trust than ever before in cyberspace, there is more scope than ever for subtle subversion of the means of control. Because states have better information than ever before about the balance of power and likely costs of great power war, there is more scope than ever before for provocative moves in the "gray zone" below the threshold of retaliatory response. Vertical moves that inflict clear and obvious harm risk serious punishment, but horizontal moves into new domains that are not clearly proscribed by a credible deterrent policy offer some promise of gain. Deterrence "fails" in low-intensity and especially non-violent disputes because it "succeeds" everywhere else.

Conclusion

Although it is possible and sometimes necessary to talk about cybersecurity and CDD separately, there is an intimate historical and conceptual connection between them. Cyberspace may be one domain among many, but all of the other domains depend on some sort of information technology for command and control. As a military operational environment, furthermore, it is notable that civilians largely invent, own, and operate much of the constitutive architecture;

as a result, cyberspace is largely out of military control. Deterrence, in practice if not in theory, has leveraged many means since long before the information age, yet its success and failure has always been a problem of what one knows or perceives, and what one can convey. Even commitment problems under supposedly perfect information still depend on information about the range of states that actors might assume in the future. It is no accident that these two policy problems have appeared together, or that a complex information technology should complicate the information challenges of strategic interaction. They are symptoms of the same underlying cause: historically increasing economic, political, and technological complexity. Exchange and conflict are two related mechanisms that ratchet up the complexity of human interaction by incentivizing an increase in variety.

This chapter has sketched an argument that is embedded in a larger research agenda on CDD.[33] We have noted the ways in which our previous work on cybersecurity has both inspired and benefited from our research on deterrence. Further work remains to be done to clarify the formal logic and empirical implications and to test key implications of the insights that result. Doing so is difficult because of the same complexity that is the subject matter of this research. Yet, in posing the problem of complexity as primarily an issue of uncertainty and the management of information, there is real potential to make new progress in both the micro and macro logic of deterrence, a topic that appeared filled out, well understood, and even stagnant to many scholars. Winning differs from warning. The fact that they have been conflated in traditional discussions of deterrence made it difficult to understand the trade-offs involved in emphasizing one or the other, and made it impossible to consider how new means might differ in accomplishing either objective.

The historical origins of information theory may point out a way in which deterrence theory can develop. Shannon's seminal 1948 article on communication examined the challenges of encoding a signal to get it *through* a noisy channel.[34] This work was an outgrowth of Shannon's wartime work in Bell Labs on encryption, described in a classified 1945 article on the challenges of disguising an encoded signal *as* noise.[35] The mathematics of obfuscated information and reliable communication are one and the same endeavor. So too deterrence has a dual aspect, which we have described in terms of winning and warning. Warning is the problem of clear and reliable signaling, which clarifies cost and power and makes war less likely. Winning is the problem of ensuring that power is sufficient to get a favored outcome in conflict, and it often relies on capabilities that must be hidden to be effective. The element of surprise is an important, but variable, complement to the possession and exercise of different capabilities. Maneuver warfare attempts to present the adversary with more problems than it can handle, tipping the relative balance of friction in one's favor. Cyber deception, like a magician's sleight of hand, exploits degrees of freedom that deterministic machines cannot detect. Whereas signaling attempts to reduce uncertainty, warfighting (and intelligence) attempts to increase it.

Shannon's unified view of clear communication and unreadable encryption suggests that winning and warning, apparently so different, need to be understood in a common framework. Warning attempts to credibly communicate through the noise, whilst winning attempts to prevail more effectively by masquerading as noise. Strategy must combine them both. The logic of encryption, moreover, may ultimately be more appropriate for the complex intelligence-counterintelligence contests that characterize modern strategic problems from cybersecurity to counterterrorism. Deterrence is no longer simply a game of chicken with the survival of civilization in the balance, if it ever was, but rather an ongoing tapestry of moves and countermoves at different timescales and levels of analysis. These intertwined and iterated games both exploit and generate systemic complexity. Classical deterrence theory provides the invaluable distinction between contests of strength and contests of resolve. A more general deterrence theory must include contests of deception as well.

Notes

* The authors wish to thank Damien Van Puyvelde, Tim Ridout, and Joshua Rovner for helpful comments. All errors are those of the authors.
1 Dorothy E. Denning, "Rethinking the cyber domain and deterrence," *Joint Forces Quarterly* 77/2 (2015): 8–15; David Elliott, "Deterring strategic cyberattack," *IEEE Security & Privacy*, 2011; Martin C. Libicki, *Cyberdeterrence and Cyberwar* (Santa Monica: RAND, 2009); Brandon Valeriano and Ryan C. Maness, *Cyber War versus Cyber Realities: Cyber Conflict in the International System* (New York: Oxford University Press, 2015); Jon R. Lindsay, "Tipping the scales: The attribution problem and the feasibility of deterrence against cyber attack," *Journal of Cybersecurity* 1 (2015): 53–67.
2 Robert Jervis, *The Meaning of the Nuclear Revolution: Statecraft and the Prospect of Armageddon* (Ithaca: Cornell University Press, 1989); Lawrence Freedman, "The First Two Generations of Nuclear Strategists," in Peter Paret (ed.), *Makers of Modern Strategy: From Machiavelli to the Nuclear Age* (New York: Oxford, 1986), 735–778.
3 Erik Gartzke and Jon R. Lindsay, "Weaving tangled webs: Offense, defense, and deception in cyberspace," *Security Studies* 24 (2015): 316–348.
4 James D. Fearon, "Rationalist explanations for war," *International Organization* 49 (1995): 379–414; Robert Powell, *In the Shadow of Power: States and Strategies in International Politics* (Princeton: Princeton University Press, 1999); Charles L. Glaser, *Rational Theory of International Politics: The Logic of Competition and Cooperation* (Princeton: Princeton University Press, 2010).
5 Bernard Brodie et al., *The Absolute Weapon: Atomic Power and World Order* (New York: Harcourt, Brace and Co., 1946).
6 Thomas C. Schelling, *Arms and Influence: With a New Preface and Afterword* (New Haven: Yale University Press, 2008).
7 Shannon Carcelli and Erik Gartzke, "Blast from the Past: Revitalizing and Diversifying Deterrence Theory," Working Paper (La Jolla: 2016).
8 Joshua Rovner, "New Concepts for Ancient Wars: Cross-Domain Deterrence in the Peloponnesian War," in Erik Gartzke and Jon R. Lindsay (eds), *Cross-Domain Deterrence: Strategy in an Era of Complexity* (forthcoming).
9 Jon R. Lindsay, *Shifting the Fog of War: Information Technology and the Politics of Control* (forthcoming), Chap. 4.
10 Jason Healey, ed., *A Fierce Domain: Conflict in Cyberspace, 1986 to 2012* (Washington, DC: Cyber Conflict Studies Association, 2013).
11 Jon R. Lindsay, "Stuxnet and the limits of cyber warfare," *Security Studies* 22 (2013): 365–404.

12 Kevin Pollpeter, "Chinese Writings on Cyberwarfare and Coercion," in Jon R. Lindsay, Tai Ming Cheung, and Derek S Reveron (eds), *China and Cybersecurity: Espionage, Strategy, and Politics in the Digital Domain* (New York: Oxford University Press, 2015).

13 William J. Lynn III, "Defending a new domain," *Foreign Affairs* 89/5 (2010): 97–108.

14 In addition to exoatmospheric nuclear tests in the early Cold War, the Soviet Union tested anti-satellite (ASAT) weapons in the 1970s and 1980s, and the United States tested an ASAT weapon in 1985 (ASM-135) and demonstrated a capability again in 2008 with an unconventional use of a RIM-161 Standard Mk 3.

15 Evan Braden Montgomery, "Contested primacy in the Western Pacific," *International Security* 38/4 (2014): 115–149.

16 It is not clear that terrorists and others are as often non-deterrable as presumed. The basic problem with the call to action in response to "non-deterrable" terrorists is that kinetic or other responses, if successful, should themselves generate deterrence. The problem may more accurately be described as uncertainty about the true cost or effectiveness of counterterrorist actions. Madelyn R. Creedon, "Space and cyber: Shared challenges, shared opportunities," *Strategic Studies Quarterly* (2012): 3–8; James A. Lewis, "Cross-Domain Deterrence and Credible Threats" (Washington, DC: Center for Strategic and International Studies, July 2010); Shawn Brimley, "Promoting security in common domains," *The Washington Quarterly* 33 (2010): 119–132; Vincent Manzo, "Deterrence and Escalation in Cross-Domain Operations: Where Do Space and Cyberspace Fit?" Strategic Forum (Washington, DC: Institute for National Strategic Studies, National Defense University, 2011).

17 Michael Nacht et al., "Cross Domain Deterrence in American Foreign Policy," in *Cross-Domain Deterrence: Strategy in an Era of Complexity* (forthcoming). See also: "A New Look at the 21st Century Cross-Domain Deterrence Initiative: Summary of a Workshop, May 19–20, 2016 at The George Washington University," http://deterrence.ucsd.edu/_files/CDDI2-Workshop-Summary-080916.pdf.

18 Alexander L. George and Richard Smoke, *Deterrence in American Foreign Policy: Theory and Practice* (New York: Columbia University Press, 1974), 399.

19 Schelling, *Arms and Influence*, 2–6.

20 US Joint Chiefs of Staff, "Deterrence," in Joint Publication (JP) 3–0: Joint Operations, August 11, 2011.

21 Certain types of military action are particularly dependent on surprise or secrecy. Threats that leave too little to chance can be undermined as a target adjusts its defensive posture to counter action anticipated in a deterrent claim.

22 Stephen D. Biddle, *Military Power: Explaining Victory and Defeat in Modern Battle* (Princeton: Princeton University Press, 2004).

23 Jon R. Lindsay, "Reinventing the revolution: Technological visions, counterinsurgent criticism, and the rise of special operations," *Journal of Strategic Studies* 36/3 (2013): 422–453; Michael Fortmann and Stefanie von Hlatky, "The Revolution in Military Affairs: Impact of Emerging Technologies on Deterrence," in T. V. Paul, Patrick M. Morgan, and James J. Wirtz (eds), *Complex Deterrence: Strategy in the Global Age* (Chicago: University of Chicago Press, 2009), 304–320.

24 Lindsay, "Tipping the scales."

25 Erik Gartzke, "The myth of cyberwar: Bringing war in cyberspace back down to earth," *International Security* 38/2 (2013): 41–73.

26 For additional exploration and justification of these arguments, please see Erik Gartzke and Jon R. Lindsay, "Thermonuclear Cyberwar," (under review).

27 John Seely Brown and Paul Duguid, *The Social Life of Information* (Cambridge: Harvard Business Press, 2000); Paul Davies and Niels Henrik Gregersen (eds), *Information and the Nature of Reality: From Physics to Metaphysics* (New York: Cambridge University Press, 2010).

28 Ronald R. Kline, *The Cybernetics Moment: Or Why We Call Our Age the Information Age* (Baltimore, MD: Johns Hopkins University Press, 2015).

29 James C. Scott, *Seeing Like a State: How Certain Schemes to Improve the Human Condition Have Failed* (New Haven: Yale University Press, 1998).

30 Thomas Rid, *Rise of the Machines: A Cybernetic History* (New York: W. W. Norton & Company, 2016).

31 James R. Beniger, *The Control Revolution: Technological and Economic Origins of the Information Society* (Cambridge: Harvard University Press, 1986); Joel Mokyr, *The Gifts of Athena: Historical Origins of the Knowledge Economy* (Princeton: Princeton University Press, 2002).

32 Jon R. Lindsay and Erik Gartzke, "Coercion through Cyberspace: The Stability-Instability Paradox Revisited," in Kelly M. Greenhill and Peter J. P. Krause (eds), *The Power to Hurt: Coercion in Theory and in Practice* (New York: Oxford University Press, forthcoming).

33 See Erik Gartzke et al., "Cross-Domain Deterrence," University of California San Diego, http://deterrence.ucsd.edu.

34 Claude E. Shannon, "A mathematical theory of communication," *The Bell System Technical Journal* 27 (1948): 379–423, 623–656.

35 Claude E. Shannon, "A Mathematical Theory of Cryptography," Technical Report (Bell Labs, September 1, 1945).

3 Crossing the Rubicon

Identifying and responding to an armed cyberattack[1]

Nerea M. Cal[*]

In the wake of 9/11, US officials raised concerns that an attack by Al Qaeda against the digital networks that control US infrastructure would prove even more devastating than the destruction of the World Trade Center towers.[2] In a meeting with corporate security executives in 2002, the director of the National Infrastructure Protection Center at the Federal Bureau of Investigation revealed that the event he feared most was "a physical attack in conjunction with a successful cyberattack on the responders' 911 system or on the power grid."[3] An attack of this kind would be doubly damaging, inflicting physical damage along with the psychological effects resulting from the inability to respond to the attack immediately.

Fortunately, an attack of this type has not occurred over the past 15 years. Nevertheless, the potential for a catastrophic cyberattack has increased significantly, due to its relatively low cost and potentially catastrophic effects. The price tag of perpetrating an attack is astonishingly cheap, with one estimate putting the cost of developing malware that can debilitate critical infrastructure as low as $10,000.[4] Yet, whilst the costs of a cyberattack have decreased, the country's dependency on digital networks has expanded to nearly every element of national security infrastructure. As Ted Koppel asserted in his fictional account of a cyberattack on the United States' electrical grid, "to be dependent is to be vulnerable."[5] Taken together, these developments spell a "hugely increased vulnerability to destruction and attack" in cyberspace.[6] A group with modest financial means and better-than-average technological skills could incur significant damage on critical infrastructure.

Despite these defensive challenges, the world's increasing dependency on digital networks also offers new opportunities for the United States to take offensive cyber action against its adversaries. For example, it is widely believed that the United States and Israel worked together to develop Stuxnet, a malicious computer worm that infected the software of a uranium enrichment plant in 2010.[7] However, notwithstanding President Obama's directive to "institutionalize cyberattacks as an integral tool of American diplomacy and war," neither policymakers nor military leaders have developed a clear framework to guide their actions in cyberspace.[8] Dubbed "the fifth domain"—in addition to the land, sea, air, and space—the prospect of warfare in the cyber realm introduces a set of complex issues with respect to international law and the law of armed conflict.[9]

Though the United States maintains that existing international law applies to warfare in cyberspace, implementing the traditional rules of armed conflict presents challenges due to the blurring of boundaries that complicate the question of sovereignty as well as attribution. Neither current international law nor US defense policy has resolved the question of what classifies as an armed attack in cyberspace nor how to adjudicate attacks perpetrated by non-state actors. The United States has a unique opportunity to clarify the ambiguities around these two issues, thus shaping international law and providing clear guidelines for military forces charged with employing offensive cyber capabilities.[10]

This chapter briefly outlines the set of international laws governing war, describes the challenges in applying them to cyberwarfare, and provides a recommendation for how to resolve these two key issues by advocating for an effects-based definition of an armed attack and providing a legal avenue for the United States to respond to cyberattacks perpetrated by non-state actors.

The rise of cyberwarfare

Whilst the feared Al Qaeda cyberattack never occurred, the frequency of nefarious cyber activity has expanded in tandem with the world's dependence on the digital networks. In 2003, Chinese hackers were able to infiltrate the systems of top US defense-related organizations, including Lockheed Martin and the National Aeronautics and Space Administration (NASA).[11] In 2007, Estonia was crippled by attacks on government websites, banks, universities, and newspapers. When it was determined that the attacks were initiated in Russia, Estonia quarantined itself from international web activity. As "the most wired country in Europe," this denial of service attack significantly affected Estonia's economy and the lives of its citizens.[12] A year later, Russian hacktivists perpetrated a similarly styled attack against Georgian information technology systems.[13] In December of 2015, more than 230,000 Ukrainians were left without electricity when hackers disabled over 30 substations as well as backup power supplies.[14] The age of cyberwarfare has arrived.

Western security experts have taken a series of measures to understand and counter the increased threat of cyberwarfare. In response to the attacks on Estonia's networks, NATO established the Cooperative Cyber Defense Center of Excellence (CCD CoE) in Tallinn, Estonia to "conduct cyber-terrorism response research and establish a standard protocol for responding to a cyber-attack."[15] The CCD CoE continues to wrestle with some of the most complex questions surrounding the role of cyberspace and cyber technologies in warfare.

The US national security establishment has also taken steps to address this threat. Recognizing that "the increase in attacks heightens the possibility that states might respond to a cyberattack with conventional military means," the Department of Defense established a new sub-unified command in 2010 to chart the way forward in the fifth domain.[16] US Cyber Command (CYBERCOM) is charged with developing operational concepts and a command and control structure to generate, employ, and integrate cyber capabilities into broader operations.[17] In his guidance to the new entity, CYBERCOM's commander, Admiral Michael Rogers, envisioned the implementation of cyber operations as "an integral part of conflict in the land, maritime, air, and space domains."[18] In May 2011, President Obama published the United States' *International Strategy for Cyberspace* in which he offered a broad policy vision and agenda to address cyber threats.[19] The creation of this command and the prioritization of cyber issues by the White House demonstrate the importance of this issue at the highest levels of US military and defense strategy.

Nevertheless, CYBERCOM remains a relatively new entity and policymakers have yet to resolve many of the complex issues that exist in this new military domain. Most notably, if cyber technologies are going to be incorporated as part of an offensive strategy, military leaders must understand what types of cyber-attacks justify a retaliatory response. Let us explore this question by presenting a hypothetical, but realistic, scenario that the United States may face in the not too distant future. Imagine hackers attacked the United States in phases, first crippling the country's banking system, then infiltrating military communications systems, and ultimately succeeding in shutting down a major city's electric grid. Should the United States consider an attack of this type an "act of war?"[20] What constitutes an "armed attack" in cyberspace? How will the United States—once it has attributed responsibility—respond to this kind of attack?

International law and war

The answers to these questions require an examination of the body of international law that outlines the conditions under which states are legally justified to enter into war. The modern concept of international law coalesced into a distinct field in the mid-seventeenth century with Hugo Grotius' publication of *The Law of War and Peace*, which maintained that international law was a set of universal legal norms by which sovereign states are bound.[21] In today's globalized and interconnected world, the importance of codifying the interaction between states into a set of agreed upon legal rules is only increasing.

As the title of Grotius' text indicates, international law developed from an attempt to codify the rules of war. Though the use of force was seen as a legitimate political tool in Grotius' time, modern principles governing the decision to use force—*jus ad bellum*—emphasize a respect for sovereignty that constrains violence.[22] The United Nations (UN) Charter serves as the main source of international law for *jus ad bellum.* Article 2(4) exhorts all members to "refrain in their international relations from the threat or use of force against the territorial integrity or political independence of any state."[23] However, Article 51 confirms the "inherent right of individual or collective self-defense" in the face of an armed attack, thus establishing the legal parameters within which the use of force is appropriate.[24] From this perspective, force is an appropriate method of defending individuals or states from the aggression of others.

International law and cyberwarfare

US policy states that "established principles of international law do apply in cyberspace."[25] Nevertheless, the unique characteristics of cyberspace present a variety of challenges to implementing this policy.[26] The law of war provides a framework for regulating only those cyberattacks "that amount to an armed attack or that take place in the context of an ongoing armed conflict." As a result, the first step to implement the law of war in cyberspace should be to clarify what cyber actions amount to an armed attack, and justify self-defense under Article 51 of the UN Charter.[27] Second, policymakers must consider how to attribute responsibility for cyberattacks and how to respond to them.

To do this, international law must be reinterpreted in a cyber context. This, in turn, requires translating a broad set of legal terms and definitions for use in cyberspace, an effort that remains in an "embryonic state."[28] Though the United States claims that current international law "affirmatively anticipates technological innovation, and contemplates that its existing rules will apply to such innovation," cyberspace convolutes the concept of traditional sovereignty, obscures the perpetrators of the attack, and complicates the ability to distinguish between combatants and non-combatants.[29] Implementing the law of armed conflict in cyberspace is, therefore, not as straightforward as the rhetoric of US policymakers would lead one to believe.

The most notable effort to grapple with the challenge of interpreting international law for cyberspace occurred in 2009, when the CCD CoE convened a group of international law experts in Tallinn, Estonia.[30] In an effort to examine how extant legal norms applied to this "new" form of warfare, this gathering resulted in the 2013 publication of the *Tallinn Manual*, which translates accepted international law into a broad set of rules for cyberwarfare. Though not formally considered international law, this manual provides the most comprehensive application of international law to cyberwarfare to date.

Defining an "armed attack"

The *Tallinn Manual* treats cyberspace as a physical domain and therefore grants states sovereignty over their cyber infrastructure "and cyber activities within [their] territory."[31] According to this treatment of cyberspace, an incursion into another state's cyber infrastructure may be considered a violation of that state's sovereignty. Whilst a violation of sovereignty certainly constitutes a breach of international law, it does not in and of itself justify an offensive response. In order for retaliation to be justified, the incursion on sovereignty must amount to an armed attack against which the attacked state has an inherent right to self-defense.

The term "armed attack" has yet to be clearly defined in the physical realm, consequently its application to cyberspace proves particularly challenging. Though international law condemns the use of force, it does not clearly define what is meant by the terms "aggression," "armed attack," and "use of force."[32]

The approach followed by authors of the *Tallinn Manual*, who draw parallels from the application of law in the physical realm, therefore faces limitations. Nevertheless, legal scholars have developed a set of approaches to evaluate whether cyberattacks reach the threshold of an armed attack. These approaches are instrument-based, effects-based, and target-based.

The instrument-based approach emphasizes the tools with which an attack is conducted, concluding that only those acts of force perpetrated using "traditional weapons with physical characteristics" can be considered armed attacks.[33] This definition results from the attempt to draw as close a parallel between cyberspace and the physical domain as possible. It aligns with the vague language of the UN Charter, which expressly forbids the use of physical military force but does not prohibit economic or political coercion.[34] According to this definition, cyberattacks would never qualify as an armed attack, regardless of the amount or type of destruction they caused, because cyber technologies are not traditional weapons. Whilst the instruments-based definition simplifies the task of identifying an armed attack, its construction is too narrow given the destructive potential of cyberattacks.[35]

The targets-based approach broadens the definition by evaluating an attack based on the type of system it targets. Any attack on critical infrastructure would be considered an armed attack "that may justify self-defense, regardless of its severity."[36] According to this definition, every phase of the hypothetical cyber-attack presented earlier would be considered an armed attack. This approach also opens the door to considering acts of cyber espionage—which are generally not considered armed attacks under current international law—as a use of force against which states have the legal right to self-defense.[37] This inclusion contradicts previous rulings by the International Court of Justice in which the "scale and effects" of the use of force must be considered when evaluating whether it rises to the level of an armed attack.[38] Finally, this approach undermines security by increasing the probability of cyberattacks escalating into larger conventional conflicts.[39] Whilst the instruments-based approach provides too constraining a definition, the targets-based approach broadens the consideration of an armed attack too widely and clashes with commonly accepted elements of international law with respect to physical attacks.

A third framework attempts to overcome the limitations of these two approaches by focusing on the consequences of cyberattacks. The effects-based definition considers a cyberattack to be an armed attack if its effect is "equivalent to that of an armed attack carried out by physical weapons."[40] For example, in the previous hypothetical scenario, if the attack on the electrical grid resulted in deaths because of a loss of power to a hospital, this could be considered an armed attack and confers a legal right to self-defense. This approach incorporates the useful parallel with warfare in the physical domain whilst recognizing the unique capabilities that cyber technologies bring to bear in modern warfare.[41]

In their efforts to develop military doctrine to address cyber challenges, the Joint Chiefs of Staff have adopted an effects-based definition, classifying a cyberattack as:

a hostile act using computer or related networks or systems, and intended to disrupt and/or destroy an adversary's critical cyber systems, assets, or functions. The intended effects of cyberattack are not necessarily limited to the targeted computer systems or data themselves—for instance, attacks on computer systems which are intended to degrade or destroy infrastructure or C2 capability. A cyber attack may use intermediate delivery vehicles including peripheral devices, electronic transmitters, embedded code, or human operators. The activation or effect of a cyber attack may be widely separated temporally and geographically from the delivery.[42]

The Joint Chiefs emphasize the effects of a cyberattack, even to the point of allowing for non-cyber means of perpetration, such as human operators to conduct attacks. This definition of a cyberattack is detailed, but it does not clarify when an attack can be considered an *armed attack* according to international law. Clarifying this question is key to determining when the United States is legally justified to retaliate.

The *Tallinn Manual*, though it only represents the opinion of legal experts, provides a foundation upon which policymakers and military leaders can formulate a more cohesive cyber defense policy, particularly regarding when and how their country will respond to cyberattacks. This framework represents the most comprehensive attempt to apply international law concepts to the still-evolving world of cyberwarfare. The international group of experts that authored the manual adheres to the effects-based approach to cyberattack and notes that "whether a cyber operation constitutes an armed attack depends on its scale and effects."[43] In the manual, the experts proceed to unpack these considerations into a fairly detailed set of guidelines by which to evaluate cyberattacks in accordance with international law.

The first condition for a cyberattack to be considered an armed attack is that it must feature a "trans-border element."[44] That is, the action must constitute a breach of sovereignty by one state into the territory of another. Since the *Tallinn Manual* eschews the instruments-based approach, the experts contend that this breach of sovereignty can occur through the use of cyber means alone, as long as the effect of the attack is grave enough to rise to the level of an armed attack.[45] Rather than focus on the means by which the attack is perpetrated, they focus on the effects of the attack and whether they are "analogous to those that would result from an action otherwise qualifying as a kinetic armed attack."[46]

The international group of experts contends further that circumstances may allow for the consideration of a series of attacks to qualify as a "composite armed attack."[47] A group of smaller-scale cyberattacks can be evaluated in the aggregate against the "scale and effects" considerations and be deemed an armed attack. Considering the scenario presented earlier, whilst the phases that affect the banking system and the military communications networks might not be classified armed attacks if conducted individually, together they can reach the threshold of an armed attack.

Responding to an attack: attribution

Whilst political leaders have acknowledged the severity of the cyber threat, they have not provided a clear and comprehensive framework by which military leaders can guide their actions in cyberspace. The Department of Defense's Law of War Manual, released in June 2015, includes a chapter on "Cyber Operations" that attempts to provide some clarification, but concedes: "precisely how the law of war applies to cyber operations is not well-settled."[48] Future criteria based on the effects-based definition should clarify the conditions that must be met for a cyberattack to rise to the level of an armed attack, and fill a critical gap in current US policy with respect to cyberwarfare.

Once a cyberattack has been categorized as an armed attack against which a state can claim the right to self-defense, leaders must identify the perpetrator. The difficulty of attributing actions in cyberspace cannot be overstated. On a physical battlefield, an enemy combatant is identified by their uniform, offensive behavior, or possession of a weapon. Cyber combatants can hide behind a web of networks, Internet Protocol addresses, and firewalls to mask their identity, location, and state affiliation. Due to the very structure of digital networks, cyber attackers can use intermediaries to mask their identity and location, "hampering law enforcement efforts to track [them] down after an attack has been made."[49] States can use these same techniques to obscure their role in facilitating or directing a cyberattack.

International law stipulates that states bear responsibility for an armed attack when it is attributable to them and constitutes a breach of an international obligation of the state.[50] Once this responsibility is established, the victim of the attack can claim the right to retaliate in self-defense. Additionally, any actions by an element considered an "organ of the state" according to that state's domestic law can also be attributable to the state even if not directly ordered by the state's leadership.[51] This prevents states from hiding behind the claim that elements of the state apparatus have gone rogue, and incentivizes states to exercise control over those entities with the capacity to inflict an attack.

Cyberattacks can be perpetrated by combatants acting either at the behest of a government or on their own initiative. Since international law applies to sovereign states, "non-state actors cannot violate the customary international law norm against the use of force," unless a direct link can be drawn between them and the state.[52] The challenge in establishing this link between non-state actors and a state significantly complicates the ability to attribute responsibility for and retaliate against cyberattacks, even if they have been deemed to rise to the level of an armed attack.

Cybersecurity experts have devised a number of techniques to trace the origin of cyberattacks. Especially in larger-scale attacks, the "volume of traffic involved allows probabilistic tracing techniques to be particularly effective."[53] Estonian officials used these trace-back techniques to link the 2007 attacks to a youth group founded by President Putin.[54] Since this youth group was affiliated with the government, it could be considered an organ of the state, therefore conferring to Russia responsibility for the attack. However, the vagueness of international law concerning attribution prevented Estonia and its allies from putting forward a legal argument for retaliation. Though one could argue that a fear of escalation with Russia precluded retaliatory action from NATO and other allies, the existence of a legal rationale for action at the time would have, at least, given more impetus to responses short of war, such as economic sanctions. As this case demonstrates, possessing the technical capability to trace an attack does not fully resolve the set of complications inherent in attributing responsibility.

Retaliation against non-state actors

The attribution of responsibility for a cyberattack is particularly difficult when an attack emanated from a non-state actor. It may be the case that an attack emanates from within a state's territory by a non-state actor that is not considered an organ of the state. Does this mean the state is abdicating its responsibility? If so, how can the attacked state respond? Though international law is unclear regarding how to treat non-state actors that perpetrate cyberattacks, treating cyberspace as physical territory can help resolve this issue of attribution and response. Specifically, the United States should endorse and adopt an approach that recognizes cyberspace as part of a state's sovereign territory. If a state either directs or provides substantial logistical or operational support to a non-state actor, it assumes responsibility for the attack. This approach would prevent states from hiding behind other-than-governmental actors in order to avoid bearing responsibility for an armed attack.

However, it may be the case that a non-state actor possesses the capacity to perpetrate an attack without state support and knowledge. For example, a terrorist organization or lone hacktivist may conduct an attack without the knowledge of the state. International law has not fully clarified how to treat such cyberattacks. Whilst the US response to the attacks perpetrated by Al Qaeda on 9/11 point to at least some acceptance of the notion that self-defense is justified against a non-state actor, the International Court of Justice has recently shown a "hesitancy to embrace the notion of armed attack by non-state actors."[55] The lack of clarity surrounding cyberattacks by non-state actors represents a significant gap in the US cyber defense policy and international law, especially given the ease with which independent actors can attain the technical capabilities to conduct cyberattacks.

The United States should take the opportunity to shape customary international law around this topic by adopting a two-tiered approach. In the first stage of this approach, the United States should afford the host nation from whose territory the attack emanated the opportunity to adjudicate the attack according to its domestic legal system as a law enforcement matter. If the host nation proves unwilling or unable to resolve the issue, the United States would then have a legal right to retaliate in self-defense.[56] This approach will deter states from attempting to conceal or deny their cyber activities by blaming a non-state actor. Additionally, the threat of outside intervention should also encourage states to constrain cyber activity originating within their borders.

Conclusion

To date, no country has claimed the right to self-defense in reaction to a cyber-attack. Even in Estonia, where the 2007 attacks nearly crippled the country financially, NATO failed to invoke its right to collective self-defense under Article V. This lack of response arguably stems more from the lack of a cohesive policy to guide military cyber operations than the belief that a response was not lawful in these circumstances. With no policy framework to guide their decision making, Estonia and her allies were constrained to implementing defensive measures that, though ultimately successful in the restoration of digital networks in the country, did not hold the perpetrators of the attack accountable nor deter future attacks.

Attacks like those conducted against Estonia (as well as Georgia and Ukraine) will continue to increase as the costs of conducting them decrease and global dependency on digital networks expands. If countermeasures are to be effective, their implementation must be guided by a thoughtful and well-articulated policy that translates international law into the cyber context. Current US defense policy does not clarify the threshold at which cyberattacks become an armed attack against which a response is justified for self-defense. The United States should adopt a cyber policy that reflects an effects-based approach to determining when a cyberattack rises to the level of an armed attack. If an attack causes a level of destruction that, in its scale and effects, would be considered an armed attack if conducted using physical means, it should be considered an armed cyberattack against which the United States has the legal right to respond in self-defense. Additionally, the United States should resolve the question of how to respond to non-state actors by allowing the states within whose territory these organizations operate to adjudicate the issue according to their domestic law before responding in self-defense.

This framework will face a number of criticisms. The international community, Russia and China especially, will claim the United States is overstepping its bounds by unilaterally developing international cyber law. Ideally, the United States should lead the effort to codify these concepts into an international cyber treaty that could "address the elusive concepts of attribution, self-defense, and enforcement" by clarifying terms and outlining responsibilities.[57] However, given the amount of time it normally takes to develop international agreements, the United States should not wait until a cyber treaty is signed to implement these recommendations, since the benefits far outweigh the costs of international criticism. Even in the absence of an international agreement, transparent and consistent behavior from the US government will help set expectations and increase predictability among states in cyberspace. Through its actions, the United States can shape international norms and legal concepts in the fifth domain.

A policy that incorporates an effects-based definition of an armed attack, holds non-state actors accountable for cyberattacks, and strives to foster international norms would also bolster a cyber deterrence strategy. An effective deterrence policy "must apply to a full spectrum of actors, from individuals to nations, from small invasions into computer systems to large-scale 'attacks' that produce significant kinetic effects."[58] In order for its deterrence strategy to truly be effective, the United States must signal its intent to follow through on its threats. The United States must adopt an interpretation of international law that allows for retaliation to cyberattacks and be willing to enact it. Ultimately, its willingness to use offensive cyber tools will reduce the overall likelihood of a large-scale cyber conflict by signaling to its adversaries that the costs of perpetrating attacks are increasing.

Notes

* Special thanks to Professor Oona Hathaway and Edward Wittenstein, whose instruction and input during my time at Yale University's Jackson Institute for Global Affairs was invaluable to the writing of this chapter.
1 This chapter originally appeared as an article in *IEEE Xplore* October 2016.
2 Toby Harnden, "Al Qaeda Plans Cyber Attacks on Dams," *Telegraph*, June 28, 2002, at www.telegraph.co.uk/news/worldnews/asia/afghanistan/1398683/Al-Qaeda-plans-cyber-attacks-on-dams.html.
3 Barton Gellman, "Cyber Attacks by Al Qaeda Feared; Terrorists at Threshold of Using Internet as Tool of Bloodshed, Experts Say," *Washington Post*, June 27, 2002, sec. A1.
4 Pierluigi Paganini, "Cost of Conducting APT Campaigns Dramatically Dropping," February 9, 2014, Security Affairs, at http://securityaffairs.co/wordpress/22056/cyber-crime/apt-cost-dramatically-dropping.html
5 Ted Koppel, *Lights Out* (New York: Crown, 2015), 6.
6 Vida M. Antolin-Jenkins, "Defining the parameters of cyberwar operations: Looking for Law in all the Wrong Places?" *Naval Law Review* 51 (2005): 133.
7 David Kushner, "The Real Story of Stuxnet," *IEEE Spectrum*, February 26, 2013, at http://spectrum.ieee.org/telecom/security/the-real-story-of-stuxnet
8 Fred Kaplan, *Dark Territory: The Secret History of Cyber War* (New York: Simon & Schuster, 2016), 217. Kaplan is referring to PPD-20, a top-secret presidential policy directive published by the *Guardian* in 2013 as part of the Snowden leaks. The author is unable to cite the document directly because of its classification level.
9 Editor, "War in the fifth domain," *Economist*, July 1, 2010, at www.economist.com/node/16478792.
10 Aaron P. Brechner, "Cyber attacks and the covert action statute: Toward a domestic legal framework for offensive cyberoperations," *Michigan Law Review* 111/3 (2012): 426.
11 Jason Richards, "Denial of Service: The Estonian Cyberwar and its Implications for US National Security," *International Affairs Review*, May 1, 2016, at www.iar-gwu.org/node/65.
12 Ibid.
13 Stephen Moore, "Cyber attacks and the beginnings of an international cyber treaty," *North Carolina Journal of International Law and Commercial Regulation* 39/2 (2014): 227.
14 Kim Zetter, "Inside the Cunning, Unprecedented Hack of Ukraine's Power Grid," *Wired*, March 3, 2016, at www.wired.com/2016/03/inside-cunning-unprecedented-hack-ukraines-power-grid/.
15 Richards, "Denial of Service."
16 Oona Hathaway et al., "The law of cyber-attack," *California Law Review* 100/4 (2012): 840.

17 Michael S. Rogers, "Commander's Guidance and Vision for US Cyber Command," June 3, 2015, at www.defense.gov/Portals/1/features/2015/0415_cyber-strategy/docs/US-Cyber-Command-Commanders-Vision.pdf.
18 Ibid.
19 Barack Obama, *International Strategy for Cyberspace: Prosperity, Security, and Openness in a Networked World* (Washington, DC: The White House, 2011).
20 Scheherazade Rehman, "Estonia's Lessons in Cyberwarfare," *US News*, January 14, 2013, at www.usnews.com/opinion/blogs/world-report/2013/01/14/estonia-shows-how-to-build-a-defense-against-cyberwarfare.
21 Mark Weston Janis, *International Law* (New York: Walters Kluwer, 2016), 1.
22 Sheng Li, "When does internet denial trigger the right of armed self-defense?" *The Yale Journal of International Law* 38/1 (2013): 182.
23 United Nations, "Charter of the United Nations," October 24, 1945, 1 UNTS XVI.
24 Ibid.
25 Harold Hongju Koh, "International law in cyberspace," *Harvard International Law Journal* 54 (2012): 3.
26 Hathaway et al., "The law of cyber-attack," 850.
27 Ibid., 821.
28 Antolin-Jenkins, "Defining the parameters of cyberwar operations," 134.
29 Koh, "International law in cyberspace," 5.
30 Michael N. Schmitt (ed.), *Tallinn Manual on the International Law Applicable to Cyber Warfare* (Cambridge: Cambridge University, 2013).
31 Ibid., 16.
32 Antolin-Jenkins, "Defining the parameters of cyberwar operations," 150.
33 Li, "When does internet denial trigger the right of armed self-defense?" 186.
34 Daniel B. Silver, "Computer network attack as a use of force under Article 2(4) of the United Nations Charter," *Computer Network Attack and International Law* 76 (2002): 88.
35 Hathaway et al., "The law of cyber-attack," 846.
36 Li, "When does internet denial trigger the right of armed self-defense?" 179.
37 Ibid., 187.
38 Schmitt et al., *Tallinn Manual*, 55.
39 Hathaway et al., "The law of cyber-attack," 847.
40 Li, "When does internet denial trigger the right of armed self-defense?" 187.
41 Ibid.
42 James E. Cartwright, Memorandum for Chiefs of the Military Services, Commanders of the Combatant Commands, Dirs. of the Joint Staff Directories on Joint Terminology for Cyberspace Operations, November 5, 2011, last modified April 22, 2016, at www.nsci-va.org/CyberReferenceLib/2010-11-joint%20Terminology %20for%20 Cyberspace%20Operations.pdf.
43 Schmitt et al., *Tallinn Manual*, 54.
44 Ibid.
45 Ibid.
46 Ibid., 55.
47 Ibid.
48 Department of Defense, *Department of Defense Law of War Manual*, June 2015, athttp://archive.defense.gov/pubs/law-of-war-manual-june-2015.pdf.
49 Richards, "Denial of Service."
50 International Committee of the Red Cross, *Articles on State Responsibility*, Art. 2, at www.icrc.org/casebook/doc/case-study/ilc-state-responsability-case-study.htm#CHAPTERIGENERALPRINCIPLES.
51 Ibid., Art. 4.
52 Stephen Moore, "Cyber attacks and the beginnings of an international cyber treaty," *North Carolina Journal of International Law and Commercial Regulation* 39/2 (2014): 244.

53 Li, "When does internet denial trigger the right of armed self-defense?" 202.

54 Duncan B. Hollis, "Why states need an international law for information operations," *Lewis & Clark Law Review* 11/4 (2007): 11.

55 Michael N. Schmitt, "Cyber Operations in International Law: The Use of Force, Collective Security, Self-Defense, and Armed Conflicts," *Proceedings of a Workshop on Deterring Cyberattacks: Informing Strategies and Developing Options for US Policy* (Washington, DC: National Academies Press, 2010), 172.

56 Li, "When does internet denial trigger the right of armed self-defense?" 205.

57 Moore, "Cyber attacks and the beginnings of an international cyber treaty," 232.

58 Eric Talbot Jensen, "Cyber deterrence," *Emory International Law Review* 26/2 (2012): 782.

4 The outlook for constraining international norms for offensive cyber operations

Brian M. Mazanec

Norms, which are shared expectations of appropriate behavior, exist at various levels and can apply to different actors.[1] In the international arena, these non-binding shared expectations can, to some degree, constrain and regulate the behavior of international actors and, in that sense, have a structural impact on the international system as a whole. For example, early in the age of nuclear weapons, Lt. Gen. James Gavin expressed the contemporary wisdom when he wrote, "Nuclear weapons will become conventional for several reasons, among them cost, effectiveness against enemy weapons, and ease of handling."[2] However, as the nuclear era advanced, a constraining norm developed that made states reluctant to possess or use nuclear weapons. International security and US national security may be enhanced by the emergence of regulative norms for offensive cyber operations (OCO, also known as cyberwarfare), similar to norms that developed in the past for these emerging-technology weapons such as nuclear, chemical, and biological weapons.

In February 2016, Director of National Intelligence James Clapper testified that many actors "remain undeterred from conducting reconnaissance, espionage, and even attacks in cyberspace because of the relatively low costs of entry, the perceived payoff, and the lack of significant consequences."[3] This is likely due in part to the current lack of consensus on constraining international norms, which will be discussed in detail in this chapter. Previously, Director Clapper testified that the growing international use of these emerging-technology weapons to achieve strategic objectives was outpacing the development of a shared understanding or norms of behavior and thus increasing the prospects for miscalculations and escalation.[4] Today, relatively early into the age of OCO, many scholars and policymakers hold a view regarding the inevitability of significant use of force in cyberspace similar to that held early in the nuclear era.[5] In expectation that norms will emerge, in May 2011 the Obama administration issued the *International Strategy for Cyberspace*.[6] One pillar of this strategy recognizes the "borderless" international dimension of cyberspace and identifies the need to achieve stability and address cyber threats through the development of international norms. In 2013, Michael Daniel, the White House cybersecurity coordinator, told computer security practitioners that diplomacy, including fostering international norms and shared expectations, is essential to prevent OCO against US economic interests. This chapter discusses how constraining norms for OCO are actually developing and offers some predictions—based on norm evolution theory for emerging-technology weapons—for how they will develop in the future.[7] Some scholars think that great powers will inevitably cooperate and establish rules, norms, and standards for cyberspace.[8] Whilst it is true that increased competition may create incentives for cooperation on constraining norms, norm evolution theory for emerging-technology weapons leads one to conclude that constraining norms for cyberwarfare will face many challenges and may never successfully emerge.

Some of these challenges were also presented by the advent of other emerging-technology weapons in historic cases such as chemical and biological weapons, strategic bombing, and nuclear weapons. An analysis of these three historic examples offers valuable lessons that lead to the development of norm evolution theory tailored for emerging-technology weapons, which can then be applied to OCO to better evaluate whether or not the authors' conclusions are well founded. This chapter first defines emerging-technology weapons and norm evolution theory, then briefly reviews the current state of international norms for OCO. Next, it illustrates norm evolution theory for emerging-technology weapons— grounded in the three historic case studies—and prospects for current norms between China, Russia, and the United States. Third, it presents a refined theory of norm development as a framework to evaluate norm emergence that contradicts the authors' thesis. This argument leads to the conclusion that a constraining international order in cyberspace is far from inevitable.

Emerging-technology weapons and norm evolution theory

Emerging-technology weapons are weapons based on new technology or a novel employment of older technologies to achieve certain effects. Given that technology is constantly advancing, weapons that initially fall into this category will eventually no longer be considered emergent. For example, the gunpowder-based weapons that began to spread in fourteenth-century Europe would clearly be classified as emerging-technology weapons in that century, and perhaps in the fifteenth century, but eventually these weapons were no longer novel and became fairly ubiquitous.[9] Chemical weapons up to the early twentieth century could be considered an emerging-technology weapon. Likewise, strategic bombing up to World War II falls into this category. Nuclear and biological weapons could be considered emerging-technology weapons during World War II and the immediate years that followed. Today, cyber weapons used to conduct computer network attack (CNA) are emerging-technology weapons. In general, norm evolution theory identifies three major stages in a norm's potential life cycle. These three stages are: (1) norm emergence, (2) norm cascade, and (3) norm internalization.[10] In the latter two phases, a norm is often codified first through customary international law (a legally binding consensus on what constitutes lawful behavior based on historic practices) and then often through binding international treaties and conventions.[11] The primary hypothesis of norm evolution theory for emerging-technology weapons is that a state's self-interest will play a significant role and a norm's convergence with perceived state self-interest will be important to achieving norm emergence and a state acting as a norm leader. This theory further states that norms are more likely to emerge when vital actors are involved, specifically key states acting as norm leaders, and norm entrepreneurs within organizations. The two primary intergovernmental bodies and organizations currently being used to promote emerging norms for OCO are the United Nations (UN) and the North Atlantic Treaty Organization (NATO).[12] Additionally, there are some other key multilateral efforts to encourage the development of cyber norms, such as the London Conference on Cyberspace (and subsequent conferences) and academic cyber norm workshops.[13]

The case for norm evolution theory

What does norm evolution theory for emerging-technology weapons predict regarding the development of constrictive international norms? The three examples of chemical and biological weapons, strategic bombing, and nuclear weapons are particularly salient historic case studies when considering norm evolution for OCO due to a variety of reasons.

Chemical and biological weapons and cyber weapons are both non-conventional weapons that share many of the same special characteristics with significant international security implications. They include challenges of attribution following their use, attractiveness to weaker powers and non-state actors as asymmetric weapons, use as a force multiplier for conventional military operations, questionable deterrence value, target and weapon unpredictability, potential for major collateral damage or unintended consequences due to "borderless" domains, multi-use nature of the associated technologies, and the frequent use of covert programs to develop such weapons.[14] Due to these characteristics, both of these weapons are also attractive to non-state actors or those seeking anonymity. The involvement of these non-state actors, as well as state actors exploiting the anonymity possible with OCO, results in a lack of clarity regarding the responsible party.

Strategic bombing—particularly with the advent of airpower as an emerging-technology weapon and the early use of airplanes to drop bombs on cities—forced states to grapple with a brand new technology and approach to warfare; as is now the case with OCO. As with chemical and biological weapons, strategic bombing shares some special characteristics with cyberwarfare. Strategic bombing made civilian populations highly vulnerable, was difficult to defend against, and used technology which also had peaceful applications (air travel and transport)—all of which can also be said about OCO today. The effort to constrain strategic bombing through normative influences was mixed and at times completely unsuccessful, which makes it particularly well suited as an exemplar of the limits of norms and how other factors may impede or reverse norm development.[15] Soon, British Bomber Command decided to pursue a policy of "dehousing" by explicitly striking German residential targets.[16]

Finally, nuclear weapons, like airpower before them and perhaps cyber weapons today, presented states with a challenge of a completely new and emerging warfighting technology. Nuclear weapons and cyber weapons, like the other emerging-technology case studies, share many of the same special characteristics with significant international security implications. These include the potential for major collateral damage or unintended consequences (due to fallout, in the case of nuclear weapons) and covert development programs. Because of these common attributes, valuable lessons can be learned regarding norm development. Additionally, a framework based on these lessons can be developed that is applicable to predicting the prospects of constraining norms as a tool to address the use of cyber weapons.

Examining how norm evolution theory, informed by the three historic case studies mentioned above, specifically applies to norms for emerging-technology weapons allows for a more informed prediction regarding the prospects of norm emergence for OCO.[17] When these three case studies are considered, the primary reason for developing constraining norms for emerging-technology weapons is the perception among powerful or relevant states that such norms are in their national self-interest. That is, a direct or indirect alignment of national self-interest with a constraining norm leads to norm emergence and the extent to which it is aligned with key or powerful states' perception of self-interest will determine how rapidly and effectively the norm emerges. The role of national self-interest as the primary ingredient leading to norm emergence also helps explain why, when challenged with violations of a young and not-yet-internalized norm, a state is quick to abandon the norm and pursue its material interest by using the previously constrained emerging-technology weapon, as seen with both chemical and biological weapons and strategic bombing in World War I and strategic bombing in World War II.

Prospects for cyberwarfare norms

The key principle of norm evolution theory for emerging-technology weapons is that norm emergence is more likely to occur when powerful, relevant actors are involved, specifically key states acting as norm leaders and norm entrepreneurs within organizations. There are a variety of intergovernmental bodies and organizations currently being used by a variety of states to promote various emerging norms for OCO. Through these organizations, a variety of actors, motivated by a number of factors and employing a range of mechanisms, have promoted various candidate cyber norms, ranging from a total prohibition on cyber weapons and warfare, to a no first-use policy, and the applicability of the existing laws of armed conflict to OCO. Norm evolution theory would thus seem to interpret this as a sign of progress for norm emergence. However, if one examines these efforts more closely, the prospects are less promising.

Powerful states, constraining norms, and self-interest

Powerful self-interested state actors play a significant role in norm emergence. Additionally, the perceived state self-interest is important for norms to emerge and for a state to become a leader of a particular norm. Successful norm emergence requires states as norm leaders and increasing multipolarity is unlikely to help. After all, there were eight great powers in 1910 and that complicated rather than fueled the convergence of a constraining norm for strategic bombing. Since there is generally less exposure and understanding surrounding cyber weapons as well as different rates of weapon adoption and cyber vulnerability, states will be reluctant to lead on the issue of norms because they may be unable to determine the utility of such weapons relative to their own interests. However, such calculations are essential if important and powerful states are going to become strong norm leaders and help promote the emerging norm. Additionally, with regards to China, Russia, and the United States—the preeminent cyber actors—an analysis of their respective cyber doctrines indicates that there appears to be a perspective that each nation has more to gain from engaging in OCO than from significantly restricting it or giving it up entirely. National investments in cyberwarfare capabilities and the development of doctrine and strategies for OCO provide insight into state perceptions of self-interest and the expectations for behavior and emerging norms for OCO. So, where do state cyberwarfare programs stand today in China, Russia, and the United States? The three key states discussed here are the most significant, both due to the breadth and sophistication of their capabilities and activities as well as the likelihood that they are serving as the model for many other nations preparing to operate in cyberspace.

Chinese interest in cyberwarfare

China's early activity and interest in OCO indicate that it likely does not consider the emergence of constraining norms in its self-interest. It has been largely unconstrained by cyber norms and is preparing to use cyber weapons to cause economic harm, damage critical infrastructure, and influence kinetic armed conflict. As such, it is unlikely to be a vocal norm leader. China is best known for its expansive efforts in conducting espionage-style cyber operations. For example, in February 2013, the US cybersecurity firm Mandiant released a study detailing extensive and systematic cyberattacks originating from Chinese military facilities of at least 141 separate US-affiliated commercial and government targets, and in May 2014, the Department of Justice indicted five Chinese military hackers for computer network exploitation (CNE) activity in the United States.[18] These attacks have led the US DoD to classify China as "the world's most active and persistent perpetrators of economic espionage" and point out that they are also "looking at ways to use cyber for offensive operations."[19] It is this latter point that is of most interest to this chapter. China is increasingly developing and fielding advanced capabilities in cyberspace whilst its interests in OCO appear to be asymmetric and strategic. For example, China's military doctrine envisions striking first with OCO during a conflict.[20] Whilst China and the United States agreed in September 2015 that they will not knowingly conduct CNE theft of intellectual property for commercial advantage, there is evidence that China is not living up to its end of the bargain.[21]

Russian interest in cyberwarfare

Like China, Russia's early OCO activity—especially the disruptive distributed denial of service attacks on Estonia and the use of OCO as a force multiplier for kinetic operations in Georgia and Ukraine—indicates that it is largely unconstrained by restrictive cyber norms and is preparing to use cyber weapons in a wide range of conflicts and against a variety of targets. It likely does not consider the emergence of constraining norms in its self-interest. As such, one would think it unlikely to be a vocal norm leader. However, Russia has been a leading proponent of a total ban on cyber weapons. This is similar to the Soviet Union's efforts early in the nuclear era to demonize US possession of nuclear weapons whilst simultaneously pursuing such weapons itself. This helps illustrate how powerful states acting in their own self-interest can inadvertently act as norm leaders despite flouting the candidate norm itself. However, Russia's confusing support for fully constraining norms for OCO (based on its behavior in the UN and proposal for an "International Code of Conduct for Information Security") may be based on its broader definition of OCO and its interest in using a constraining norm to prevent what it perceives as "propaganda" inside Russia and in its near abroad.[22] But its position may also be disingenuous, as it was when supporting the Biological Weapons Convention in the early 1970s whilst simultaneously launching a massive, illicit, biological weapons program.[23] To achieve any real convergence among the main cyber actors, the authoritarian interest in constraining free speech must be addressed, which could deflate Russian support. This is because Russia's current conception of cyber conflict includes information operations and persuasion via a free and open media. Further, Russian doctrine now states that future conflict will entail the "early implementation of measures of information warfare to achieve political objectives without the use of military force, and in the future to generate a favorable reaction of the international community to use military force."[24]

US interest in cyberwarfare

Whilst China is perhaps the noisiest and Russia the most secretive when it comes to OCO, the United States is the most sophisticated. The United States is in the process of dramatically expanding its military organization committed to engaging in OCO and regularly engages in these operations.[25] However, unlike Russian attacks and Chinese planning, it appears to exercise restraint and avoid targeting nonmilitary targets. This seems to indicate that the United States is acting as a norm leader for at least a certain category of constraining cyber norms, although its general "militarization" of cyberspace may be negating the norm-promoting effects of this restraint. Whilst the United States has recently developed classified rules of engagement for OCO, it has articulated few, if any, limits on its use of force in cyberspace or response to hostile OCOs.[26] For example, the May 2011 *International Strategy for Cyberspace* states that the United States "reserves the right to use all necessary means" to defend itself and its allies and partners, but that it will "exhaust all options before [the use of] military force."[27] Additionally, the former US Deputy Secretary of Defense, William Lynn, clearly asserted that "the United States reserves the right, under the law of armed conflict, to respond to serious cyberattacks with an appropriate, proportional, and justified military response."[28] Ultimately, US behavior and interest in cyberwarfare indicate that it does not consider the emergence of robust constraining norms for OCO as a priority relative to its self-interest.

Secondary factors affecting norm emergence[29]

Norm evolution theory for emerging-technology weapons also recognizes secondary reasons for norm development, some of which are examined below in more detail.[30]

Coherence with existing dominant norms unlikely

Should current trends continue, the outlook for coherence with existing norms is not favorable when applied to OCO. First, cyber norms will have difficulty achieving coherence with, and grafting onto, existing norms. Unfortunately, the success of a norm candidate for emerging-technology weapons also will depend in large part on the ability to achieve coherence by connecting the new weapon type to an existing category and, thus, beginning the process of grafting the new norm onto existing norms. Whilst cyber weapons and OCO have some commonalities with certain weapons—particularly unconventional and emerging-technology weapons—overall, they are truly unique. In fact, they are so unique as to operate in their own new, man-made and changeable domain outside the normal domains of land, sea, air, and space. As such, cyber norms lack obvious coherence with many prominent norms and, thus, it is difficult for norm entrepreneurs to graft the candidate norms to existing norms. For example, cyber weapons do not align with the characteristics of nuclear weapons that led to constraining nuclear norms, such as the sheer destructiveness of a single weapon and the assuredness of that destruction.[31] Cyber weapons are truly unique. Perhaps the best option for success is the humanitarian norm underlying the existing laws of armed conflict, particularly the norm regarding the protection of civilians and minimization of collateral damage.[32] This is precisely what NATO's *Tallinn Manual on the International Law Applicable to Cyber Warfare* attempts to achieve by arguing that the laws of armed conflict apply to OCO.[33] However, the lack of agreement on key terms and confusion over the spectrum of hostile cyber operations make coherence and grafting complex and difficult.[34]

Too late to preemptively establish norms for cyberwarfare

Another challenge for norm emergence is that a prospective constraining norm will be more successful if the candidate norm can be permanently and preemptively established before the weapon exists or is fully capable or widespread. With OCO, the train has already left the station, so to speak. Between 2006 and 2013, James Lewis and the Center for Strategic and International Studies identified 16 significant CNA-style cyberattacks.[35] These included major attacks around the globe, occurring in the former Soviet states of Estonia and Georgia to Iran and Saudi Arabia. The opportunity for permanent preemptive establishment of a norm has long since passed.

Differing perspectives on future capability and threat inflation

There will be challenges for the emergence of a constraining norm for OCO arising from both differing perspectives as to future capability as well as the prospect for threat inflation. Whilst it is true OCO have been demonstrated to some degree (e.g., Stuxnet, etc.), the hidden and secretive nature of cyberspace make the actors and their intent unclear, thus limiting the true demonstrative value of recent cyberattacks. Issues of attribution create competing theories and arguments as to future effectiveness and strategic impact. As a case in point, some (including former US Secretary of Defense Leon Panetta) argue that OCO poses a major threat and warn of a "cyber Pearl Harbor" or "cyber 9/11" moment when critical infrastructure is attacked. Others have argued that statements such as Panetta's are pure hyperbole and that OCO poses no such dire threat and that it in fact may not even constitute warfare as properly defined.[36] In the December 2013 edition of *Foreign Affairs*, Thomas Rid argued that not only is cyberattack not a major threat, but that it will in fact "diminish rather than accentuate political violence" by offering states and other actors a new mechanism to engage in aggression below the threshold of war.[37] Erik Gartzke argued further that cyberwarfare is "unlikely to prove as pivotal in world affairs … as many observers seem to believe."[38] However, cybersecurity is a huge and booming business for IT-security firms, with industry market research firms predicting that the global cybersecurity market will grow from $106.32 billion in 2015 to $170.21 billion by 2020.[39] IT-security expert Bruce Schneier has alleged that these firms benefiting from cyber growth have, along with their government customers, artificially hyped the cyber threat.[40] Some critics have gone so far as to refer to this dynamic as "cyber doom" rhetoric or a "cybersecurity-industrial complex" similar to the oft-derided "defense-industrial complex."[41] Norm evolution theory applied in this case indicates that these vastly different perceptions—both within the West and even more broadly when including China and Russia—of the impact and role of OCO in international relations and conflict will impair norm emergence, as was the case early in the twentieth century when the role and impact of strategic airpower was highly contested.

Defenseless perception impact

The notion that cyber weapons cannot be defended against will fuel interest in a constraining norm but also limits the effectiveness of reciprocal agreements and can lead to weapon proliferation. As a result, once convention-dependent norms are violated, intense domestic pressure can build for retaliatory violations of the norm. Defenses against cyber weapons are largely viewed as inadequate. A report from DoD's Defense Science Board reported in January 2013 that the United States "cannot be confident" that critical IT systems can be defended from a well-resourced cyber adversary.[42] The nature of cyberspace, with intense secrecy and "zero-day" vulnerabilities, makes defense particularly difficult and fuels interest in other strategies to manage the threat, including constraining international norms. This explains the broad range of actors and organizations involved in early norm promotion and is a positive factor for the successful emergence of norms for OCO. However, the experience of norms for emerging-technology weapons with similar perceptions regarding the weakness of defenses also indicates that whilst this may fuel interest in cultivating norms, they will be fragile. This experience also indicates that the most successful norms will apply to use and not proliferation as actors will continue to develop and pursue the weapons as they believe they cannot rely on defenses and seek deterrence-in-kind capabilities. Further, if an early norm is violated, given the inability to defend against continued violations, there may be domestic pressure to respond in kind, leading to a rapid erosion of the norm. Should early cyber norms be violated, such domestic pressure for a response in kind could build. In fact, the Iranian attack on Saudi Aramco in August 2012 is largely viewed as one of Iran's responses to Stuxnet.[43] The challenge of attribution in cyberspace may accentuate this dynamic by making retaliatory responses even easier than with prior emerging-technology weapons.

Unitary dominance and delayed proliferation and adoption

Weapon proliferation and adoption will play a significant role in norm emergence, as it will influence state interest in constraining norms. For OCO, there is not the kind of unitary dominance of a single actor as there was with the US monopoly in the early nuclear age—giving the United States significant influence on norm emergence regarding nuclear restraint. Additionally, given the ongoing proliferation of cyber weapons, the multi-use nature of the technology and the relatively low cost of entry, delays in proliferating cyber weapons is unlikely. However, there will likely be varied rates of adoption of cyber weapons, with some nations such as the United States, China, Russia, and Israel possessing the most sophisticated cyber warheads.[44] Experience with norm development for emerging-technology weapons indicates that states with powerful cyber weapons are more likely to resist the emergence of any constraining norms. This is especially true with strong bureaucratic actors, such as the National Security Agency (NSA) in the United States or the Federal Agency of Government Communications and Information in Russia, potentially advocating for permissive norms. Whilst the Russians have been major advocates in the UN for a total prohibition on cyber weapons, their interest may be driven by a perception that the United States is the dominant cyber power or, perhaps more cynically, it could be akin to the Soviet Union's disingenuous early promotion of the constraining biological weapon and nuclear norms whilst simultaneously pursuing biological and nuclear weapons. Regardless, the varied rates of adoption and development of cyber capabilities indicate that there will be divergent perspectives on constraining norms, making consensus difficult.

Ultimately, if current trends continue, norm evolution theory for emerging-technology weapons predicts that the emergence and early development of constraining norms will be challenged and may not occur at all. Key states—especially China, Russia, and the United States—are unlikely to perceive the emergence of robust constraining norms in their self-interest. Further, limited options for coherence and grafting, inability to preemptively establish a prohibition, lack of unitary dominance, increased proliferation and adoption of cyber weapons, and the lack of powerful self-interested state actors converging on a candidate norm present serious hurdles for norm emergence. However, the connection with the idea that cyber weapons cannot be adequately defended against as well as industry and government hyping of the threat have spurred significant general interest in constraining norms for OCO—leading to a rise of many actors and organizational platforms, such as most Western nations active in the UN, NATO, and the G-20. To move past this point and achieve success, a consensus on cyber norms will need to be built, which does not seem inevitable at this point or in the near future.

Secondary factors affecting prospects for norm cascade and internalization

Whilst norm evolution theory for emerging-technology weapons predicts low odds for constraining OCO norms, should norms emerge it is worth briefly examining what the theory predicts about achieving norm cascade and internalization. These latter two phases in the norm life cycle are important if a norm is to have a structural impact on the international system. If a constraining cyber norm emerges and approaches a norm cascade, then a tipping point may actually be more likely. Certain indicators are important to achieving a norm cascade, such as potential technological improvements that mitigate the attribution challenge, the unconventional characterization afforded to cyber weapons, and the expansive international arms control and disarmament bureaucracy. However, should the norm cascade occur, internalizing it will be less likely largely due to secrecy and the multi-use nature of cyber technologies which pose their own barriers to internalization and blunt international pressure for conformity and private-sector support. As a result, norm internalization is likely to be most successful for norms governing usage rather than development, proliferation, and disarmament. Table 4.1 summarizes the implications of the various hypotheses

Table 4.1 Norm evolution theory for emerging-technology weapons' implications for norms for cyberwarfare[45]

Primary hypothesis	Implications for cyber norms
Direct or indirect alignment of national self-interest with a constraining norm leads to norm emergence, and the extent to which it is aligned with key or powerful states' perception of self-interest will determine how rapidly and effectively the norm emerges.	Negative

Secondary hypotheses for norm emergence	Implications for cyber norms
1 Coherence and grafting with existing norms.	Negative
2 Permanently establishing a norm before the weapon exists or is fully capable or widespread.	Negative
3 Undemonstrated emerging-technology weapons.	Negative
4 Connections with the idea that the weapon can't be defended against.	Positive
5 Initial weapon proliferation/adoption.	Negative

Secondary hypotheses for norm cascade	Implications for cyber norms
1 Improvements in technology.	Positive
2 Characterizing the weapon type as unconventional or otherwise granting it a special status.	Positive
3 Public demonstrations of the weapon type, enabled by real-time media.	Negative
4 The international arms control and disarmament bureaucracy and the increasing regulation and legalization of armed conflict.	Positive

Secondary hypotheses for norm internalization	Implications for cyber norms
1 Internalization of aspects of a norm governing usage rather than aspects governing development, proliferation, and disarmament.	Positive
2 Congruent support and involvement from the public and private sectors.	Negative
3 Secrecy and the multi-use nature of the technology.	Negative
4 International pressure for conformity, enabled by real-time media coverage of the weapon's use.	Negative

of norm evolution theory for emerging-technology weapons when applied to cyberwarfare.

Leaks further impair states supporting a constraining norm

The Snowden leaks may have introduced more distrust than already existed among adversaries and allies alike to complicate and hamper a convergence of norms among states. When reporting on classified documents provided by Edward Snowden began, including documents outlining offensive cyberattacks, suddenly the spotlight was on US cyber activity and the breadth and nature of its secret offensive actions in cyberspace thus far.[46]

The purported revelations regarding the extent of the NSA cyber intelligence collection efforts led some US allies such as Germany and Finland to begin to construct their own independent IT infrastructure, such as fiber-optic cables.[47] Additionally, France has launched its own data counter-surveillance efforts and Brazil's president cancelled a state visit to the United States and decried the NSA activities as "an assault on national sovereignty."[48] This led David DeWalt, chairman of cybersecurity firm FireEye, to predict that there will be increasing "cyber Balkanization" with more cyber nationalism and less international cooperation.[49] The current Snowden leaks alone will likely have an impact on the evolution of constraining OCO norms; however, more leaks are likely coming. Future leaks could fracture state interests and increase national secrecy of cyber weapon programs and distrust of US intentions and those of other powerful cyber actors. This type of effect was evidenced by a Russian government source claiming in late 2013 that "Washington has lost the moral authority" in cyberspace and that support for the Russian UN First Committee cyber resolution—titled "Developments in the Field of Information and Telecommunications in the Context of International Security"—was growing and the cyber-focused UN Group of Government Experts becoming more Russian-friendly.[50] It appears that powerful support from self-interested actors has not converged on a comprehensive constraining norm for OCO and recent developments may make such a convergence less likely.

Conclusion

Cyberwarfare is still in its relative infancy, and there are multiple possibilities for how this new mode of warfare will evolve over the coming decades. However, reasonable conclusions can be drawn regarding the prospects for the emergence of a constraining norm for OCO based on norm evolution theory for emerging-technology weapons.[51] The theory indicates there are many hurdles facing the development of constraining norms for OCO and predicts that if current trends continue, constraining norms for OCO will have trouble emerging and may not ever reach a norm cascade. This is principally due to the fact that powerful state actors are unlikely to perceive a convergence between a robust constraining norm and their self-interest. Whilst the norm evolution theory for emerging-technology weapons predicts grim prospects for the evolution of constraining cyber norms, the threat of cyberwarfare is not diminishing. Realizing that constraining norms are unlikely to develop into a regime that could successfully manage and contain the threat is helpful as it allows policymakers to instead focus on more fruitful strategies for addressing this growing threat.

Notes

1 Ronald L. Jefferson, Alexander Wendt, and Peter J. Katzenstein, "Norms, Identity, and Culture in National Security Policy," in Peter J. Katzenstein (ed.), *The Culture of National Security: Norms and Identity in World Politics* (New York: Columbia University Press, 1996), 54.
2 James M. Gavin. *War and Peace in the Space Age* (New York: Harper, 1958), 265.
3 James R. Clapper, "Worldwide Threat Assessment," February 9, 2016, 3, at www.dni. gov/files/documents/Intelligence%20Reports/HPSCI%20WWTA%20Remarks%20 as%20delivered%2011%20April%202013.pdf.
4 Ibid., 1–3.
5 Offensive cyber operations are cyber operations intended to project power by the application of force in and through cyberspace. For examples of scholars and policy-makers who hold these views, see: Gary McGraw, "Cyber war is inevitable (unless we build security in)," *Journal of Strategic Studies* 36/1 (2013): 109–119; Kevin Downey, "Top Story: NSA Warns That Cyberwar in US is Inevitable," *Komando*, at www.komando.com/happening-now/349702/top-story-nsa-warns-that-cyberwar-in-u-s-is-inevitable/all.
6 White House, International Strategy for Cyberspace: Prosperity, Security, and Openness in a Networked World, May 2011, at www.whitehouse.gov/sites/default/files/ rss_viewer/international_strategy_for_cyberspace.pdf.
7 Brian Mazanec, *The Evolution of Cyber War: International Norms for Emerging Technology Weapons* (Lincoln: Potomac Books, 2015).
8 James W. Forsyth Jr. and Billy E. Pope. "Structural causes and cyber effects: Why international order is inevitable in cyberspace," *Strategic Studies Quarterly* 8/4 (2014): 113–130.
9 John Norris, *Early Gunpowder Artillery: 1300–1600* (Marlborough, UK: Crowood Press, 2003).
10 Martha Finnemore and Kathryn Sikkink, "International norm dynamics and political change," *International Organization* 52/4 (1998): 887–917.
11 Gary Brown and Keira Poellet, "The customary international law of cyberspace," *Strategic Studies Quarterly* 6/3 (2012): 132.
12 Many of the norms being discussed in the UN deal with peaceful use of cyberspace and not norms for OCO during or leading up to an armed conflict.
13 For example, see: United Kingdom Foreign and Commonwealth Office, "London Conference on Cyberspace: Chair's Statement," November 2, 2011, at www.gov.uk/ government/news/london-conference-on-cyberspace-chairs-statement; and Roger Hurwitz, "A Preliminary Report on the Cyber Norms Workshop," October 2011, at http:// citizenlab.org/cybernorms/preliminary_report.pdf.
14 Gregory Koblentz and Brian Mazanec, "Viral warfare: The security implications of cyber and biological weapons," *Comparative Strategy* 32/5 (2013): 418–434.
15 Charles K. Webster and Noble Frankland, *The Strategic Air Offensive against Germany: 1939–1945* (HM Stationery Office, 1961), 143–145.
16 Tami D. Biddle, "Air Power," in Michael Howard et al. (eds), *The Laws of War: Constraints on Warfare in the Western World* (New Haven: Yale University Press, 1994), 152.
17 Mazanec, *The Evolution of Cyber War*.
18 William Wan and Ellen Nakashima, "Report Ties Cyberattacks on US Computers to Chinese Military," *Washington Post*, February 19, 2013, at http://articles.washington-post.com/2013-02-19/world/37166888_1_chinese-cyber-attacks-extensive-cyber-espionage-chinese-military-unit; US Department of Justice Office of Public Affairs, "US Charges Five Chinese Military Hackers for Cyber Espionage Against US Corporations and a Labor Organization for Commercial Advantage," May 19, 2014, at www.justice.gov/opa/pr/us-charges-five-chinese-military-hackers-cyber-espionage-against-us-corporations-and-labor.

19 Anna Mulrine, "China Is a Lead Cyberattacker of US Military Computers, Pentagon Reports," *Christian Science Monitor*, May 18, 2012, at www.csmonitor.com/ USA/Military/2012/0518/China-is-a-lead-cyberattacker-of-US-military-computers-Pentagon-reports.
20 Jon R. Lindsay, Tai Ming Cheung, and Derek S. Reveron (eds), *China and Cybersecurity: Espionage, Strategy, and Politics in the Digital Domain* (Oxford: Oxford University Press, 2015), 142.
21 Editor, "China Already Violating US Cyberagreement, Group Says," *CBS News*, October 19, 2015, at www.cbsnews.com/news/crowdstrike-china-violating-cyber agreement-us-cyberespionage-intellectual-property/.
22 United Nations General Assembly, "A/66/359," September 14, 2011, at www.citizen-lab.org/cybernorms/letter.pdf.
23 Milton Leitenberg, Raymond A Zilinskas, and Jens H Kuhn, *The Soviet Biological Weapons Program: A History* (Cambridge: Harvard University Press, 2012).
24 Roland Heickerö, "Emerging Cyber Threats and Russian Views on Information Warfare and Information Operations," *Swedish Defence Research Agency* (2010): 27.
25 Jason Healey, "How Emperor Alexander Militarized American Cyberspace," *Foreign Policy*, November 22, 2013, at http://foreignpolicy.com/2013/11/06/how-emperor-alexander-militarized-American-cyberspace/.
26 The fact that these rules are classified also suggests that the United States is not particularly keen at this stage to communicate its own norms publicly. Security in this case appears to be more important than acting as a norm leader.
27 White House, *International Strategy for Cyberspace*, May 2011, 14; Ellen Nakashima, "In Cyberwarfare, What Is an 'Imminent' Threat?" *Washington Post*, March 11, 2013, A2.
28 William J. Lynn III, "The Pentagon's cyberstrategy, one year later," *Foreign Affairs*, September 28, 2011.
29 The designation of primary or secondary factors are relative designations based on the role each played in the emergence of norms for chemical and biological weapons, nuclear weapons, and strategic bombing. Measuring or quantifying the role each factor played is difficult.
30 Such as: coherence and grafting with existing norms; permanently establishing a norm before the weapon exists or is fully capable or widespread; threat inflation regarding the possible effects of the weapon often by the private sector via industry and lobbying groups; the idea a weapon cannot be defended against will fuel interest in a norm; unitary dominance of a single actor with the particular weapon type gives that actor significant influence in norm emergence for that weapon type; and delays in proliferation (often due to technological barriers) can create added time for a constraining norm to emerge.
31 Patrick Cirenza, "Cyberweapons Aren't Like Nuclear Weapons," *Slate*, March 15, 2016, at www.slate.com/articles/technology/future_tense/2016/03/cyberweapons_are_not_like_nuclear_weapons.html.
32 Martha Finnemore, "Cultivating International Cyber Norms," in Kristin M. Lord and Travis Sharp (eds), *America's Cyber Future: Security and Prosperity in the Information Age* (Washington, DC: Center for a New American Security, 2011), 99.
33 Michael N. Schmitt, *Tallinn Manual on The International Law Applicable to Cyber Warfare* (Cambridge: Cambridge University Press, 2013).
34 Brown and Poellet, "The customary international law of cyberspace," 141.
35 Based on author's analysis of: James Lewis, "Significant Cyber Events since 2006," Center for Strategic and International Studies, July 11, 2013, at http://csis.org/publication/cyber-events-2006.
36 Thomas Rid, *Cyber War Will Not Take Place* (Oxford: Oxford University Press, 2012).
37 Ibid.

38 Erik Gartzke, "The myth of cyberwar: Bringing war in cyberspace back down to earth," *International Security* 38/2 (2013): 42.
39 Editor, "Global Forecast to 2020," *Markets and Markets*, at www.marketsandmarkets. com/PressReleases/cyber-security.asp.
40 Bruce Schneier, "Threat of 'Cyberwar' Has Been Hugely Hyped," *CNN*, July 7, 2010, at www.cnn.com/2010/OPINION/07/07/schneier.cyberwar.hyped/.
41 Jerry Brito and Tate Watkins, "Loving the Cyber Bomb? The Dangers of Threat Inflation in Cybersecurity Policy," *Mercatus Center: George Mason University* (April 26, 2011) at http://mercatus.org/publication/loving-cyber-bomb-dangers-threat-inflation-cybersecurity-policy; Russia Today, "Is Cyberwar Hype Fueling a Cybersecurity-Industrial Complex?" February 16, 2012, at http://rt.com/usa/security-us-cyber-threat-529/.
42 United States Department of Defense. *Defense Science Board Task Force Report: Resilient Military Systems and the Advanced Cyber Threat* (January 2013), 1.
43 Nicole Perlroth, "In Cyberattack on Saudi Firm, US Sees Iran Firing Back," *New York Times*, October 24, 2012, A1.
44 As evidenced by the examination of customary state practice of cyberwarfare reviewed earlier in this chapter.
45 Reproduced from Brian M. Mazanec, *The Evolution of Cyber War: International Norms for Emerging-Technology Weapons* by permission of the University of Nebraska Press. Copyright 2015 by the Board of Regents of the University of Nebraska.
46 Barton Gellman and Ellen Nakashima, "'Black Budget' Details a War in Cyberspace," *Washington Post*, August 30, 2013, A1; Kurt Eichenwald, "How Edward Snowden Escalated Cyber War With China," *Newsweek*, November 1, 2013, at www. newsweek.com/how-edward-snowden-escalated-cyber-war-1461.
47 Tero Kuittinen, "NSA Spying Has Triggered a Crazy Chain Reaction of Countermeasure," *BGR*, December 16, 2013, at http://bgr.com/2013/12/16/nsa-spying-finland-fiber/.
48 Ibid.; Kathleen Hennessey and Vincent Bevins, "Brazil's President, Angry about Spying, Cancels State Visit to US," *Los Angeles Times*, September 17, 2013, at http://articles.latimes.com/2013/sep/17/world/la-fg-snowden-fallout-20130918.
49 David DeWalt, "Going There: The Year Ahead in Cyber Security," February 5, 2014, at http://recode.net/2014/02/05/going-there-the-year-ahead-in-cyber-security/.
50 Paul Meyer, "Cyber Security Takes the UN Floor," ICT4 Peace Foundation, November 11, 2013, at http://ict4peace.org/?p=3000.
51 Forsyth and Pope, "Structural causes and cyber effects," 123.

5 Developing an international cyberspace governance framework

Comparisons to outer space

*Tim Ridout**

As humanity develops technologies that enable it to accomplish new feats and reach previously inaccessible places, new forms of conflict typically follow. New potentialities, such as those that emerged regarding cyberspace in recent decades, often lead to struggles over distribution of gains, competition for resources, and disputes about how to guide and restrain novel human activities. This chapter seeks insights for cyberspace from processes of developing international governance frameworks for outer space.

Cyberspace is distinct from land, sea, air, and outer space because it requires human-made electronics in order to exist, which can be constantly redesigned and reprogrammed. Although other domains can be altered to some degree, cyberspace's greater capacity to morph, grow, and be shaped by different groups with varying agendas adds layers of complexity. The threat landscapes associated with each domain also differ significantly, but systemic human factors that lead to disputes, conflict, and war, change little across space and time. Among them are the mutual fear and suspicion inherent in the security dilemma;[1] questions about who determines rules of behavior in the international system;[2] authority and control, particularly relating to jurisdiction, liability, and dispute resolution;[3] negative externalities;[4] desires to preserve one's identity, culture, and way of life as well as in-group, out-group frictions;[5] free rider and collective action dynamics;[6] historic grievances; and unrestrained ambition. However, the physics of different domains vary, limiting what is technically feasible and dictating how certain desired outcomes can and cannot be achieved. In other words, people fight with each other for many deeply ingrained reasons, but the specific ways they do so change over time.

As philosopher John Dewey observed in 1935:

> We are always dependent upon the experience that has accumulated in the past and yet there are always new forces coming in, new needs arising, that demand, if the new forces are to operate and the new needs to be satisfied, a reconstruction of the patterns of old experience.[7]

In this sense, the Internet, wireless and space-based communications, fiber optics, and increasingly powerful computers, sensors, transmitters, and algorithms that enable all sorts of previously unthinkable feats are new forces in society that require "a reconstruction of the patterns of old experience."

Today, world society is experiencing disputes as well as forms of crime and conflict between states, non-state actors and states, and among non-state actors operating in cyberspace, with increasingly damaging and potentially escalatory effects. Due to their novelty and the diminished importance of geography and distance in cyberspace, the structures of human government are having difficulty adapting. Analyzing outer space as a point of comparison for cyberspace is instructive due to the similar institutional frameworks that existed when these two domains first generated broad concern. The challenges posed by outer space and modern cyberspace confronted humanity when the primary political bodies of human government were states, loosely woven together by regional organizations and the United Nations, which remains so today. Transnational networks, non-governmental organizations, and multinational corporations have become increasingly influential in managing human affairs since World War II, but the monopoly on the legitimate use of force, the power to make and enforce laws and treaties, and the power to tax continue to reside with states.

The term "cyberspace" generates some confusion, but it has recently been adopted by many state institutions and appears to be entering the broader lexicon. This chapter adapts information operations professor Daniel Kuehl's definition of cyberspace, defining it as:

> a global domain whose distinctive and unique character is framed by the use of electronics and the electromagnetic spectrum to capture or create, store, modify, exchange, and exploit information via interdependent and interconnected networks to produce kinetic and information effects.[8]

The electromagnetic spectrum exists all around us and is a natural phenomenon, but when electronics utilize it to transmit to each other it can be considered part of cyberspace.

Outer space is conceptually easier to grasp than cyberspace. This chapter defines it as the space beyond earth's atmosphere and in between other celestial bodies. However, precisely delineating where outer space begins from earth's perspective can be difficult and has implications for space vehicles and satellites. These objects rely on cyberspace to communicate information and transmit operational instructions between each other and earth-based command centers, utilizing radio waves. In fact, cyberspace has become essential to operations in all other domains.

Most technologies have multiple uses. Some are designed for military purposes, whereas others are initially designed for commercial or social purposes, but how these technologies are ultimately used and perceived depends to a degree on political circumstances. Despite a proliferation of international institutions and efforts to strengthen international law since World War II, a mutual perception of threat and the potential for escalation are often necessary for states to negotiate on contentious political issues with security implications. In order to comprehend new threats and opportunities such as those presented by cyberspace or outer space, one must understand the relevant scientific aspects of the domain and the technologies that permit its use. In the case of outer space, these include physics, engineering, rocketry, and propulsion, among others. For cyberspace, they also include physics and engineering, but with a greater focus on the electromagnetic spectrum, computational sciences, microchip manufacturing, and software engineering. One must also contemplate how utilizing these domains alters interpersonal, societal, and international dynamics. This is necessary to develop mutually understood international behavioral norms and laws that enjoy broad legitimacy, and that allow for peaceful, coordinated, and productive use of the domain whilst also punishing transgressors.

Through a comparative analysis focused on security concerns, this chapter argues that the process of developing such international governance frameworks is characterized by the complex interplay of strategic rivalry, technological advancement, economic ambitions, security concerns, and international dialogue. Competitive pressures drive development of technologies and tactics which, in turn, opens up new possibilities for various actors to engage in conflict. Moreover, desires to employ new technologies for economic and social benefits drive their development and adoption, which may unintentionally create vulnerabilities in societies. New capabilities and behavioral changes sometimes increase tensions and elicit responses from other actors, which can fuel security dilemma dynamics. International institutions, interaction, and strategic dialogue among allies, rivals, and neutral parties help develop mutually understood terminology, situation definitions, conceptual frameworks, and norms through both analogic and inductive reasoning, whilst domestic political systems and economic considerations shape preference formation at the international level. Importantly, these processes are iterative and never complete. After illustrating broader contexts whilst drawing on examples and theoretical work to describe and explain patterns, trends, and trajectories,[9] the chapter concludes that work at the UN on cyberspace is less robust than it was for outer space, which slows preference formation and fragments dialogue.

Outer space geopolitical context, threats, and opportunities

The 1950s through 1980s were characterized by intense military, economic, and political competition between the United States and the Soviet Union, with proxy wars and near-confrontations but also periods of détente. This bipolar power structure divided the world into states that were either aligned with one of the superpowers or non-aligned. The North Atlantic Treaty Organization (NATO) linked the United States and its Western European allies, whereas the Soviet Union relied on the Warsaw Pact to bind Eastern European countries to it.

In the early outer space years, geopolitical tensions combined with uncertainty about technical possibilities and related military doctrines to generate fears of worst-case scenarios, primarily related to nuclear weapons because the possibility of their delivery through outer space was contemplated by political and military leaders from the beginning.

The Soviet launch of Sputnik in October 1957, the first human-made satellite to reach orbit, marked a turning point when theoretical discussions about human activity in outer space became reality. The same missile technology that delivered Sputnik to outer space could be used to send missiles through outer space and hit cities and military installations from a previously unimaginable distance. Prior to the Soviet launch of the first intercontinental ballistic missile (ICBM) in August 1957, the most effective way to deliver a nuclear warhead was by airplane or cruise missile. Bombers took longer to reach their targets and cruise missiles required greater proximity. These limitations allowed for more advanced warning and the possibility of shooting down bombers or destroying nearby missile launchers, a feat easier than intercepting an ICBM due to its speed and altitude. In 1960, the United States successfully launched the first submarine-launched ballistic missile (SLBM), adding a third effective delivery platform to nuclear arsenals. The Soviet Union sent the first man into outer space in 1961, followed by the United States in 1962, which opened new theoretical possibilities for space-based warfare.

Though the development of missile technologies was primarily driven by militarized superpower competition, satellites promised immense possibilities for global communications and remote sensing. Once the capacity to put them in orbit was developed, governments and telecommunications companies quickly sought to use them for scientific and commercial purposes, further stimulating the development of missiles, satellites, and space vehicles. But there was no governance framework in place to manage the new domain. For example:

> In 1960 AT&T filed with the Federal Communications Commission for permission to launch an experimental communications satellite with a view to rapidly implementing an operational system. The US government reacted with surprise—there was no policy in place to help execute the many decisions related to the AT&T proposal.[10]

After the advent of satellites, ICBMs, and SLBMs, it took years of debate, experimentation, strategic analysis, and learning before states formed preferences regarding the outer space domain. As Professor James Clay Moltz observed, the United States and Soviet Union tested nuclear weapons nine times in outer space between 1957 and 1962, emitting damaging electromagnetic pulses and energy apart from the blasts themselves.

> By the fall of 1962, however, the two sides had begun to recognize that nuclear testing and unfettered military competition in space had self-damaging consequences for both sides and increased the possibility of nuclear war. The Cuban Missile Crisis stimulated a process of mutual learning that had already begun with regard to space.[11]

Meanwhile, US civilian strategists had been developing new understandings of nuclear deterrence throughout the 1950s and 1960s that took into account the latest missile technologies, and influenced leadership and broader debates about outer space. Dubbed the "Wizards of Armageddon" by journalist Fred Kaplan,[12] they engaged in dialogue with Soviet strategists and helped advance common understandings of strategic dynamics whilst nuclear warheads were detonated around the world. Nuclear arms control treaties were also negotiated at the UN in an effort to reduce testing and proliferation. This led to the 1963 Limited Test Ban Treaty and the 1970 Nuclear Non-Proliferation Treaty. The initial outer space governance framework was laid down in this tense, militarized context in which fears of mass destruction were quite real.

Outer space debates, concepts, and codification of norms

The UN Committee on the Peaceful Uses of Outer Space (COPUOS) was formed as an ad hoc committee in 1958 and made permanent in 1959. It contains a scientific and technical subcommittee and a legal subcommittee. States haggled over the committee's balance between "East," "West," and non-aligned as well as mutually acceptable negotiating and voting procedures. Consisting of 24 member states in 1959, COPUOS prepared and presented numerous resolutions adopted by the UN General Assembly prior to completing the Outer Space Treaty (OST) in 1967. Years of debate and non-binding resolutions allowed governments to work toward consensus before committing to a binding treaty. The OST laid down core principles upon which outer space governance is built, including legal classification, liability, jurisdiction over objects and personnel, prohibition on placing weapons of mass destruction, and notification of activities. It is thin on details and was never intended to be the last step in rule-making processes. As historian Walter McDougall put it, "space technology was moving very quickly; international legal committees move slowly. As specific uses and interests emerged, then nations could hammer out temporary conventions. But of the general charter for space, the spirit, not the letter, was the essence."[13]

Beginning in 1959, the UN International Telecommunications Union (ITU) was empowered to regulate use of outer space radio spectrum, and it began implementing physical spacing rules in 1971 to avoid radio frequency interference for satellites using geostationary orbital slots.[14] Coordinated management of these rival resources is necessary to avoid overcrowding and collision as well as to control satellites and space vehicles.

UN and bilateral discussions were informed by debate among political and military elite, international lawyers, scientists, private telecommunications companies, and others about potential implications of specific situation definitions and norms. Strategic thinking and ambitions were intertwined with rule-making. Classifying outer space, regulating satellites, and delimiting between airspace and outer space were all informed by scientific realities, existing and potential capabilities, and the incentive structure that different definitions and rules would create. M. J. Peterson referred to this as "the interplay of interest calculations and analogic reasoning."[15]

Early debates on outer space were speculative and dialectic due to novelty and uncertainty. A quote from a 1957 article by international lawyer Myres McDougal is illustrative:

> With regard to outer space and customary international law, both Mr. Jenks, in a general way, and Professor Cooper, more specifically, have expressed the thought that the principle of the freedom of the seas appears to be the most relevant analogy…. For a recoverable satellite it suffices to mention that there is, of course, the possibility of unauthorized entry into traditional airspace of underlying states as well as of damage, and apprehension of damage, to structures on the earth.[16]

The urgency of building an outer space governance framework led to a decision to classify outer space by analogic rather than inductive reasoning. The perceived imminence of nuclear war made slow, inductive processes undesirable at the time. Airspace analogies would have extended state jurisdiction over their territory into outer space. Soviet leaders initially favored this approach because they were concerned about US spy satellites over their territory, which could mean a loss of advantage in terms of intelligence gathering because US society was more open than Soviet society.[17] If airspace analogies were used, this would have established a right to shoot down satellites over territory, even during peacetime.[18] Scientifically, extending airspace above territory made little sense because earth's position is continuously shifting relative to specific portions of outer space.

High seas analogies implied defining outer space as a commons, including for spy satellites and in support of earth-based military activities. These analogies by themselves also meant the Moon and celestial bodies would be treated like islands, subject to appropriation into state domain by whoever established effective control, which could have led to intense competition. Such analogies were eventually adopted for outer space, but were supplemented with analogies from the 1959 Antarctic Treaty with regards to the Moon and other celestial bodies, which prohibited "any measures of a military nature, such as the establishment of military bases and fortifications, the carrying out of military maneuvers, as well as the testing of any type of weapons."[19] This avoided creating a costly and destabilizing incentive structure and was also inspired by real-world similarities. As Peterson put it:

> both Antarctic explorers and astronauts needed a level of supply requiring large support teams and budgets. The relatively long distance from other continents and the difficulty of the climate meant that military and other installations would be hard to defend from attack.[20]

Delimiting a boundary between airspace and outer space was also debated. In scientific terms, there is no clear line dictated by nature where airspace ends and outer space begins. Concentrations of gases in earth's atmosphere gradually thin out to the end of the exosphere at roughly 10,000 km distance from earth, at which point the airless void of outer space begins. However, delimitation in legal terms aids in questions of jurisdiction and establishing rules for distinct types of spaces. Some suggested the Kármán line of 100 km above sea level. This line is used by NASA and the World Air Sports Federation to determine "space flight" and is a rough estimate of the point below which significant lateral thrust is needed to maintain aerodynamic lift. However, "such 'lines' were a function of velocity and therefore of technology, and were in no way innate."[21] If the delimitation were too high, satellites with an orbit dipping below it could be shot down. If it were too low, states would lose sovereign control over part of their airspace, which could lead to intrusive actions. Since few parties wanted to constrain future operations as capabilities advanced, the question was left undecided and remains so today.

Other issues included questions of liability, jurisdiction, coordination, and control. These were resolved in principle by assigning international responsibility and liability over objects and people to the states to which they were registered. For non-governmental entities, states retained jurisdiction over their activities depending on their nationality, whereas responsibility for activities of international organizations were jointly borne by the organizations and the states comprising them.[22] Subsequent treaties on the return of astronauts and space objects, liability, registration, and the Moon entered into force between 1968 and 1984, which further fleshed out principles adopted in the OST.[23] Though the Moon Treaty has technically entered into force, only 17 countries—and no major space powers—have ratified it, so it is generally not considered a meaningful source of space law.

The OST and subsequent treaties lacked enforcement mechanisms, but they codified principles that had emerged through years of debate and state practice. Political scientists Koremenos, Lipson, and Snidal find that:

> Uncertainty is a frequent obstacle to cooperation, as is "noise," the difficulty of observing others' actions clearly. States are naturally reluctant to disclose vital information that could make them more vulnerable. Reducing uncertainty among participants is a major function of institutions.[24]

Thus, among the most important functions of the OST was to reduce uncertainty in a volatile international environment by providing agreed upon definitions and general behavioral guidelines. Moreover, treaty negotiations entailed purposeful interaction and strategic dialogue.

The emotional, affective, and cognitive effects of greater clarity are significant because threat perception and anxiety have linkages to uncertainty,[25] which is a primary driving force behind the security dilemma. These more granular understandings of the human mind provided by modern neuroscience offer additional insight into group and individual behavior in security dilemma dynamics and the long-observed problem of "other minds." For example, international politics professor Robert Jervis noted in 1976:

Because statesmen believe that others will interpret their behavior as they intend it and will share their view of their own state's policy, they are led astray in two reinforcing ways. First, their understanding of the impact of their own state's policy is often inadequate—i.e. differs from views of disinterested observers—and, second, they fail to realize that other states' perceptions are also skewed.[26]

All actors were initially unsure how to treat the outer space domain and its associated set of threats and opportunities. Uncertainty about goals, intentions, and strategic thinking of an adversary is typically destabilizing, but especially so when new technologies have recently altered the strategic landscape and rendered existing mental frameworks outdated. When the implications of agreeing to be bound by certain rules are unknown, there is an incentive to avoid making commitments whilst continuing to experiment with newfound capabilities. These experiments with destructive capabilities by adversaries and potential adversaries constitute threatening stimuli, which inevitably trigger a state of heightened vigilance in human brains[27] and can fuel security dilemma anxieties if intentions are uncertain. Thus, aside from the benefits of reaching agreed upon rules and mutually understood concepts that helped guide policy, processes of creating an outer space governance framework helped mitigate security threats by accelerating strategic learning and state preference formation through dialogue. Of course, international governance frameworks must be continuously refined.

Refining the outer space governance framework

As trends and incidents in outer space have generated new concerns, additional agreements, guidelines, and state practices have sought to reduce security risks and strengthen outer space governance. Efforts have focused on the threats of anti-satellite weapons (ASATs), proliferation of missile technology, and space debris.

The Anti-Ballistic Missile (ABM) Treaty was signed in 1972 between the Soviet Union and United States as the recent development of multiple independent targetable re-entry vehicles (MIRVs) threatened to create a costly and destabilizing situation. With MIRVs, several nuclear warheads could be mounted on one ICBM, which could split off and hit multiple targets as the missile descended from outer space, making it harder for missile defense systems to shoot them down. Even without MIRVs, improving the accuracy of missile technology increased the chances of shooting down incoming ICBMs with missile interceptors and created an incentive to manufacture more ICBMs and warheads to ensure that some would reach their targets. MIRVs meant that missile defense systems would have to be even more robust. By allowing only two missile defense sites per country and obligating both sides not to interfere with national technical means of verification, the Treaty helped increase trust and assurance of nuclear deterrence. It also prohibited sea-, air-, and space-based ABM systems, further limiting strategic competition.

As technological change and proliferation continued, concerns about spreading missile technology led the G-7 countries[28] to create the Missile Technology Control Regime (MTCR) in 1987, a voluntary effort to limit export of missiles and components. The initiative eventually expanded to 34 members. MTCR's track record is mixed, but it has served as a forum for dialogue and norm development, such as defining "a nuclear-capable ballistic missile as one that could carry a 500-kilogram payload to a range of 300 kilometers."[29]

In 2002, with growing concerns about regimes such as Iran and North Korea, MTCR members established the International Code of Conduct against Ballistic Missile Proliferation (ICOC). The voluntary ICOC is open to all states and currently has 138 members, with India being the latest to join in June 2016. In addition to establishing controls on technology related to WMD-capable ballistic missiles, it includes transparency and confidence-building measures such as annual declarations and the imperative to "exchange pre-launch notifications on their Ballistic Missile and Space Launch Vehicle launches and test flights."[30] The ICOC calls on members to ratify the OST, Registration Convention, and Liability Convention, seeking to reinforce existing principles.

Significant concerns about outer space emerged when China conducted a kinetic ASAT test against its own defunct weather satellite in 2007, hitting it with a missile, which created significant space debris. Though the Soviets conducted numerous ASAT tests between 1968 and 1982, no one had done so since the United States in 1985. The Chinese test "galvanized long-held US military fears about the vulnerability of the satellites it relies on for global power projection."[31] This was followed by a US ASAT demonstration, which shot down an unresponsive de-orbiting intelligence satellite in 2008, citing a safety risk if the satellite's hydrazine tank leaked or exploded over a populated area. The maneuver occurred low enough in the atmosphere for debris to quickly de-orbit and burn up; the debris it did create posed a threat, and some was launched higher than the point of destruction, but it was less dangerous overall than the Chinese test. This could have been designed to strengthen norms about notification and consultation, to demonstrate how to responsibly conduct an ASAT, to signal to Chinese leaders about US capabilities, or a combination of reasons. As Moltz noted, "whatever the true reason, Washington conducted the world's first advance consultation under Article IX of the Outer Space Treaty."[32]

Aside from risks posed by intentional satellite destruction, degradation, or incapacitation through ASATs, accumulated space debris from decades of activity in outer space is a growing concern. Spent rockets, defunct satellites, and even paint flecks threaten operational satellites through collision. Major world space agencies formed the Inter-Agency Space Debris Coordination Committee in 1993, which created debris-mitigation guidelines eventually adopted by the UN in 2008. These guidelines outline best practices for collision avoidance, reducing debris creation during operations, and end-of-life procedures to remove satellites from optimal orbits, etc. In 2009, an accidental collision between the operational Iridium 33 communications satellite and the defunct Kosmos 2251

Russian spy satellite added more space debris and highlighted the need to improve coordination, early warning, and adherence to best practices.

Another initiative, the Prevention of an Arms Race in Outer Space (PAROS) process, has sought since 1981 to advance discussions at the UN Conference on Disarmament and through transparency and confidence-building measures. PAROS includes a 2008 Sino-Russian proposal for a Treaty on the Prevention of the Placement of Weapons in Outer Space and the Threat or Use of Force Against Outer Space Objects. It grew out of Chinese and Russian fears after US withdrawal from the ABM Treaty in 2002, which undermined the strategic logic of nuclear deterrence. Their fears were compounded by a 2006 National Space Policy that stressed US freedom of unilateral action. This action-reaction feedback loop is bringing strategic, militarized competition in outer space to the fore again, especially as geopolitical tensions have increased in recent years.

In 2008, the European Union proposed a Code of Conduct for Outer Space Activities, which provides detailed rules for specific situations. It has gone through numerous drafts and was endorsed in principle by the United States in 2012, pending modifications. Though imperfect, as European space policy analyst Lucia Marta noted in 2010, "a Code today can facilitate the adopting of a Treaty tomorrow, or even the creation of customary international law."[33] Indeed, international lawyers Francis Lyall and Paul Larsen argued in 2009 that certain elements of the OST have become customary international law, noting that numerous agreements "relating to space activities all proceed on the basis of the general principles of space law."[34] Such international norms are starting to emerge for cyberspace, but clear general principles of cyberspace law have, so far, remained elusive.

Cyberspace geopolitical context, threats, and opportunities

Cyberspace has existed for over a century and has played a supporting role in warfare in the form of radar jamming, communications interception, remotely piloting aircraft, and precision-guided munitions, etc. As Kuehl notes, cyberspace has been around since the invention of the telegraph in 1837,[35] and has been expanding in size and complexity ever since. Cyberspace lacks a pivotal moment like Sputnik, although revelations beginning in 2013 of widespread surveillance and other activities by the US National Security Agency (NSA) is a significant milestone that captured public attention and stimulated further work on cyberspace.

For simplicity, this chapter considers the invention of the World Wide Web in 1989 as the beginning of the modern cyberspace era because it enabled the commercialization and growth of the Internet in society. The Internet is the most integral piece of cyberspace because it enables one global, interoperable network of computers and other electronics to exist through its shared protocols, root servers, unique names and numbers, and coordinated management. Separate computer networks exist, but distinct public networks for different states have not been created, although levels of content filtering and activity monitoring vary.

The modern cyberspace era was initially characterized by the end of the Cold War and a period of triumphalist sentiment in the "West." The Warsaw Pact crumbled, but NATO expanded eastward as did the European Union. In recent years, however, geopolitical tensions have grown. The 2014 Russian invasion and annexation of Crimea, followed by support for separatists in Eastern Ukraine, brought NATO-Russia relations to their most tense since the Cold War. Chinese military strategy and modernization of forces have focused on anti-access/area-denial capabilities in response to a sense of encirclement, which has led US strategists to develop the Air/Sea Battle Concept, arguably stoking a security dilemma as both sides boost capabilities and put war plans on paper.[36] Though it is the job of militaries to prepare for all contingencies, perceptions of threat often grow when potential adversaries become aware of an opposing party's new plans and capabilities. The 2011 Arab Spring revolts against dictatorships in the Middle East and North Africa and subsequent government crackdowns ushered in greater instability, violence, and ungoverned spaces in those regions. They also generated fears of similar uprisings among Russian and Chinese leadership, especially given the efficient coordination among citizens within and across Arab societies enabled by modern cyberspace through social media and mobile devices.[37] These and other conflicts present an array of existing and potential threats apart from the death and destruction that has already occurred, and cyberspace is one of many domains through which they play out. Current thinking about cyberspace is partially conditioned by these recent events and the geopolitical context. Moreover, nuclear, biological, and chemical weapons remain significant concerns.

As with outer space, human activity in cyberspace is shaped by the broader political and technological environment. Geopolitical rivalry, threats posed by non-state actors, domestic politics, and desires to stay one step ahead of potential adversaries drive development of increasingly sophisticated computer network attack and surveillance capabilities. However, rather than a "Sputnik moment" that marked a clear *before* and *after* space flight, whose security implications were immediately clear because of the kinetic and nuclear implications of rockets and space vehicles, the security implications of cyberspace gradually sunk into public consciousness. Whereas early strategic thinking about outer space was primarily driven by fears of potential worst-case scenarios involving nuclear weapons, modern cyberspace has been shaped by numerous instances of actual harm in addition to fears of potential worst-case scenarios.

In terms of actual harm, examples include the "I Love You" virus, unleashed by a 24-year-old Filipino man in 2000, which infected roughly 50 million computers and caused an estimated $10 billion in damage.[38] Increasingly frequent corporate data breaches and identity theft throughout the 2000s raised awareness of dangers. Chinese hackers, some with links to the People's Liberation Army, have for years been stealing personnel records, intellectual property, weapon designs, and other data from US computer networks. The 2007 distributed denial of service (DDoS) attacks on Estonia, which temporarily disabled financial, media, and government websites in the country, demonstrated a new type of threat. The attacks are widely assumed to have been at least partially directed by the Russian state, and they ushered in what political scientist Lucas Kello called "a wholly new type of social and economic disturbance."[39] Operation Olympic Games, the assumed United States-Israeli cyberattacks that caused physical destruction in Iran's nuclear facility at Natanz and other locations, began to leak out in 2010 as the Stuxnet virus spread to computers around the world. The 2012 Shamoon cyberattacks, believed to have been conducted by Iran in retaliation for Olympic Games, destroyed roughly 30,000 computers at Saudi Aramco, the state-owned oil company of US ally Saudi Arabia. The 2014 cyberattack on Sony Pictures Entertainment in the United States stole and published proprietary information and internal communications in addition to destroying computers and servers, which the United States publicly accused North Korea of orchestrating and imposed economic sanctions in retaliation.[40]

With regards to potential worst-case scenarios, US President Barack Obama explained in February 2015:

> We're hugely vulnerable. We've started with critical infrastructure. That's an area where heavy involvement with those industries—whether it's Wall Street and the financial sector, utilities, our air-traffic control system—all of that, increasingly, is dependent on the digital base that they're working off of.[41]

In his 2015 book, *Lights Out*, journalist Ted Koppel highlighted a long-held fear that cyberspace could be used to knock out the US electric grid for weeks or months, resulting in mass death and destruction. He also pointed to concern among US military planners that an electromagnetic pulse attack, perhaps through high-altitude detonation of a nuclear weapon over US territory, could result in "destruction of electronic equipment over an extremely wide area."[42] Of course, US offensive cyberspace capabilities are assumed to be the best in the world, so US political and military leaders are acutely aware of what may be achievable. Moreover, other states are equally if not more vulnerable than the United States, depending on the degree to which their economies and societies rely on modern cyberspace.

As in the early outer space years, demonstrations of capabilities and provocative actions have led to reactions, mutual learning, and dialogue regarding cyberspace. The US electric grid's vulnerability has been known for over a decade, but public awareness and policy responses have grown as hackers linked to Iran, Russia, China, and non-state actors such as Daesh are discovered penetrating computer systems that operate the grid and lay the groundwork for a potential cyberattack.[43] The 2007 DDoS attacks on Estonia accelerated the creation of the NATO Cooperative Cyber Defence Centre of Excellence (CCDCoE) in 2009.[44] The speed of protestor mobilization demonstrated by the Arab Spring led Russia, China, and other less open states to tighten control of information flowing through their portions of cyberspace and also proposed in September 2011 an International Code of Conduct for Information Security at the UN,[45] which was updated in 2015.

Iran and North Korea have likely learned from US cyberattacks, including ones believed to have been conducted under Olympic Games such as Stuxnet, Flame, Wiper, and Duqu. The 2012 Shamoon and 2014 Sony Pictures cyber-attacks appear to have been inspired by the Wiper cyberattack on Iran's oil industry. As journalist Kim Zetter explained:

> Regardless of whether Iran is behind the Shamoon attack, there's no ques-tion that it and other nations learn from cyberattacks launched by the US and its allies. Common cybercriminals also study Stuxnet and the like to learn new techniques for evading detection and stealing data.[46]

Soon after the 2013 NSA leaks began, many governments pushed for data localization in an effort to protect their citizens and sovereignty. This would have required major tech companies to store data for their nationals within their territory. But European calls for "technological sovereignty," Brazil's temporary flirtation with data localization in the context of Marco Civil legis-lation,[47] and similar initiatives around the world often betrayed a lack of tech-nical understanding of cyberspace akin to the early outer space years because *where* data is stored matters less for data security and privacy than *how* it is stored and transmitted. However, territorial location and related laws matter for data storage when it comes to authorized access through due process, as highlighted by the so-called Microsoft Ireland warrant case that grabbed head-lines in 2015 and early 2016.[48] Other reactions included creation in January 2014 of the Global Commission on Internet Governance (GCIG), chaired by former Swedish Foreign Minister Carl Bildt.[49] In December 2013, US-based tech companies announced the Reform Government Surveillance coalition, seeking to pressure the US and other governments to update laws and practices regarding surveillance.[50]

Demonstrated capabilities and growing awareness of threats and opportunities have helped drive a cyber arms race that included more than five dozen countries seeking military cyber operations as of 2015.[51] Unlike outer space, lower barriers to entry mean that weaker states and non-state actors can have significant impact in cyberspace. The complexity of modern cyberspace and the vast spectrum of conflict it enables make it a more difficult domain to apprehend than outer space. When cyberspace was primarily a means to communicate information quickly across distances through networked electronics, disruption to those systems did not present a significant security threat. However, cybersecurity concerns have grown as it has become clear that a range of actors can hack directly into modern systems through an ever-expanding global, interoperable computer network and remotely issue commands to computer-operated machinery, weaponry, and infrastructure that can cause physical destruction. Moreover, growing depend-ence on cyberspace opens new vectors for attack and theft whilst also increasing the magnitude of harm to society that can be inflicted through cyberspace.

Even as dangers grow in cyberspace, desires to utilize it for commercial, sci-entific, and social purposes drive technological advancement and adoption, as with satellites and missile technology. For example, MIT scientist Alex Pentland has helped develop the discipline "social physics," which utilizes cyberspace to map billions of human interactions in organizations and societies to track the flow of ideas and identify patterns. With the knowledge garnered, he hopes to "begin to build a society that is better at avoiding market crashes, ethnic and religious violence, political stalemates, widespread corruption, and dangerous concentrations of power."[52] Manufacturing could increasingly be customized through 3-D printing, placing a higher proportion of value-added in digital design and distributed services relying on cyberspace.[53] Significant potential also exists for the Internet of Things, smart grids, cloud computing services, and smart cities. By computerizing and adding sensors to nearly everything and connecting them to the global network that is the Internet, it would be technically possible to significantly reduce inefficiencies in energy usage, traffic patterns, and financial markets whilst also opening new social and commercial possibilities.

As with outer space, these and other possible future scenarios affect behavior today, both in terms of ambition to innovate and commercialize as well as protect against emerging threats and prepare for worst-case scenarios. Though the cyberspace governance framework is more advanced today than the outer space framework was in 1960 when ambitions to commercialize satellites for telecommunications emerged, it is a patchwork of specific conventions and agreements that have been adopted as opportunities and threats have arisen. It has not kept pace with the increasing size and complexity of modern cyberspace.

Cyberspace debates, concepts, and emerging norms

Much like the early outer space years, many governments do not have good understandings of modern cyberspace's scientific and technical properties or clear preferences regarding aspects of its use. Potential threats and opportunities are poorly understood, as are the ways modern cyberspace has altered social and strategic dynamics. There is no well-established lexicon. Cyberspace classification and situation definitions are poorly formed and there is no clear set of agreed principles governing its use that enjoys international political legitimacy.

Whereas the ITU was empowered to manage outer space radio frequencies and orbital slots, the Internet Corporation for Assigned Names and Numbers (ICANN) is the primary technical body for the Internet. Created in 1998, ICANN manages the domain name system and is responsible for "Internet Governance," a term often confused with debates about norms and laws regarding cyberspace. ICANN operates through a multi-stakeholder governance system that includes "owners and operators of servers and networks around the world, domain name registries, regional IP address allocation organizations, standards organizations, Internet service providers, local and national governments, noncommercial stakeholders, business users, intellectual property interests, and others."[54] The US government transitioned ICANN to the global Internet multi-stakeholder community in October 2016 by allowing the Internet Assigned Numbers Authority functions contract with the US National Telecommunications and Information Administration to expire, although ICANN remains incorporated under the laws of California.

Given the Internet's central role in modern society, questions about its engineering are inherently political. As Internet-enabled cyberspace continues to supplant previous means of carrying out basic social functions in areas such as banking, commerce, healthcare, and government services, cyberspace is increasingly required to participate in society; thus, age-old questions of legitimacy, representation, and preference-aggregation are more prevalent. Unlike the multistakeholder model, the UN is based on multilateral engagement between states, although states are free to appoint experts of any background as representatives on UN committees. Lu Wei, Chinese minister of the Cyberspace Administration until June 2016, has offered the predominant Chinese view on the competing models:

> These two alternatives are not intrinsically contradictory. Without "multilateral," there would be no "multi-stakeholders." Exaggerating our disagreements due to difference in concepts is neither helpful to the China–US Internet relations nor beneficial to global governance and development of the Internet."[55]

US preference for the multi-stakeholder model could be explained by the logic of a "two-level game" described by political scientist Robert Putnam:

> At the national level, domestic groups pursue their interests by pressuring the government to adopt favorable policies, and politicians seek power by constructing coalitions among those groups. At the international level, national governments seek to maximize their own ability to satisfy domestic pressures, whilst minimizing the adverse consequences of foreign developments.[56]

The US position seems clearly influenced by the libertarian ethos of people that built the Internet and spread it commercially, which is mistrustful of government and values freedom to innovate over order and security.

Aside from disagreement over Internet governance, ambiguity regarding situation definitions, lexicon, and strategic dynamics in cyberspace inhibits efforts to lay down principles. General Michael Hayden, former Director of the NSA and the CIA, argued in 2011, "our most pressing need is clear policy, formed by shared consensus, shaped by informed discussion, and created by a *common* body of knowledge. With no common knowledge, no meaningful discussion, and no consensus … the policy vacuum continues."[57] A similar sentiment was echoed by the current NSA Director and Commander of Cyber Command, Admiral Mike Rogers, in February 2015: "The concepts of deterrence in the cyber domain are still relatively immature. We clearly are not, I think, where we need to be."[58]

The *Tallinn Manual on the International Law Applicable to Cyber Warfare*, published by CCDCoE in 2013, is an effort to create situation definitions and apply the Law of Armed Conflict and International Humanitarian Law to cyber-space.[59] Though criticized as insufficient to address the novel challenges of cyber conflict and for its lack of input from Russia and China,[60] the *Tallinn Manual* has informed cyberspace debates regarding international conflict. International lawyer Michael Schmitt, editor of the manuals, argued in a 2015 article with Sean Watts that states have largely ceded debates to non-state entities on how international humanitarian law applies in cyberspace, indicating inchoate prefer-ences and a desire not to constrain operations prematurely.[61]

A shared lexicon is lacking within countries as well as internationally. In common parlance in the United States and elsewhere, different people and professional communities use terms such as *online, the Internet, the virtual world, digital technologies, the web, information and communications technolo-gies* (ICTs), *cyberspace, information security, cybersecurity, network security,* and so on. Many of these terms refer to similar concepts, but consensus on appropriate verbiage and definitions is lacking.

Different concepts also exist within cyberspace debates. One source of confu-sion and disagreement is over *cyberspace/cybersecurity* and *information space/ information security*. In Russian and Chinese conceptions, information space includes the cognitive effects of information on the population and the resultant social effects. "The Chinese view 'information space' as a domain, or landscape, for communicating with all of the world's population. This chimes with the Russian view of this space including human information processing, in effect cognitive space."[62] Thus, *information security* in this conception refers not only to computer, network, and data security; it also encompasses information intended for human consumption—i.e., content. Therefore, questions of public morals, coordinating action between citizens, and government criticism are included, whereas the concept of *cybersecurity* leaves these aside. Ironically, US-based tech companies frequently invoke *information security*, but their con-ception focuses on protecting information from theft, alteration, and destruction. Once that information is intentionally sent by its owner into public cyberspace, they would be loath to see it controlled by anyone, especially a government.

Within the *information space* debate, Professors Andrey Krutskikh and Anatoly Streltsov stressed in 2014 the need for clarifying definitions internation-ally. They referred to *information war* as defined in the 2009 Agreement between the Governments of the Member States of the Shanghai Cooperation Organiza-tion in the Field of Ensuring International Information Security, which includes "mass psychologic brainwashing to destabilize society and state, as well as to force the state to taking decisions in the interest of an opposing party."[63] Krut-skikh and Streltsov discussed disruption of air control systems, missile defense, and critical infrastructure, which are included in *cybersecurity* debates. They also referred to the unlawful use of ICTs in which "physical damage is difficult to assess since losses are often intangible," noting the damage caused by mass theft and publication of information.[64]

Despite different terminology and concepts, democratic societies control certain types of information sent through cyberspace, such as those involving defamation of character, incitement to violence, providing material support to criminal or terrorist groups, and Holocaust denial. They are more permissive about free expression, but they monitor and control their information space. Indeed, Daesh's use of cyberspace to raise money and engage directly with Americans has led the FBI to increasingly monitor Twitter, prompting questions such as: when do "retweets" become criminal acts?[65] Given that modern cyberspace emerged in the United States, the Internet and business models that have built computer operating systems, software, and social media platforms reflect US democratic ideology and culture, a source of friction in managing global cyberspace. Thus, more authoritarian societies tend to slow or block US-inspired models. As Timothy Thomas argued in 2001, "Russia lost an ideology and is working hard to ensure that Russian culture, identity, and spirit do not also disappear along with it."[66]

Given differing views on information space, more authoritarian societies perceived Secretary of State Hillary Clinton's 2010 "Internet Freedom" speech as provocative. An agenda that includes "supporting the development of new tools that enable citizens to exercise their rights of free expression by circumventing politically motivated censorship"[67] can be seen as fomenting revolution within more closed societies that have a less permissive culture toward freedom of expression and assembly.[68]

Regarding classification, a 2014 GCIG paper by political scientist Joseph Nye used inductive and analogic reasoning to conceptualize cyberspace. It exhibited the same speculative, dialectic style characterizing articles such as the one by Myres McDougal in 1957:

> The cyberspace domain is often described as a public good or a global commons, but these terms are an imperfect fit. A public good is one from which all can benefit and none should be excluded, and while this may describe some of the information protocols of the Internet, it does not describe the physical infrastructure, which is a scarce proprietary resource located within the boundaries of sovereign states and more like a "club good" available to some, but not all. And cyberspace is not a commons like the high seas, because parts of it are under sovereign control. At best, it is an "imperfect commons" or a condominium of joint ownership without well-developed rules.[69]

Whereas Nye's discussion sought to understand social dynamics within the domain (classification questions), Lu Wei has sought to establish clear jurisdiction over portions of the domain that correspond to territorial boundaries (delimitation questions). Conveying the official position of the Chinese government, he has argued that "cyber sovereignty" must dictate management of the global Internet.[70] Former government officials Michael Chertoff and Paul Rosenzweig, writing for GCIG in 2015, offered another perspective on jurisdiction based on the assumption of an open, borderless Internet. They proposed a:

> choice-of-law rule based on either: the citizenship of the data creator; the citizenship of the data subject; one based on the location where the harm

being investigated has taken place; or one based on the citizenship of the
data holder or custodian.[71]

These debates are similar to haggling over classification and delimitation of
outer space in the 1950s and 1960s, but the complexity of cyberspace dynamics
appear to make slower, inductive processes more likely than analogic ones.

The primary UN body charged with developing a framework for cyberspace
is the Group of Governmental Experts on the Developments in the Field of
Information and Telecommunications in the Context of International Security
(GGE). It is roughly equivalent to COPUOS in its early years but, unlike
COPUOS, the GGE has not been charged with laying the groundwork for a
formal treaty and is not permanent.

The GGE first met in 2004. At the conclusion of its third iteration in 2013, it
issued a report determining that international law, particularly the UN Charter, is
applicable in the "ICT environment."[72] The GGE's 2015 report used the term
"cyberspace" for the first time and elaborated on how international law applies
to cyberspace and the ICT environment, including recommending that states
develop voluntary norms. Though the GGE's work is not binding, it constitutes
an effort to build an international governance framework for cyberspace, elements of which could be codified in a treaty at some point.

Among the most significant recent advances is the norm against state-
sponsored theft of information for commercial advantage. In September 2015,
the United States and China agreed that neither will "conduct or knowingly
support cyber-enabled theft of intellectual property, including trade secrets or
other confidential business information, with the intent of providing competitive
advantages to companies or commercial sectors."[73] The G-20 affirmed this principle at the November 2015 summit, in addition to endorsing the GGE's 2015
report and affirming that international law applies to cyberspace.[74] In May 2016,
the G-7 followed suit at its summit, utilizing similar language.[75]

The US agreement with China was preceded by the May 2014 indictment of
five members of the People's Liberation Army for economic espionage and trade
secret theft by the US Department of Justice.[76] This was followed by the threat of
economic sanctions against Chinese companies and individuals who benefited
from such theft in the lead-up to the September 2015 summit between President
Obama and Chinese President Xi Jinping.[77] By June 2016, at least one independent
report indicated that Chinese intrusions into US networks had dropped significantly.[78] The US government has acknowledged that it has seen a change in activity, but debate continues as to how long it will last.[79] Thus, the threat of public
exposure, sanctions, and damage to the US–China relationship appears to have
incentivized Chinese leadership to support the norm against cyber-enabled theft
for commercial advantage, with many other countries affirming it soon after.

Another emerging international cyberspace norm is that the same rights that
people enjoy offline must also be protected online.[80] It can be found in the UN
resolution presented by Brazil and Germany in 2013 on The Right to Privacy in
the Digital Age, in the 2015 draft of the International Code of Conduct for

Information Security, and the 2014 EU Human Rights Guidelines on Freedom of Expression Online and Offline, to name a few. Another emerging norm involves state responsibility for activities originating within their territory. As the 2015 GGE report put it, states "should not knowingly allow their territory to be used for internationally wrongful acts using ICTs."[81] Of course, verifying whether states are aware of and have the capacity to halt these acts is difficult. Regardless of difficulties of implementation, the existence of these norms would help guide policy and facilitate dispute resolution by providing principles upon which to base specific actions.

Recommendations: toward a UN cyberspace treaty

Although cyberspace debates suffer from inchoate state preferences, lack of a shared lexicon, and uncertainty, processes of developing a cyberspace governance framework built on mutually understood international behavioral norms and laws is slowly advancing through an interdependence of strategic rivalry, technological advancement, economic ambitions, security concerns, and international dialogue.

Based on the lessons of history, it seems necessary to begin negotiations on an international cyberspace treaty at the UN. As with the OST, a cyberspace treaty would not be a panacea, nor would it be the end of rule-making processes. Concluding one would inevitably take years or decades, but putting in place core principles that outline a cyberspace governance framework from which future cyberspace law can derive would be valuable.

Negotiating a cyberspace treaty at the UN would facilitate purposeful interaction and idea exchange among states. Given geopolitical tensions partially fueled by novel forms of conflict in cyberspace, working together on a common project would be constructive, providing a focal point in the world's primary global political body to slowly arrive at common understandings. It could stimulate work in other forums with cyberspace components, encouraging all stakeholders to transmit preferences to state leaders whilst accelerating updates to legal frameworks within states. Negotiations could also facilitate strategic learning and discipline the cyberspace lexicon such that concepts of deterrence and awareness of potentially escalatory dynamics could mature more quickly. The GGE serves this purpose to a degree, but its ad hoc nature and ambiguity about its future signals a lack of importance from which COPUOS did not suffer, making it easier for states to engage in "forum shopping,"[82] which fragments dialogue and leads to confusion. In this context, a distinction should be made between concepts of *Internet governance* (focused on technical management of one piece of cyberspace) and *cyberspace governance* (focused on the totality of the space created by networked electronics and the electromagnetic spectrum).

The legitimacy of a UN cyberspace treaty would generate greater "buy-in" around the world and would codify core principles that emerge from state practices and normative debate. Moreover, if and when a cyberspace treaty is concluded, it would create a shared reference of higher law that could be drawn

upon to guide future action, resolve disputes, and address new challenges. Negotiating it could also reduce uncertainty about how to manage potential threats
and worst-case scenarios, mitigating security dilemma dynamics.

A cyberspace treaty would have to consider the implications that might arise
from uses of networked artificial intelligence, greater computerization of human
bodies through mechanical limbs and organ-regulating devices such as heart
monitors, direct brain-to-brain communication via the Internet,[83] and so on. It
would have to address questions of jurisdiction, liability, and control, including
how to manage threats posed by non-state actors. It would need to be simple
enough so average citizens could comprehend the basic principles yet broad
enough to allow for future interpretation and evolution as technologies and
norms change.

As we struggle with the challenges of modern cyberspace, wisdom from the
early outer space years is worth revisiting:

> Particular subjects may be dealt with by formal agreement.... The remainder
> of what a future historian will—only in that future—be entitled to call "The
> Law of Space," when law is conceived as the community's expectations about
> the ways in which authority will and should be prescribed and applied, will
> undoubtedly grow by the slow building of expectations, the continued accre-
> tion of repeated instances of tolerated acts, the gradual development of assur-
> ances that certain things may be done under promise of reciprocity and that
> other things must not be done on the pain of retaliation.[84]

Cyberspace governance frameworks will inevitably evolve over time and will be
shaped by myriad actors and institutions, but without core principles and mental
frameworks to help governments and other organizations understand where to
focus energies and invest resources, it will be hard for anyone to adjust to the
challenges of modern cyberspace.

Notes

* I would like to dedicate this chapter to the memory of Dr. William C. Martel, author
   of *Victory in War* and beloved professor at the Fletcher School of Law and Diplomacy. Cyberspace and outer space were both strong interests of his, and he did much
   to get his students thinking about these issues in a systematic way. Though this analysis, its conclusions, and any errors it may contain are my own, I would not have
   been thinking about these questions if it were not for Dr. Martel.
1 John Herz, "Idealist internationalism and the security dilemma," *World Politics* 2
   (1950): 157–180; Robert Jervis, "Cooperation under the security dilemma," *World
   Politics* 30 (1978):167–212; Charles Glaser, "The security dilemma revisited," *World
   Politics* 50 (1997): 171–201; and Adam Liff and G. John Ikenberry, "Racing toward
   tragedy? China's rise, military competition in the Asia Pacific, and the security
   dilemma," *International Security* 39 (2014): 52–91.
2 Robert Gilpin, *War and Change in World Politics* (New York: Cambridge University
   Press, 1981): 34–35.
3 Stephen Krasner, *Sovereignty: Organized Hypocrisy* (Princeton: Princeton University
   Press, 1999): 10–42.

4 Ronald Coase, "The problem of social cost," *Journal of Law and Economics* 3 (1960): 1–44.
5 Richard Ned Lebow, "Identity and international relations," *International Relations* 22 (2008): 7–8.
6 Mancur Olson, *The Logic of Collective Action: Public Goods and the Theory of Groups* (Cambridge: Harvard University Press, 1965).
7 John Dewey, *Liberalism and Social Action* (Amherst: Prometheus Books, 1963), 55.
8 Daniel Kuehl, "From Cyberspace to Cyberpower: Defining the Problem," in Franklin Kramer, Stuart Starr, and Larry Wentz (eds), *Cyberpower and National Security* (Washington, DC: National Defense University Press and Potomac Books, Inc.), 28.
9 In doing so, it necessarily simplifies a more complex reality.
10 David Whalen, "Communications Satellites: Making the Global Village Possible," NASA, http://history.nasa.gov/satcomhistory.html.
11 James Clay Moltz, "The past, present, and future of space security," *Brown Journal of World Affairs* 16 (2007): 188–189.
12 Fred Kaplan, *The Wizards of Armageddon* (New York: Simon & Schuster, 1983).
13 Walter McDougall, *The Heavens and the Earth: A Political History of the Space Age* (New York: Basic Books, 1985), 419–420.
14 Robert Oslund, "The Geopolitics and Institutions of Satellite Communications," in Joseph N. Pelton, Robert J. Oslund, and Peter Marshall (eds), *Communications Satellites: Global Change Agents* (New York: Routledge, 2004), 126.
15 M. J. Peterson, *International Regimes for the Final Frontier* (Albany: State University of New York Press, 2005), 68.
16 Myres McDougal, "Artificial satellites: A modest proposal," *The American Journal of International Law* 51 (1957): 75–76.
17 William Burrows, *This New Ocean: The Story of the First Space Age* (New York: The Modern Library, 1999), 338–339.
18 Peterson, *International Regimes for the Final Frontier*, 50.
19 Antarctic Treaty, Art. I (1).
20 Peterson, *International Regimes for the Final Frontier*, 56.
21 McDougall, *The Heavens and the Earth*, 186.
22 Treaty on Principles Governing the Activities of States in the Exploration and Use of Outer Space, including the Moon and Other Celestial Bodies, Arts. VI–VIII.
23 The four other UN treaties include the Agreement on the Rescue of Astronauts, the Return of Astronauts and the Return of Objects Launched into Outer Space (1968); Convention on International Liability for Damage Caused by Space Objects (1972); Convention on Registration of Objects Launched into Outer Space (1976); and Agreement Governing the Activities of States on the Moon and Other Celestial Bodies (1984).
24 Barbara Koremenos, Charles Kipson, and Duncan Snidal, "The rational design of international institutions," *International Organization* 55 (2001): 766.
25 See, for example: Dan Grupe and Jack Nitschke, "Uncertainty and anticipation in anxiety," *Nature Reviews Neuroscience* 14 (2013): 488–501.
26 Robert Jervis, *Perception and Misperception in International Politics* (Princeton: Princeton University Press, 1976), 69–70.
27 Dean Mobbs et al., "The Ecology of Human Fear: Survival Optimization and the Nervous System," *Frontiers in Neuroscience* 9 (2015): 9.
28 Canada, France, Germany, Italy, Japan, the United Kingdom, and the United States.
29 Waheguru Pal Singh Sidhu, "Looking Back: The Missile Technology Control Regime," *Arms Control Today*, April 2, 2007, www.armscontrol.org/act/2007_04/LOOKINGBACK.
30 International Code of Conduct against Ballistic Missile Proliferation, Art. IV.i.3 (2002).
31 Theresa Hitchens, "Debris, traffic management, and weaponization: Opportunities for and challenges to cooperation in space," *Brown Journal of World Affairs* 16 (2007): 179.

32 James Clay Moltz, *Crowded Orbits: Conflict and Cooperation in Space* (New York: Columbia University Press, 2014), 148.
33 Lucia Marta, "The Hague Code of Conduct against Ballistic Missile Proliferation: 'Lessons Learned' for the European Union Draft Code of Conduct for Outer Space Activities," *European Space Policy Institute Perspectives* 34 (2010): 2.
34 Francis Lyall and Paul Larsen, *Space Law: A Treatise* (Farnham: Ashgate Publishing, 2009), 79.
35 Kuehl, "From Cyberspace to Cyberpower: Defining the Problem," 30.
36 Ayush Midha, "Lessons in Avoiding a US–China War: Rethinking the Air/Sea Battle," *Harvard Political Review*, December 17, 2015, http://harvardpolitics.com/united-states/lessons-avoiding-u-s-china-war-rethinking-airsea-battle/.
37 Jonathan Pollack, "Unease from Afar," in Kenneth M. Pollack et al., *The Arab Awakening* (Washington, DC: Brookings Institution, 2011), 298–304; Bruce Etling, "The Russian Media Ecosystem and the Arab Spring," Internet & Democracy Blog at Harvard University's Berkman Center, May 18, 2011, http://blogs.law.harvard.edu/idblog/2011/05/18/russian-media-ecosystem-arab-spring/; Chrystia Freeland, "Arab Spring, Russian Winter," *Reuters*, December 16, 2011, http://blogs.reuters.com/chrystia-freeland/2011/12/16/arab-spring-russian-winter/.
38 Mark Landler, "A Filipino Linked to 'Love Bug' Talks About His License to Hack," *New York Times*, October 21, 2000, C1.
39 Lucas Kello, "The meaning of the cyber revolution," *International Security* 38 (2013): 24.
40 Carol Lee and Jay Solomon, "US Targets North Korea in Retaliation for Sony Hacks," *Wall Street Journal*, January 3, 2015, www.wsj.com/articles/u-s-penalizes-north-korea-in-retaliation-for-sony-hack-1420225942.
41 Barack Obama, "The Re/Code Interview," interview with Kara Swisher, February 13, 2015, http://recode.net/2015/02/15/white-house-red-chair-obama-meets-swisher/.
42 Ted Koppel, *Lights Out: A Cyberattack, A Nation Unprepared, Surviving the Aftermath* (New York: Crown Publishers, 2015), 21.
43 Joseph Marks, "ISIL Aims to Launch Cyberattacks on US," *Politico*, December 29, 2015, www.politico.com/story/2015/12/isil-terrorism-cyber-attacks-217179; Siobhan Gorman, "Electricity Grid in US Penetrated by Spies," *Wall Street Journal*, April 8, 2009, A1.
44 Robert McMillan, "NATO to Set Up Cyber Warfare Center," *Network World*, May 15, 2008, www.networkworld.com/article/2279535/lan-wan/nato-to-set-up-cyber-warfare-center.html.
45 See, for example: Timothy Farnsworth, "China and Russia Submit Cyber Proposal," *Arms Control Today*, November 2, 2011, www.armscontrol.org/act/2011_11/China_and_Russia_Submit_Cyber_Proposal.
46 Kim Zetter, "The NSA Acknowledges What We All Feared: Iran Learns from US Cyberattacks," *Wired*, February 10, 2015, www.wired.com/2015/02/nsa-acknowledges-feared-iran-learns-us-cyberattacks/.
47 Tim Ridout, "Marco Civil: Brazil's Push to Govern the Internet," *Huffington Post*, October 22, 2013, www.huffingtonpost.com/t-a-ridout/brazils-push-to-govern-the-internet_b_4133811.html.
48 Orin Kerr, "Does It Matter Who Wins the Microsoft Ireland Warrant Case?" *Washington Post*, July 23, 2015, www.washingtonpost.com/news/volokh-conspiracy/wp/2015/07/23/does-it-matter-who-wins-the-microsoft-ireland-warrant-case/.
49 Michelle Dobrovolny, "Commission Seeks New Ways to Govern the Internet," *SciDev.Net*, July 29, 2014, www.scidev.net/global/icts/news/commission-seeks-new-ways-to-govern-the-internet.html.
50 Jon Swartz, "Tech Giants Team Up in Anti-Snoop Coalition," *USA Today*, December 10, 2013, 1B.
51 Shane Harris, "China Reveals Its Cyberwar Secrets," March 18, 2015, www.thedailybeast.com/articles/2015/03/18/china-reveals-its-cyber-war-secrets.html.

52 Alex Pentland, *Social Physics* (New York: Penguin Books, 2014), 17.
53 Alfredo Valladão, *Masters of the Algorithms: The Geopolitics of the New Digital Economy from Ford to Google* (Washington and Rabat: The German Marshall Fund of the United States and OCP Policy Center, May 2014).
54 Lennard Kruger, *The Future of Internet Governance: Should the US Relinquish Its Authority Over ICANN?* (Washington, DC: Congressional Research Service, May 2015), 1.
55 Lu Wei, "Cyber Sovereignty Must Rule Global Internet," *The Huffington Post*, December 15, 2014, www.huffingtonpost.com/lu-wei/china-cyber-sovereignty_b_6324060.html.
56 Robert Putnam, "Diplomacy and domestic politics: The logic of two-level games," *International Organization* 42 (1988): 434.
57 Michael Hayden, "The future of things 'cyber,'" *Strategic Studies Quarterly* 5 (2011): 5.
58 Michael Rogers, remarks at "Cybersecurity for a New America" Conference, Washington, DC, February 23, 2015.
59 A second edition, *Tallinn 2.0*, was published in February 2017.
60 See, for example: Ashley Deeks, "Tallinn 2.0 and a Chinese View on the Tallinn Process," *Lawfare*, May 31, 2015, www.lawfareblog.com/tallinn-20-and-chinese-view-tallinn-process.
61 Michael Schmitt and Sean Watts, "The decline of international humanitarian law opinio juris and the law of cyber warfare," *Texas International Law Journal* 50 (2015): 223–224.
62 Keir Giles and William Hagestad II, "Divided by a Common Language: Cyber Definitions in Chinese, Russian and English," in Karlis Podins, Jan Stinissen, and Markus Maybaum (eds), *5th International Conference on Cyber Conflict* (Tallinn: NATO CCD COE Publications, 2013), 7.
63 Shanghai Cooperation Organization, *Agreement between the Governments of the Member States of the Shanghai Cooperation Organization in the Field of Ensuring International Information Security [unofficial translation]*, Yekaterinburg, June 16, 2009, Annex 1.
64 Andrey Krutskikh and Anatoly Streltsov, "International law and the problem of international information security," *International Affairs: A Russian Journal of World Politics, Diplomacy and International Relations* 6 (2014): 67–68.
65 See, for example: Ryan Reilly, "FBI: When It Comes to @ISIS Terror, Retweets = Endorsements," *The Huffington Post*, August 7, 2015, www.huffingtonpost.com/entry/twitter-terrorism-fbi_55b7e25de4b0224d8834466e.
66 Timothy Thomas, "Information Security Thinking: A Comparison of US, Russian, and Chinese Concepts," *Foreign Military Studies Office Publications* (2001): 4.
67 Hillary Clinton, "Remarks on Internet Freedom," The Newseum, Washington, DC, *US Department of State transcript*, January 21, 2010.
68 Richard Andres, "Inverted militarized diplomacy: How states bargain with cyber weapons," *Georgetown Journal of International Affairs: International Engagement on Cyber IV* (2014): 124.
69 Joseph Nye, "The Regime Complex for Managing Global Cyber Activities," *Global Commission on Internet Governance Paper Series: No. 1* (May 2014), 6.
70 Wei, "Cyber Sovereignty Must Rule Global Internet."
71 Michael Chertoff and Paul Rosenzweig, "A Primer on Globally Harmonizing Internet Jurisdiction and Regulations," *Global Commission on Internet Governance Paper Series: No. 10* (March 2015), 2.
72 UN Res A/68/98, "Group of Governmental Experts on Developments in the Field of Information and Telecommunications in the Context of International Security," June 24, 2013.
73 White House, "FACT SHEET: President Xi Jinping's State Visit to the United States," *Press Release*, September 25, 2015.

74 "G20 Leaders' Communiqué, Antalya Summit, 15–16 November 2015," 6, paragraph 26.

75 "G7 Ise-Shima Leaders' Declaration: G7 Ise-Shima Summit, 26–27 May 2016," 14.

76 Devlin Barrett and Siobhan Gorman, "US Charges Five in Chinese Army with Hacking," *Wall Street Journal*, May 19, 2014, www.wsj.com/articles/SB1000142405 2702304422704579571604060696532.

77 Ellen Nakashima, "US is Crafting Sanctions on China," *Washington Post*, August 31, 2015, A1.

78 David Sanger, "Chinese Curb Cyberattacks on US Interests, Report Finds," *New York Times*, June 20, 2016, A9.

79 Nafeesa Syeed, "US Cyber Deal with China Is Reducing Hacking, Official Says," *Bloomberg*, June 28, 2016, www.bloomberg.com/news/articles/2016-06-28/u-s-cyber-deal-with-china-is-reducing-hacking-official-says.

80 See, for example: Henry Rõigas, "An Updated Draft of the Code of Conduct Distributed in the United Nations – What's New?" *InCyder News* (CCDCoE), February 10, 2015.

81 United Nations, "Report of the Group of Government Experts on Developments in the Field of Information and Telecommunications in the Context of International Security," A/RES/70/174: Art. III.13.c.

82 See, for example: Frank Baumgartner and Bryan Jones, *Agendas and Instability in American Politics* (Chicago: University of Chicago Press, 1993); and Alastair Johnston, "The Social Effects of International Institutions on Domestic (Foreign Policy) Actors," in Daniel Drezner (ed.), *Locating the Proper Authorities* (Ann Arbor: University of Michigan Press, 2003), 145–196.

83 See, for example: Andrea Stocco et al., "Playing 20 Questions with the Mind: Collaborative Problem Solving by Humans Using a Brain-to-Brain Interface," *PLOS ONE*, September 23, 2015, http://journals.plos.org/plosone/article?id=10.1371/journal.pone.0137303.

84 Myres McDougal and Leon Lipson, "Perspectives for a law of outer space," *The American Journal of International Law* 52 (1958): 420.

Part II

Conceptualizing cybersecurity

6 Traditional military thinking in cyberspace

The need for adaptation

*Jan Kallberg**

The application of traditional military strategy and operational concepts to cyberspace can mislead, resulting in spurious assessments and unfavorable outcomes. Four tenets of the cyber world present profound challenges for the application of traditional military strategies in cyber conflicts. The cyber world is characterized by the following: a lack of object permanence, which undermines the concept of maneuver; limited or absent measurement of effectiveness in offensive cyber; conflicts that are executed at computational speed, removing the time window for meaningful strategic leadership; and anonymity that makes the parties to the conflict unknown. Thus, the application of traditional military thinking in cyber is likely to lead to incorrect conclusions regarding strategic achievements and abilities in the pre-conflict stage, increasing the risk of strategic failure in actual conflict.

As noted military strategist Edward N. Luttwak once stated, strategies without the ability to execute are pointless exercises.[1] Established military thinking is appealing as an explanatory model for the outfall of cyber conflicts for two reasons. First, it is already in place. For generations, the training and education of military officers, political scientists, and the political elite have focused on the works of Carl von Clausewitz, Sun Tzu, Antoine-Henri Jomini, B. H. Liddell-Hart, Heinz Guderian, and other traditional thinkers whose theories are considered timeless and universal. This focus on *Masters of War* has created a path dependency that renders political, institutional, and bureaucratic organizations unable to adapt under the pressure of change.[2] Second, since alternative strategic theories designed explicitly for cyber have not been established, traditional military thinking becomes the default formulator of strategy.[3] In some quarters, the concepts of cyberwar (and cyber conflicts leading to war), have been rejected under the belief that they do not fit traditional military thinking, and thus do not meet the traditional military framework for destruction and capture of physical items.[4] Over time, domain-specific strategic fundamentals for cyber will emerge based on the experiences and inferences identified in a major cyber conflict. Whilst the lack of major state cyber conflicts to date has delayed the development of cyber theory, an identification of the unique characteristics of cyber prior to this can help lay a foundation for strategic development in this realm. This chapter emphasizes four unique characteristics of cyberspace: the lack of physical target permanence; the difficulty in measuring effectiveness; computational speed; and anonymity. These characteristics challenge traditional military concepts such as command and control and create a need to develop specific military strategies.

Limited object permanence

One major challenge in the application of traditional military thinking to cyberspace is object permanence. The main body of traditional military thinking was consolidated under the framework of the art of war during the Napoleonic era of the late eighteenth and early nineteenth centuries. At that time, the major nation states created war colleges and adopted a scientific approach through which warfare could be studied and taught using theories on how to conduct successful campaigns that would lead to victory. From these theories emerged detailed types of battlefield maneuvers, orders of battle, and strategies for achieving superiority by improving one's position to be able to fire on the enemy and reach a decisive outcome.

Over time, the study of war has become a viable science. This science leverages theoretical and intellectual constructs to advance a common body of knowledge that can be handed down to successive generations of officers. Strategy and the concept of maneuver are embedded within the study of war. The ability to maneuver over terrain to seek battlefield advantage is instrumental to military schooling and doctrinal training. The focus on maneuver developed in four stages over the past 400 years.[5] During the Thirty Years War, the Swedish king, Gustavus Adolphus, introduced light cavalry and horse-drawn artillery for quickly exploiting and flanking slow-advancing quadrants of pikemen and musketeers deployed by the Catholic League. Two hundred years later, Napoleonic tactics increased the focus on exploiting opportunities by introducing rapid cavalry charges as a form of maneuver. These advances were significantly challenged by trench warfare during the First World War. Rapid maneuver was reintroduced during the German invasion of France in 1940 as *Blitzkrieg* (Lightning War). *Blitzkrieg* used highly mobile mechanized units to strike deeply into enemy formations with maneuverability to take advantage of tactical and operational opportunities. The concepts of *Blitzkrieg* were further refined and advanced in the 1980s through the introduction of air–land warfare. Air–land warfare leverages air assets to enable ground forces to maneuver and relocate quickly. Over the course of 400 years, maneuver warfare has developed as a central feature of military thinking. The underlying assumption embedded in maneuver warfare is that objects are physically tangible. Tanks, soldiers, and other instruments of war do not disappear, change form or reappear in absent physical signs. It would be inconceivable to Napoleon that assets could disappear, reappear, and change form absent physical telltale signs. Stealth and surprise are part of kinetic war, but the complete reconstitution of a military unit, weapon system, or other asset in a novel and wholly unpredictable form, as is the case with malware, distributed denial of service attacks and other operations occurring in cyberspace, challenges conventional thinking. Under traditional military thinking, maneuver is dependent on the arrangement of limited assets and fixed terrain. The present cyber environment is different. In cyberspace, the enemy can emerge and evolve without fixed positions or assets. Both the terrain and the assets within that terrain have no defined shape, they are amorphic.

Napoleonic generals operated within a framework in which they could decide where to fight the battle (terrain), when to fight the battle (time), and possess reasonable knowledge of both one's own and opposing force's assets (resources). Terrain, time, and resources provided a reasonably predictive framework to assess outcomes. Even when maneuver increased in speed through the utilization of *Blitzkrieg* tactics, the variable components associated with war remained limited in scope.[6] Cyberspace operations challenge these fixed notions of terrain, time, and resources. States can create, change, move, duplicate, and eliminate objects at much faster raters than strategists can define maneuvers. The variability of the cyber environment limits strategists' ability to make fixed assumptions associated with time, terrain, and resources.

Despite rapid changes in both physical and information terrain, some measures of permanence exist in cyberspace. The underlying infrastructure of cyberspace, the domain name system and root servers, terrestrial and undersea cables, electric grids, and satellites are temporally fixed terrain. The execution of cyberwar occurs across physical and information spaces, where physical permanence can be limited.[7] Although an argument can be made that the information infrastructure of hardware, cables, switches, hubs, and servers that are part of the seven layers (physical, data link, network, transport, session, presentation, and application) of the Open Systems Interconnection model,[8] constitutes a permanent physical presence, the actual engagement in cyber of these assets is largely digital. The first two layers of the Open Systems Interconnection model constitute the physical infrastructure, but not the battle space. Armor warfare uses tanks or other mechanized systems to achieve the projection of force. The physical presence of a tank and its projection of force is inseparable from its spatial and temporal place. In contrast, in cyber, the physical infrastructure can be the system to which force is directed or the environment within which force is directed. As systems are combined in overlapping systems of systems frameworks, a system might be an intended target or the vector by which force is achieved in connected systems. This reality creates a need to think beyond first-order effects (e.g., a malware shuts down a computer), to consider second- (that computer controlled the patient records system of a hospital) and third-order effects (patients are provided the wrong dosage of medications and some patients die) that extend military thought beyond an initial action-reaction pair to other consequences, often unforeseen or difficult to predict. Traditional military thinking is not designed to address the lack of physical target permanence. Consequently, a direct application of traditional military thinking in cyber is more likely to fail than be successful.

Measuring effectiveness

In cyberspace, actual battle damage can occur within layers of networks and, increasingly, through a kaleidoscope of nodes and digital interchanges. An attacker in cyberspace has limited ability to verify, assess, and take action, based on information gained from a previous attack and its aftermath. Even if the origin of an attack is assessed and validated, the defender has limited ability to see the actual damage a counter-strike could achieve. Likewise, when the problem is reversed, attackers must assess the effects of an attack on the defender not only in action-reaction but in cascading effects across systems and assets. Networks are typically only visible and assessable on the perimeter, to a limited number of functions performed. The actual depth, layout, and capacity of the networks is hidden behind firewalls, internal defensive measures, and areas of denied access. The complexity faced by both attackers and defenders as to the actual impact of their cyber operations undermines traditional military thinking.

Since the invention of the bow and arrow in prehistoric times, armies have fought from a distance by firing weapons, observing the effect, and adjusting their aim to maximize lethality. The French Napoleonic general storming the thin red line of British troops could see how the enemy's lines became thinner following each volley. He could discern a relatively accurate assessment of effectiveness in real time, forcing a retreat if the British remained standing after the French Guards lost their battlefield thrust. In this framework, measurable results provide the necessary information for further decision making and battle assessment. Cyberspace must necessarily contain a feedback loop to provide accurate measures of effectiveness.[9]

The absence of measures of effectiveness in cyberspace supports decisions that lead to escalation due to incomplete information on objective attainment.[10] An attacker that is unsure about the actual effect they are having on a target is more likely to continue attacking, escalating the engagement in an attempt to achieve mission objectives. An attacker pursuing limited goals, with limited information, has greater difficulty in verifying when these goals are reached. The limits of knowledge in cyberspace can lead to hostilities beyond goal achievement, and increase the possibilities of collateral damage. The absence of verifiable and reliable measures of effectiveness strains the value of traditional military thinking in cyberspace.

Computational speed execution

The notion of cyber conflict is relatively new but one thing is clear: the value of time in the cyber domain cannot be overstated. Today and tomorrow, politicians and military leadership will struggle to impact on real-time events occurring at computational speed. Leadership must engage in anticipatory planning in the pre-conflict phases to hope to have control and impact during conflict periods.

Digital interchanges are rapid and the speed in which these engagements are executed is likely to increase over time. Key to speed in cyber conflict is automation. Humans slow the execution of cyber conflict. Early-stage cyber-attacks by humans that manually pick tools to penetrate networks, using trial and error to find the right tool to utilize, are slow, predictable, and inefficient. Manual cyberwarriors require an abundance of time to execute a major cyberattack, but this is changing due to technological advances.

Machine learning and artificial intelligence will enable cyberwarriors to make faster decisions and switches between approaches to more rapidly achieve goals. Machines are becoming better at identifying and isolating their vulnerabilities and incoming threats. Systems are increasingly able to adapt to changes in the network to provide better security. These technological advances are removing humans from the loop. Cyber interchanges will soon occur between machines in disparate systems, each operating within constrained parameters defined by code and network topology. This is not merely the realm of science fiction. Today, automated stock trading, e-commerce, and a variety of online services operate with limited human support. Just as the predictive and reactive aspects of commerce and finance are automating, so too are cyber defenses.

One of the major weaknesses in cyber defense planning is the perception that there is time to lead a cyber defense whilst under attack. In a future automated and premeditated attack, human response times will be inadequate to account for automated systems operating at computational speeds. In this near future, political and military decision makers will be unable to engage in real-time leadership as their decision timeline will be too slow; the battle could be lost before they make their first move. A premeditated attack is planned for a long time, maybe years, and if automated, the execution of a massive number of exploits will be limited to minutes or seconds. Future cyber defense will need to rely on artificial intelligence that can assess, act, and mitigate at computational speed.

In an environment where digital interchange occurs at computational speed, the only thing that governments can do is to prepare, give guidelines, set rules of engagement, and disseminate knowledge to ensure a cyber resilient society. In a resilient society, every stage of a system's production, from hardware to software to installation and maintenance, should be prepared for survival in the face of sustained, targeted attacks. Prefabricated defensive measures, whilst offering general defensive preparation and resilience, can be reverse engineered based on probes and prior attacks' TTPs. If cyber defenses can be assessed early in a probing phase of a cyber conflict, they are more likely to fail when an attack moves beyond probes. Yet, because the defender does not know that their systems are vulnerable, these bulwarks of defense become the weapons of offense.

The development of digital conflict at computational speed is troublesome for traditional military thinking, strategy, and leadership. Military units are designed to be led by an officer, who, through the support of technical systems and information, assesses the situation, makes decisions, and determines future courses of action. Military leadership executes national defense strategies through a political process that takes time. Although smaller tactical decisions might need minimal time, operational, strategic, and grand strategic decisions require increasingly large blocks of time. Can cyber, as an area of conflict, function under leadership interactions within traditionally long time periods, or will future cyber conflict necessitate the devolution of decisions to the tactical (network operator or machine) level? If tactical input is automated, cyber engagement risks losing its structure and becoming a chain of reactions to ongoing events without the possibility of any major coordination or strategic intent.

Rapidly executed cyberattacks, especially those that are well prepared, organized, and premeditated, diminish the ability of defenders to mount a robust cyber defense. Such attacks can be compared to fighting without any access to command and control, air defenses without access to ground control, or Airborne Warning and Control System command under which pilots of armed fighter jets are instructed to make all tactical decisions without coordination or control in relation to other defense assets, including the decision to fire. The decisions in all these situations would be made within frameworks of theater rules of engagement, which determine TTPs before a situation occurs.

Even if commanders address the physical–virtual complexities of the cyber domain, machine-speed attacks challenge conventional concepts of human battlefield leadership. If attacks are not premeditated, but rely on harvesting vulnerabilities in an ongoing conflict, the time frames are larger. Giving more time to offensive and defensive forces might limit worst-case outcomes and foster more robust defensive decision making. Planning is absolutely essential to conflict in cyberspace.

Anonymity

Anonymity is well researched and understood as a complicating factor in cyber operations. The lack of proper identification in cyberspace undermines one's ability to engage in defensive actions both within cyberspace and across other domains.[11] Anonymity also increases the risk of cyber friendly fire, in which entities engage friendly targets due to their inability to distinguish between friend and foe.[12] The use of proxies in cyber operations adds complexity to the concept of anonymity in cyberspace. Several countries in the developing world have a growing Internet presence and commercial computer capacity, but their focus is on economic growth and satisfying an emerging market, and security concerns are not properly addressed, allowing third party states to leverage their infrastructure for false flag attacks.[13] In traditional military theory, the enemy is identifiable and can be engaged. This might not always be the case in cyberspace.

Command and control

The unique character of cyberspace questions the relevance of the traditional models used to guide military action. In the 1960s, John Boyd developed one of the most common models used to represent military command and control: the

OODA loop. Boyd's model assumes that military command and control follows four steps: observe, orient, decide, and act (OODA).[14] The OODA loop requires the ability to assess ongoing events (as in the initial step, "Observe"), but with anonymity, computational speed in cyber execution, and lack of physical permanence, the observations feeding the loop are likely to be inaccurate, if not spurious. The "Orient" stage in the OODA loop—reaction to the unfolding events and positioning for better outcome—assumes a maneuver space with favorable positions, but the lack of permanent physical structures in a digital environment results in ever-changing terrain leading to disorientation rather than reorientation. The "Decide" stage, absent accurate information from the first two stages, results in a constrained decision calculus that leads to ineffectual actions in the final stage. Computational speed exacerbates the inability to assess and act (or react), as increasingly shorter time frames in future cyber conflicts challenge significant human deliberation. In sum, the reality of cyber conflict challenges common conceptions of command and control and requires new ways of thinking.

Harnessing cyber operations

Critics of cyber-unique strategies and concepts note that cyber operations are an enabler of war, and not a distinct form of war. If cyber operations are considered merely tools that enable other military operations, and not utilized as weapons of strategic intent, then cyber operations can simply be integrated in grand strategy and there is no need for cyber operations to achieve decisive outcome in an exclusively cyberwar fighting domain.[15] This argument reduces cyber operations to an enabler of either traditional weapons or traditional forms of war and is likely to be challenged by the expansion of the domain's growing importance. Cyber operations and the ability to conduct a conflict in cyberspace will escalate and become more sophisticated over time. The belief that cyber is peripheral to war, and not a discrete form of war, assumes that the conditions under which wars are fought are permanent. History has shown with sufficient clarity that warfighting abilities constantly emerge, develop, and change. The assumption that the characteristics of the surrounding environment are static has repeatedly led to defeat. The French disaster of June 1940, for example, was largely the result of the French refusal to conduct armored warfare. Even if French tanks outnumbered German tanks, the refusal had a direct, tactical implication. The French considered tanks to be peripheral, mere enablers for the infantry. To the French, tanks were primarily fire support vehicles for the infantry, or transportable machine gun nests, and the French High Command prohibited tanks from operating independently of the infantry. The fact that the French lacked radio communications between tanks reflects the assumption that such coordination was unnecessary because tanks merely followed the infantry. As battles started to unfold, and French commanders realized the need to engage German tanks, the French tanks—equipped with neither radio communications nor armor-piercing capability—were at a significant disadvantage in any tank-on-tank confrontations. The logic that tanks were simply support for the infantry created path dependency that constrained alternative approaches. This resulted in damaging limitations on military effectiveness and eventual defeat.

A refusal to consider cyber weapons a freestanding form of war, and instead force them into the concepts and formations of the past, could limit the opportunity embedded in these capabilities, analogous to the French army's failure in 1940 to utilize armor. A path-dependent approach, seeking to attach new weapons to an earlier form of war, removes the strategic surprise and supremacy that a military technical revolution can offer. Specific strategies need to be developed to harness cyber power to its full extent.

Each strategy relies on a fundamental, overarching framework that explains why things are the way we perceive them, structures assumptions for how to operate, and provides a pathway to reach strategic objectives. Theory provides the intellectual underpinnings for predicting the outcomes leading to these objectives. Traditional military thinking faces serious challenges today, leading to questions regarding the applicability of established military strategies in cyberspace, and whether, if these strategies are applied, they could lead to defeat instead of a decisive, positive outcome.

Cyber operations are not only an enabler for joint operations, but also a strategic option for confronting adversarial societies. The current alternative to strategic cyber operations is to attack the adversary using cyber, where exploitation opportunities occur. This approach is likely to degrade parts of the adversary's information infrastructure, but will not achieve strategic goals. If an adversarial society is unaffected by a cyber conflict, the conflict itself has not reached a decisive outcome. Decisive outcomes lead to policy change through partial or full submission to foreign will by the targeted society.[16] A decisive outcome in cyberspace is reached either by removing military capacity through cyberattacks or destabilizing the targeted society. The removal of military capacity is likely temporary in comparison to societal destabilization that jeopardizes an entire regime, yet both can help achieve victory.

Conclusion

The application of traditional military principles in strategic decision making in cyber conflicts assumes the existence of battle space attributes that are largely absent in cyberspace. As cyberspace evolves as a battle space and contested area, new, innovative strategic principles for this realm must be developed to address the core four concerning tenets of cyber combat: lack of physical permanence; lack of relevant measures of effectiveness; computational speed in execution; and anonymity. In this unique context, cyber-relevant strategies are increasingly likely to rely on artificial intelligence and preset actions as computational speed in execution and challenges to situational awareness rise in importance.

Military leaders assume that those under their command can be provided adequate training and resources, and will be sufficiently led in conflict. The very notion of leadership in cyber conflict is challenged by its speed and complexity. Mitigating factors in cyberspace challenge conventional military leadership models and can result in poor judgment and tactical errors.

Despite being challenged by cyber operations, the military must necessarily develop robust capacity to operate in cyberspace. The uniqueness of cyber operations and the domain itself limit the applicability of traditional military models for strategic, operational, and tactical success. Future military cyber forces need to be able to operate in an environment that lacks physical permanence, robust measures of effectiveness, is challenged by computational speed and is replete with anonymous actors. Militaries must develop unorthodox approaches, innovate and adapt, which militaries have often found challenging under the best of circumstances.

Notes

* The views expressed herein are those of the author and do not reflect the official policy or position of the Army Cyber Institute, the United States Military Academy, the Department of the Army, or the Department of Defense. No rights reserved. This work was authored as part of the Contributor's official duties as an Employee of the United States Government and is, therefore, a work of the United States Government. In accordance with 17 USC 105, no copyright protection is available for such works under US law.
1 Edward N. Luttwak, *The Grand Strategy of the Roman Empire: From the First Century AD to the Third* (Baltimore: JHU Press, 1979).
2 Paul Pierson, "Increasing returns, path dependence, and the study of politics," *American Political Science Review* 94/2 (2000): 251–267. On classical strategic thought, see: Michael Handel, *Masters of War: Classical Strategic Thought* (London: Frank Cass Publishers, 2000).
3 Kenneth Geers, "Strategic cyber defense: Which way forward?" *Journal of Homeland Security and Emergency Management* 9/1 (2002): 1–10; Thomas Rid, "Cyber war will not take place," *Journal of Strategic Studies* 35/1 (2012): 5–32.
4 C. B. Greathouse, "Cyber War and Strategic Thought: Do the Classic Theorists Still Matter?" in Jan-Frederik Kremer and Benedikt Müller (eds), *Cyberspace and International Relations* (Berlin: Springer, 2014), 21–40.
5 William S. Lind, *Maneuver Warfare Handbook* (Boulder: Westview Press, 1985); John Boyd, "Patterns of Conflict," presentation, December 1986, at www.ausair power.net/JRB/poc.pdf.
6 Heinz Guderian, *Panzer Leader* (Cambridge: Da Capo Press, 2001).
7 B. T. Williams, "The joint force commander's guide to cyberspace operations," *Joint Force Quarterly* 73/2 (2014): 12–19.
8 William Stallings, *Handbook of Computer-Communications Standards; Vol. 1: The Open Systems Interconnection (OSI) Model and OSI-Related Standards* (New York: Macmillan Publishing Co., 1987).
9 Asmeret B. Bier, "A Cognitive and Economic Decision Theory for Examining Cyber Defense Strategies." Sandia National Laboratories (Albuquerque, NM: Sandia Laboratories, 2014), at http://prod.sandia.gov/techlib/access-control.cgi/2014/140442.pdf.
10 Martin C. Libicki, *Cyberdeterrence and Cyberwar* (Santa Monica, CA: RAND Corporation, 2009).
11 Pauline C. Reich et al., "Cyber warfare: A review of theories, law, policies, actual incidents—and the dilemma of anonymity," *European Journal of Law and Technology* 1/2 (2010): 1–58.

12 T. E. Carroll, F. L. Greitzer, and A. D. Roberts, "Security informatics research challenges for mitigating cyber friendly fire," *Security Informatics* 3/1 (2014): 1–14.
13 Jan Kallberg and Steven Rowlen, "African nations as proxies in covert cyber operations," *African Security Review* 23/3 (2014): 307–311.
14 Frans P. B. Osinga, *Science, Strategy and War: The Strategic Theory of John Boyd*
(Abingdon: Routledge, 2007).
15 Colin S. Gray, *Making Strategic Sense of Cyber Power: Why the Sky is Not Falling*
(Carlisle: Army War College – Strategic Studies Institute, 2013); M. C. Libicki, "Why
cyber war will not and should not have its grand strategist," *Strategic Studies Quarterly* 8/1 (2014): 23–39.
16 Jan Kallberg, "Strategic cyberwar theory—A foundation for designing decisive strategic cyber operations," *Cyber Defense Review* 1/1 (2016): 101–116.

7 Public health and epidemiological approaches to national cybersecurity

A baseline comparison

Aaron F. Brantly*

This chapter leverages the concepts of big data analysis, public health modeling and disease prevention, tracking, and remediation to examine the current state of the field of cybersecurity and assess where new technologies and policies are leading in terms of solving significant national security issues presented by cyberspace. Much of the terminology of cyber threats finds its roots in biology with terms such as virus, Trojan, worm, etc. Many of the ways malware spreads closely parallel biological pathogens. Medicine provides cyber researchers with a rich history of data collection, analysis, and application dating back hundreds of years. This rich history from the use of common statistical methods, combined with new data collection and aggregation techniques, offers a unique and powerful perspective on solving pressing national cybersecurity problems. This chapter is focused on building a robust comparative analysis between cybersecurity and public health and epidemiological models.

The history of public health lends itself to the study of novel solutions for combating malicious behavior in cyberspace. Humanity has been fighting disease and illness for as long as recorded history. The established record on combating microscopic organisms parallels, in both comedy and error, the trials and tribulations which modern cybersecurity researchers face. Although the time horizon of problems faced by cyber experts comprises only about 60 years, the lessons upon which they can draw to identify, assess, and treat viruses, Trojans, worms, and other malicious and unintentional behaviors in cyberspace date back millennia in public health. This chapter examines the history of progress in public health with a focus on the spread of pathogens and draws out parallels useful for network administrators and policymakers, to combat an increasingly dynamic problem set. This is not a completely new line of inquiry. Instead, it is one that has been found to be helpful in limited applications, as will be examined below. However, few analyses have fully leveraged the rigor of public health and epidemiologic study as a guide for cybersecurity. This chapter begins a process of remediation by providing a brief historical context of public health and epidemiology before focusing on modern methods and analyzing their applicability to the study of issues in cyberspace.

By engaging in cross-disciplinary analysis, cybersecurity researchers can learn new analytic techniques and practices. Researchers can then build new sets of "best practices" and enhance the heuristic framework in which solutions to complex problems are discovered. Single focus or stovepiped disciplinary analysis constrains the possibility for novel solutions and can result in "analytic lock-in." Leveraging analytic techniques associated with public health can provide novel insights into existing cybersecurity practices. Public health and epidemiological (EPI) modeling are useful for comparative purposes because they focus on not only the forensic biological, genetic, or molecular attributes of pathogens, but also on a combination of factors that include the human/societal behavioral attributes, environmental factors, and systemic modeling of incidents in the assessment, treatment, prevention, and mitigation of disease. No single factor alone should be considered absent the systemic relationships that factor has within a broader causal matrix. Whilst human thought lends itself to linear thinking in the form of direct cause and effect, relationships are often nonlinear and nonparametric. By focusing on novel epistemological frameworks, the study of cybersecurity can advance its heuristical core and thereby enable new solutions to old problems. At its most basic, cross-disciplinary analysis allows for the challenging of established practice.

The evolution of public health and epidemiology: a very short introduction

Public health is a contested modern concept. The origins of the study of health in communities dates back to the aggregation of individuals into clans and subsequently into broader societal groupings.[1] The aggregation of individuals into communities necessitated increasingly complex structures to prevent the spread of disease. The clustering of individuals results in sanitation constraints associated with excrement and other forms of human-generated waste. Early on, public health and disease were the subjects of philosophy and theurgy, or rituals. The comprehension of complex systems, invisible to the naked eye, were unimaginable. Hippocrates (460–370 BCE), commonly referred to as the "Father of Western Medicine," is credited with shifting the study of public health away from mysticism to patient-oriented empiricism.[2] Whilst Hippocrates' empirical study is not directly comparable, the shift in the study of complex phenomena away from philosophy and theurgy to empirical analysis proved to be radical and established a pathway for future advances.

One of the first scholars to formally codify public health methodology was Avicenna (Ibn Sina), a tenth-century Persian philosopher.[3] His 14-volume *Canon on Medicine* began what would become a millennia-long process of understanding the relationships of pathogens and human society. Numerous other scholars who both helped and hurt the study of public health and the spread of disease followed Avicenna. However, it was not until John Graunt, a London haberdasher, established the "Bills of Mortality" and later a book entitled the *Natural and Political Observations Mentioned in a Following Index, and Made Upon the Bills of Mortality*, that rigorous mathematically rooted methodology began to impact the field. Since then, public health has evolved from a philosophy to a science including the use of inductive and deductive logic.[4]

John Graunt is the starting point for a substantive comparative relationship between cybersecurity and public health management. It is in the establishment of rigorous methodologies rather than the conjecture that the applicability of public health becomes more directly relevant to the study of alternative phenomena such as cybersecurity. William Farr, an officer in the General Register Office of England, wrote "Diseases are more easily prevented than cured and the first step to their prevention is the discovery of their exciting causes."[5] This sentiment expanded the scope of public health beyond the treatment of disease, and oriented the field toward prevention.

The modern study of disease derives its effectiveness from thousands of years of trial and error. Yet what separates historical public health methods from their modern counterparts is the rigor of the scientific method. This invariably leads to a discussion of multicausality. It is possible to view multicausality as a pie where the factors combine to result in an effect. Any given slice of the pie is an independent causal variable, influencing the probability of the function. Yet this independent variable does not operate in isolation. Instead, it combines with other slices to form a complete causal mechanism that explains incident (case) occurrence. The consensus in modern public health leads researchers to focus on both genetic and environmental factors. The impact of these broad categories can differ based on circumstance. For instance, a man killed in a car accident died upon impact of the car with a tree. Whilst the cause of death is seemingly apparent, the explanation fails to take into consideration that the man was driving whilst under the influence of alcohol. It is therefore also possible to attribute the cause of the crash to alcohol consumption. It is equally possible that this individual was genetically predisposed to alcoholism, further complicating the causal relationships. Had the man been treated for a genetic predisposition for alcohol it is possible that the crash might have been avoided. Three relatively simple attributes associated with a fatal car crash alone cannot provide an epidemiologist with a direct or linear causal chain of events, nor can it adequately facilitate the mitigation of future events.

It is as much the scientific method as it is the way of thinking about causality that affects the potential for success. One of the more famous structures of causality originated with Sir Austin Bradford Hill, a British epidemiologist who, building on the canons of inference established by John Stuart Mill, wrote the causal criteria known as the "Causal Criteria of Hill," which is often referred to as the "classic framework."[6] Hill's criteria include the strength, consistency, specificity, temporality, biologic gradient, plausibility, coherence, experimental evidence, and analogy related to any form of disease.[7] Whilst the terms used lack in their apparent application to other domains, a changing of terminology can increase their pertinence and guide the creation of more robust causal models.

Current EPI and public health relies on surveillance. Surveillance, unlike the basic application of the scientific method or Hill's causal criteria, implies an active and continuous process of examination. Although health surveillance is not a modern concept and can be traced back to the fourteenth- and fifteenth-century practice of excluding infected ships from entering Venetian ports, the modern concept is attributed to William Farr, the first compiler of abstract (statistician) in the General Register Office.[8] There are two primary conceptual frameworks for EPI prediction. The first, the public health surveillance system, collects and warehouses data that enables an understanding of public health issues and places an emphasis on the pathology, calculation of risk, identification of vectors, and treatment interventions.[9] The second is the calculation of risk reduction, i.e., how we minimize the post hoc effect of a disease outbreak.[10] The two models differ in their focus. Whilst the former is proactive, the latter is more likely to be reactive. An early formal definition of EPI surveillance as:

> ... the epidemiological study of a disease as a dynamic process involving the ecology of the infectious agent, the host, the reservoirs, and the vectors, as well as the complex mechanisms concerned in the spread of infection and the extent to which this spread occurs....

establishes a dynamic and robust conceptualization.[11] Although debates over the role of research and other nuanced aspects of the definition surfaced, the fundamental attributes of the definition remain generally applicable.

Arguably, one of the greatest historical successes of public health and EPI was the eradication of smallpox. The declaration on May 8 1980 at the thirty-third World Health Assembly marking the eradication of smallpox was the first time in the history of mankind that man had vanquished a disease.[12] The process of smallpox analysis and treatment was both reactive and proactive. However, the final eradication of smallpox is closely associated with reactive risk reduction strategies through processes of immunization and the creation of herd immunity. Millennia of illness had plagued humankind and only relatively recently were EPI and public health able to eradicate a disease. This was not the first time eradication of a disease had been attempted. Yet the outcome differed and ushered in a new era, one in which it was at least theoretically possible to eradicate disease. Using this as a guide, what follows in the next section are the attributes of public health and EPI focusing on both surveillance and a mitigation of risk. These categories are directly compared to cybersecurity approaches.

Thinking big and small: building multicausal models for understanding complex phenomena

The principles of cybersecurity for critical infrastructure protection as outlined by the National Institute of Standards and Technology (NIST) comprise a five-function core, each with multiple subcategories.[13] The primary functions of the framework are identification, protection, detection, response, and recovery. Together, they inform a security posture for critical infrastructure protection. The organization of these functions and their constituent categories form a risk-based framework for safeguarding digital systems. The NIST framework is the government standard; a policy document placing all organizations with a role in critical infrastructure on a similar footing. Beyond broad policy documents and macro-infrastructure protection, individuals seeking to become leaders in information technology security often earn a certified information systems security professional certificate, known as a CISSP. The CISSP, among a smorgasbord of other similar certifications, functions within a risk-based framework. The core of the CISSP method is the CIA triad, which stands for Confidentiality, Integrity, and Availability.[14] The goal of network engineers and IT professionals is to maintain the confidentiality of information within the strictures of privacy or classification requirements, the integrity of that information in that it is accurate and reliable, and the availability of information and assets when they are called for. Both the NIST and CIA models are applicable to, and can be seen as, the base model for a more robust EPI- or public health-based model for cybersecurity.

As highlighted in the previous section, EPI and public health contain risk-based structures designed to minimize the spread of pathogens. Much like them, the majority of cybersecurity tenets rest in business processes rooted in the maintenance of the CIA triad and attempt to minimize vulnerabilities. Access controls, security architecture and design, conventional physical and environmental security, encryption, business continuity, and disaster planning are all extremely valuable aspects of the maintenance of cybersecurity. Each arguably adds substantively to a rigorous causal matrix and parallels in many ways the modeling structures found within public health.

The application of EPI models to cybersecurity is not novel. In 2013, two computer scientists, David Parker and Csilla Farkas, in a response to proposed Department of Homeland Security cyber budgetary requests, wrote a thought piece explaining the potential use of EPI models to quantitatively assess risk potential and foster more targeted interventions against cyberattacks.[15] Their analysis focused primarily on public health surveillance systems with an emphasis on a base EPI model known commonly by its acronym SEIR, or Susceptible, Exposed, Infectious, and Recovered. Their suggestion was the creation of a similar modeling system for cyberspace, coined the Cyber Security Surveillance System.[16] Even more interesting than the comparative analysis of the SEIR model to cybersecurity was their reference to the World Health Organization's (WHO) guidelines for the development and implementation of surveillance systems.[17]

The impact of cross-disciplinary study resides in the WHO guideline documents as much as it is in the statistical models of public health and EPI. The WHO guidelines stipulate that an effective surveillance system is constituted by the following continuously ongoing functions:[18]

- detection and notification of health events
- collection and consolidation of pertinent data
- investigation and confirmation (epidemiological, clinical and/or laboratory) of cases or outbreaks

- routine analysis and creation of reports
- feedback of information to persons providing data
- feed-forward (i.e., the forwarding of data to more central levels).

Moreover, an effective surveillance system is useful, efficient, flexible, representative, and simple. The WHO standards are transnational and include case definitions, surveillance types, data elements to be collected, minimum analyses and routine reports, and data-driven decision making. Health surveillance systems consider every type of health-related issue and extend across species to provide advanced warning of potential issues before they reach human populations. Data sources for health surveillance are numerous and typically include: mortality data, morbidity data (case reporting), conventional EPI reporting, laboratory reporting, individual case reporting, epidemic field investigations, surveys, animal reservoir and vector distribution studies, demographic data, environmental data, hospital and medical care statistics, general practitioners, public health laboratory reports, disease registries, drug and biologics utilization and sales data, absenteeism, health and general population surveys, and news reporting.[19] The list, whilst not exhaustive, is comprehensive and indicates the depth of study and the range of causal factors included in public health analysis.

Cybersecurity surveillance, like health surveillance, needs to be exhaustive in its efforts to reduce incidence rates.[20] Currently, cybersecurity surveillance modeling is inconsistent across organizations and entities within both the public and private sectors. This creates a patchwork of regimes, each of which has different strengths and weaknesses, but each lacking in holistic and dynamic coverage. Public health has identified multiple avenues for the potential spread or contraction of disease. Vector-borne diseases, defined as illnesses caused by pathogens and parasites in human populations, are only a limited subset of disease in much the same way that viruses, Trojans, and worms constitute only a subset of cybersecurity issues.[21] Just as vector-borne disease is only a subset of the broader study of disease, malware-borne cybersecurity problems are a subset of a larger systemic problem(s). Whilst the impact of vector-borne disease and vectored malware are significant, they form only part of a broader process of health and security affecting cyberspace or human populations. Human attributes associated with the cybersecurity failures are as fundamental to ensuring cybersecurity as are the antivirus, firewall, and other defensive measures implemented by governments and organizations.[22]

The public health and EPI surveillance frameworks established by the WHO and the Centers for Disease Control (CDC) establish a comparable rule-based system that focuses on the minimization and the potential eradication of disease.[23] Their direction and standardization across operational entities, from local physicians and health clinics to nation states, establishes a rigorous and consistent framework for action. However, what is most important is the realization that the control of disease is a systemic process involving the monitoring of incidence from the lowest to the highest levels of operation. Moreover, the control of the disease does not occur solely through the development of vaccines or medications but also the retraining of societies broadly to establish practices that facilitate health. Although the literature in cybersecurity is growing increasingly robust, this robustness is often limited to specific types of analysis.

Poor behavior by citizens in times of health crisis can lead to cascading implications based on the type of disease. Kello's assessment of cyberspace—as a series of overlapping terrains of operation consisting of: (1) the Internet (all connected computing devices); (2) websites comprising the World Wide Web accessible through URL; and (3) computing devices segregated from the Internet in isolated networks—simplifies the extent of cyberspace. This simplification highlights the integrated connection between actions in one terrain and their implications in another.[24] Kello's construct of three overlapping terrains is not entirely dissimilar from the Department of Defense's (DoD) construct of cyberspace as constituting three layers.[25] The DoD's layered approach is comprised of a Physical Network Layer, a Logical Network Layer, and a Cyber-Persona Layer. Each of these layers plays a role in DoD cyberspace operational planning. An increasingly nuanced layered approach to the needs of cybersecurity experts or operators provides deeper insight into the origin of problems and their possible solutions. Yet, the disease vulnerability surface associated with either the terrain or layers should not be seen as entirely dichotomous.

Focusing operations or policy on one layer, rather than focusing on the interrelation of the layers, overlooks many of the attributes of the spread of disease, whether in cyberspace or in health and EPI. Research conducted on behalf of the United States Computer Emergency Response Team found that 40 percent of corporations and government entities in the United States indicated their greatest concern was the unintentional or accidental jeopardizing of security.[26] The unintentional exposure of individuals and corporate or government assets to risk is not unique to cybersecurity. Research in the field of cognitive psychology has demonstrated time and time again that human beings cannot understand intuitively systemic risk.[27] Individuals working in first responder positions in a large American city who participated in a training on digital hygiene were surprised to find out that their home behavior in cyberspace could lead to the compromise of their critical systems at work through inadvertent processes. In the last few years alone, well-established organizations such as Target, Home Depot or TV5Monde have come to realize that inadvertent behaviors supposed to increase the efficiency or simplicity of life can result in fundamental compromises in security.[28]

During the 2014 Ebola outbreak in the United States, a nurse caring for an Ebola victim traveled from Texas to Ohio before being tracked down by the CDC.[29] Ebola, a virus requiring Biosafety Level 4 containment, is an extremely virulent pathogen. The nurse who traveled did not have malicious intent, yet her actions resulted in the potential for the expansion of a deadly epidemic. The same unintentional behavior in cyberspace is a regular occurrence. In 2008, a service member or contractor in Iraq, likely unknowingly, inserted a USB thumb drive into a classified machine. The drive contained a malicious script called Agent.btz. The malicious code spread rapidly throughout DoD networks. The infection, which resulted in a point-source progressive infiltration of DoD systems, can be examined from the moment the USB drive was inserted into a classified machine, much like the car accident described in the first section. Yet, starting the examination at this point fails to account for the spread of the malware. Whilst the search for patient zero never reached fruition, the process of learning from the virus proved to be a starting point for a change in policy and operational capability development.[30] Just as the prevention of disease is far easier than the eradication of disease, the same is largely true in cyberspace. The next section focuses on the development of a cyber surveillance framework using the building blocks of public health and EPI within the constraints of cyberspace to develop a model that focuses on both the prevention of cybersecurity issues before they arise and their eradication once discovered. The overlap is not perfect, yet many of the same issues associated with privacy, civil rights, human rights, corporate and government security are prevalent across the two disciplines.

A foundation for cybersecurity surveillance for systemic protective measures

This discussion serves as an extension and expansion of Parker and Farkas' work on risk modeling using EPI frameworks. Whereas their model focuses predictive risk modeling, this discussion is holistic and seeks to foster normative shifts in approaches to complex systemic issues. This is done by leveraging both all-source intelligence for risk modeling and response mechanisms, systemic behavioral change based on available threats as well as opportunities to obviate threats before they arise. An ideal surveillance system must be useful, efficient, flexible, representative, and simple. Such a system for cybersecurity must be more than asset-focused and instead focus on the interaction of assets within a networked environment and the relationship of assets and networks of assets and the human users. The resulting construct thus encompasses four dimensions: Human, Hardware, Software, and Systems of Systems.[31]

Human: Humans invent computers, write codes to exploit them, use computers, establish authentication mechanisms, store, distribute, and create information on digital systems. Not all behaviors of computers and networks are the result of human interaction, but a large majority are. Human interactions with technical systems are social and psychological constructs often culturally and normatively constructed. Every individual from hardware and software engineers to the end users approach the computer with differing levels of foundational knowledge that allows them to leverage digital tools to accomplish goals and objectives. These goals and objectives differ from person to person and influence the manner in which human–computer interaction is conducted. For some, it is the creation of novel programs and for others it is the communication on Facebook between two friends. Often, the goals and objectives of an individual overlap. A software engineer can also check Facebook or Twitter whilst working on a coding project. From this perspective, there is a high degree of variability present within cyberspace both between and within individuals. This includes individuals engaging in "unhealthy practices"; just as an individual's decision to smoke can have health consequences, an individual's decision to visit certain websites can have financial or privacy considerations.

Individuals of differing socioeconomic, sociocultural, or political back-grounds assess differently levels of risk about the spread and susceptibility to disease.[32] The same is true in cyberspace. Individuals with different economic backgrounds often have widely divergent levels of educational attainment.[33] It is also likely that individuals with lower socioeconomic status are more likely to purchase less expensive or older computing devices more vulnerable to malware; they are also less likely to have surplus funds to purchase antivirus software and are less likely to conduct thorough research on proper digital hygiene or be exposed to training.[34] Whilst this area of research is lacking in formal studies, there is some ongoing research in the field looking at socioeconomic status and susceptibility to cybercrime. Moreover, the general sentiment at Army Cyber Command, US Cyber Command, and the Department of Homeland Security indicates that there is a lack of education and training adequate to meet the demand for cybersecurity. There are multiple studies further indicating a correla-tion between education and economic status, thus making the inductive leap between economic status and cybersecurity plausible as a potential factor for inclusion in dynamic modeling. Yet socioeconomic status or education alone cannot begin to account for the proliferation of inadvertently caused vulnerabili-ties. In fact, economic status might actually have a nonlinear relationship with vulnerability. This is due to the fact that individuals in the lowest socioeconomic distributions of society are less likely to own computers or multiple devices in general, thereby reducing their threat surface. There are seemingly infinite vari-ations across individuals, making the prediction of behavior extremely difficult. Yet it is the consideration of multiple causal mechanisms that makes public health and EPI surveillance models so robust.

In 1854, John Snow, an English physician, received credit for convincing the Board of Guardians of Saint James' Parish to remove the pump handle from the Broad Street pump in Golden Square after coming to the conclusion that fouled water was likely a causal factor in a significant cholera outbreak that year.[35] By isolating patterns of behavior and honing down the focus, it is often possible to find the point source of a disease outbreak. At other times when a point source is obscured, it is possible to isolate the behavioral patterns that lead to certain out-comes. In cyberspace, such behavioral patterns can be as simple as individuals clicking on unknown links, thereby exposing their computer to a potential mali-cious actor; it can be the systemic failure to add complexity to passwords or the placement of relevant data on publicly available sites that makes social engineer-ing or the guessing of passwords or other credentials significantly easier.

As much as society is reliant on computers, many of the woes faced in cyber-space are a direct result of human behavior. Sometimes the behavior is the result of cognitive biases; sometimes it is the result of complexity, and sometimes it is the result of ignorance. By isolating human–computer interactions and focusing on the behavioral attributes of users, as well as the developers and engineers designing products, cybersecurity can manipulate the failings of human inter-actions with computing devices.[36] The process of constraining behavior or guiding it can follow what Jonathan Zittrain refers to as a non-generative process.[37] Zit-train indicates that non-generative processes can stifle innovation. Products such as Apple's iPhone and iPad limit the ability of a user to harm the device as well as to innovate. The non-generative nature of certain devices significantly miti-gates the potential harm such devices can do. Whilst even these relatively non-generative devices have potential security issues, these issues pale in comparison to those of more generative platforms such as Google's Android, often referred to as the largest target for mobile malware.[38] Just as keeping humans segregated in sterile cells might prevent all spread of disease, it would also limit their shared potential. Using surveillance to isolate those behavioral patterns which result in the greatest damage would begin a process of cyber health management.

Behavior can be identified in multiple ways and pattern recognition has been a staple of modern network defenses within organizations and the government for some time. The use of intrusion detection systems and other similar plat-forms helps to generate pattern data and rapidly identify anomalous behavior before it becomes too serious. Other software- and hardware-based behavioral analysis platforms collect data from multiple networks and build large exclusion lists based on aggregated data across customer sets. What these systems fail to account for are the systemic problems caused by extra-network assets and the unintended actions of individuals inside and outside network perimeters.

Whilst it might be mandatory for restaurant employees to wash hands after using the toilet when at work, a failure to do so upon leaving a place of employ-ment can result in a return vector of a pathogen by an employee who is diligent whilst on the clock but careless off the clock. An employee who follows security protocols whilst in the office by not clicking on inappropriate or unknown links might inadvertently bring in an infected USB thumb drive to share a picture with a co-worker, or plug in an infected phone with the intention of charging it. Even if all on-the-clock actions are followed and no USBs or external devices are introduced into an ecosystem, an employee's careless behavior on social media or with home email can result in the compromise of employment-based assets through social engineering, similar password selection, personally identifiable information, or any number of unintentional actions that open the doors of a company to potential exploitation.

Beyond potential unintentional accidents, there are also wide ranges of inten-tional threats that come from digital system use both at work and at home. Much as certain populations are more likely to engage in reckless behavior behind the wheel of a car or in a wide range of other situations, certain individuals are more likely to engage in deliberate acts that result in damage. Intentionally caused medical issues tracked through public health surveillance also provide insight into the spread of disease. Likewise, intentionally caused cybersecurity vulnerabilities can provide clues to the behavior of malicious actors. US-CERT, in coordination with Carnegie Mellon University and the Software Engineering Institute, high-lighted in a survey of 557 respondent organizations that approximately 37 percent significantly damaging cyber incidents were the result of insiders.[39] Whilst a fair percentage of this group was unintentional, a large portion was due to intentional theft.

Single organizational tracking of human behavior provides disconnected snapshots within limited samples of populations. Whilst cross-organizational behavior challenges information-sharing laws and policies, privacy constraints, and other rules and regulations, the potential benefit from big data aggregation of data on human interactions within corporate networks might facilitate increasingly robust probabilistic models that can inform policy development, software and systems engineering, and network architecture.[40] The present state of the data on individual behavior is improving, yet lacks a level of comprehensiveness necessary to make significant advances in security. This is evident in DoD, corporate and academic information assurance training that focuses on non-digital behaviors to predict the level of risk associated with digital environments. Information is not a panacea for cybersecurity, but just as in EPI and public health surveillance, the goal is to use it to begin putting the causal pieces of the puzzle together to foster a more dynamic response. Beyond information on human behavior, this puzzle should include data on the design and implementation of hardware, software, and systems of systems. In each of these issue areas, parallels can be made between the management and surveillance of these systems and public health and EPI models.

Hardware: Hardware impacts every aspect of the cyber environment. Cyberspace, often thought of as a purely virtual environment, is in reality both virtual and physical. The DoD layers of cyberspace approach in Joint Publication 12 Cyberspace Operations highlights the physical nature of the environment as well as its virtual (logical) and human dimensions. It is possible to track both disease and hardware. The life expectancy, resilience, complexity, physical security, and requirements of hardware differ from machine to machine and device to device. Environmental attributes and resource constraints within and beyond nations, global manufacturing processes, and a multitude of attributes influence the innovation, development, construction, and implementation of new hardware solutions and the continued use of old ones. These constraints limit the ability to fully implement Hardware Security Development Lifecycle (HSDL) processes. HSDL is the incorporation of security at all stages of hardware development.[41]

Constructing a surveillance framework that incorporates in an HSDL everything from research and development through post-sale implementation and use is critical to the management of incidence and prevalence rates of malware within and across organizations. Structural features, design, chipsets, radios, random-access memory, material attributes, port inclusion, and more can serve to constrain or free users, software, and network usage. Hardware choices result in ramifications beyond intended use or design specifications. A comprehensive understanding of life-cycle development processes parallels a public health understanding of natural and unnatural case fatality rates. The cyberspace equivalent of a natural case fatality—a fault in a product caused by physical component failure due to usage or defective manufacturing or other non-intentionally induced failures—is as important as intentionally induced failures.

Just as there are significant degrees of genetic variation among human populations necessitating the study of tailored genetic and molecular solutions to complicated diseases such as Alpha 1-antitrypsin deficiency, there is also a wide array of computer hardware configurations necessitating tailored solution sets, such as Application Specific Integrated Circuits or Field Programmable Gate Arrays, to name but a few.[42] Knowing what hardware is in use, where it is used, its age, its vulnerability level, and its intended and current purpose can facilitate the development of risk profiles for organizations. Moreover, hardware systems are often located in areas with limited contact with other software, hardware, systems, or human interactions. Contact might be so infrequent that it leads to a failure to consider interactions, resulting in negative effects when contact inadvertently or intentionally occurs with either malicious or benign software, persons, or unpredictable environmental conditions. Infrequently accessed systems can at times be lost within modern accounting mechanisms within the offices of chief information officers. These accounting systems are devoted to accurate accounting of hardware assets through regular audits. Yet, accurate accounting becomes increasingly difficult with the expansion of organizations, the sale of organizations, the transition or transfer of staff, or through deliberate or unintended neglect.

The purpose of this discussion on the fundamental attributes of hardware within a cybersecurity surveillance system is to extend the thought processes of the reader to the impact of hardware on general cybersecurity. The manipulation of hardware post-design through customized physical modifications or modifications in firmware/software can result in implications that affect the other macro-level functional areas within this construct. Whereas in public health and EPI modeling, the objects of study largely revolve around organics with degrees of genetic differences, hardware in cyberspace revolves around an innovative and evolving process of creation, resulting in new hardware types each imbued with inherent strengths and weaknesses. Whilst the level of complexity per unit might be less on an individual unit basis, the combined complexity of hundreds, thousands, or millions of different hardware types each with different tolerances, results in an approximate level of aggregate complexity comparable to genetic diversity.[43]

Discussions on the fundamental nature of hardware design security are growing in frequency and have become almost standard in the design and innovation process for all embedded systems.[44] Life-cycle discussions, continued analysis, research and consistent systematic monitoring of active systems provide the rough equivalent of general public health surveillance and make possible statistical analysis in much the same way that the SEIR EPI model tracks disease. Big data analysis might not provide 100 percent coverage solutions, but it can provide subsets of reliable diverse data that facilitate predictive modeling for both cybersecurity and public health. Anticipating or reacting to problems before they become extreme, in this case identifying hardware patterns that result in compromise, needs to be combined with human surveillance to enhance cybersecurity.

Software: If hardware represents the bones of computers, then software is the blood and tissues that make them behave the way they do. As noted by many coding experts and standards bodies, security in software begins during the development process.[45] Comparing Public health and EPI models to software development is extremely difficult. The genetic instructions written into millions of lines of code each proscribing the function of a piece of hardware or an application constitute an immense weakness in comparing surveillance for public health and EPI and cybersecurity.

Although a large majority of the cybersecurity community focuses on post hoc malware intrusions, the true problems associated with cybersecurity reside within a level of systemic complexity that makes the ultimate prevention of malware intrusions what game theorists would refer to as a "best shot versus weakest link" scenario.[46] The probability of an absence of vulnerabilities is virtually zero. An anecdote provided by Robert O'Harrow in his book on zero-day vulnerabilities illustrates the challenges of protecting against all vulnerabilities.[47] O'Harrow tells of a hacker who seeks out vulnerabilities by trying to force scripts to malfunction. He describes testing the iPhone for weeks, using automated scripts to find a single flaw in the coding that makes it vulnerable to exploitation. There are comparable examples of biologists and geneticists attempting repeatedly to engineer or develop pathogens to cause or remedy disease or illness, but the volume of attempts is unlikely to equate to the billions of combinations conducted as quickly or as efficiently as hackers. In contrast, hackers can try to disrupt the coding schema of a supposedly secure software program through automated processes or using suites of malware or penetration modules.

Surveillance systems for public health and EPI models can and do focus on finding genetic or systemic flaws within human biology. Often, these flaws span large populations and are found primarily through post hoc analysis using both inductive and deductive logic to determine a causal relationship between a diseased state and the risk factors which led to that state. In cyberspace, the surveillance needs to begin at inception. Biologists cannot seek out a creator to understand why a genetic sequence formed in a specified pattern the same way that a cybersecurity specialist can seek out the programmer or team of programmers that wrote or designed a specific set of software. The process of creating secure code requires a reconstitution of the logical processes that underpin surveillance systems for public health and EPI. Whereas the latter are necessarily confined to analysis of flaws and vulnerabilities within existing systems, cybersecurity experts can, from the point of initial concept development, focus on what the Department of Homeland Security refers to as a Secure Software Development Life Cycle Process (SSDLC).[48] The inclusion of policy mechanisms such as laws on liability or tax incentives to enhance or mitigate the effects of the delivery of code that is insufficiently vetted for vulnerabilities, informs the life-cycle approach to surveillance. More robust SSDLC processes, whether based on Microsoft's SDLC model or on any number of other models, facilitate a dynamic early-stage analytical approach to risk.

Beyond focusing on the development and continued use of software, a vast majority of the surveillance systems associated with cybersecurity, much like their public health and EPI counterparts, focus on pathogens or malware. The average number of lines of code within software platforms is significantly higher than the number of lines of code in the average malware script. Whilst the former ranges in the hundreds of thousands to tens of millions, the average length of code for malware has remained relatively static at approximately 125.[49] Antivirus, firewall and network security vendors make it their living to identify these lines of code and weed them out of network traffic entering into controlled systems or networks. They analyze the code forensically and break it down, determine the signature and then, in much the same way that a vaccine works at inoculating a human population, they propagate the signature out across their systems to inoculate their clients. The hope is that they are able to catch and identify malware before it spreads across a significant portion of their client base, so that their inoculation is both beneficial to their clients and provides a financial benefit to the company.

The post hoc analysis and subsequent inoculation against potential malware or pathogens works well with pathogens with relatively low reproduction numbers, or R0. The inoculation of infected machines, as in their biological counterparts, can and often does minimize the extent of an infection. Yet, if the spread of the disease or malware has a high R0, or the malware/pathogen is abnormal in that it actively attempts to obscure itself within a target system or host, such as the Stuxnet virus, then post hoc analysis can be a slow and arduous process that results in high case fatalities either in humans or machines respectively. Active surveillance of the ebb and flow of malware types, their evolution and their ability to affect targeted systems generally approximates the EPI models. Large-scale analysis of these patterns can begin to mitigate the best-shot–weakest-link failings of software development by providing more efficient post-development patching and remediation solutions. Furthermore, large-scale analysis of malware use patterns can also save developers time in testing by helping them to focus on categories of potential vulnerabilities, and getting the biggest bang for the buck on testing. Thus, the life-cycle process can be improved both at the beginning and the end stages of software use.

Just as in the discussion on hardware, it is important to consider the generative and non-generative nature of software design within the constraints of human behavior. Code that might be "secure enough" for one audience might leave another less technically adept user group extremely vulnerable to exploitation. Understanding the interactions across areas of surveillance between human, hardware, and software fosters a dynamic and nuanced approach to cybersecurity. Instead of constraining a single approach into a single category, surveillance should be extended across all categories with an emphasis on multicausality. The power of public health and EPI models of surveillance for cybersecurity associated with software offers a vast number of additional avenues of exploration which cannot be addressed in this section alone. Despite failing to be all-inclusive in addressing the application of public health and EPI to software development, use, and vulnerabilities, the section provided a base level cross-disciplinary approach to software surveillance for addressing cybersecurity concerns. The next section further complicates the surveillance model approach by adding systemic complexity.

Systems of systems: The decision to use the term "system" rather than "network" is deliberate. Whilst the Internet is comprised of networks of networks, the networks are comprised of sociotechnical systems defined by the human, hardware, and software elements within them. Absent these, the building blocks of the Internet are missing. Rather than obfuscate the units into a larger typology, the focus here is on interaction of systems in larger and larger clusters. Just as in public health, where it is unproductive to speak about pathogens as a global pathogen, it is unhelpful to speak about cyberspace or the Internet broadly. Likewise, it is unhelpful to aggregate to the term network, as there are multiple types of networks. Whereas the lower-level units examined above each constituted a unit for examination, it is the aggregation of those units that creates systemic vulnerabilities.

When changing the level of analysis from the individual to the aggregate, nuance is lost. By examining the variation in levels of incidence,[50] prevalence,[51] case fatality,[52] and reproduction number[53] in a systems of systems environment, behavioral patterns of malware, the actors behind malware, and other intentional or accidental incidents become more readily apparent.[54] Therefore, by using pathogen dispersion models, cybersecurity experts can enhance an understanding of malware spread and impact. It is possible to develop advantages, through thorough understanding of both system and systems of systems constraints.

Within this system of systems concept there are two broad ways of examining the environment. The first is from the top down, network to unit. The second is from the bottom up, unit to network. With sufficient nuance at each level of analysis, each provides novel solutions for potential prevention, inoculation, or remediation. This holistic public health or EPI framework for understanding cyberspace is currently being implemented on an ad hoc basis and is in a testing stage at the Defense Advanced Research Projects Agency.[55] The discussion below summarizes the main concepts of this chapter and highlights advances in information sharing that are forwarding a dynamic holistic approach to national cybersecurity.

Conclusion

Information is the lifeblood of good public health and EPI surveillance, and good surveillance is crucial to the eradication or minimization of disease within populations. The cyber community is catching up. Executive Order (EO) 13636, Improving Critical Infrastructure Cybersecurity, and EO 13691, Promoting Private Sector Cybersecurity Information Sharing, are both aimed at developing frameworks for systems of information sharing similar to public health surveillance systems. EO

13636 specifically focuses on rigorous analysis of particular critical infrastructure with an emphasis on the financial and energy sectors. These sectors are pushed to develop rigorous analyses of network infrastructure, assets, recovery plans and, lastly, they are encouraged to contribute information to Information Sharing and Analysis Centers (ISACs).

Since sector-specific ISACs are constrained to sector-specific organizations identified within EO 13636, many organizations fall outside or cross over sector-specific categories. Just as a zoonotic pathogen can spread from animal to human populations, so too can malware from one type of organization to another. To fill in the gaps, EO 13691 promotes generalized information sharing through the creation of sector or community specific Information Sharing and Analysis Organizations (ISAOs). These organizations are designed to be inclusive, actionable, transparent, and trusted. Any organization, from any sector—including for-profit, non-profit, technically adept, and novice alike—can participate in ISAOs.[56] Furthermore, ISAOs will be run in consultation with an ISAO standards organization to be developed with or coordinated by the Secretary of Homeland Security. EO 13691 also builds upon the Homeland Security Act of 2002 with the creation of the National Cybersecurity and Communications Integration Center (NCCIC). The order requires the NCCIC to engage in continuous collaborative and inclusive coordination with ISAOs on the sharing of information related to cybersecurity risks and incidents. Furthermore, the NCCIC is directed to address the risks and incidents by strengthening national information security systems.

The movement of integration originated by the Executive Office is only one thrust in a coordinated effort to begin developing a systematic process of cybersecurity surveillance for national security purposes. Whilst the motives associated with these developments are largely benign, they are likely to encounter many of the same concerns of state encroachment on civil liberties as early public health and EPI surveillance and information-sharing systems. Moreover, the process of developing a systematized public health and EPI framework for the surveillance of threats to cybersecurity is likely to require consistent fine-tuning, in both the public and private sectors in the decade to come. When moving the nation toward a national cyber health system for cybersecurity, it is pertinent to remember that the majority of public health and EPI surveillance systems are quite novel and came to fruition only after millennia of individuals and groups tried to create a system for tracking disease in human populations. Whilst the timeline for cybersecurity is likely to be significantly shorter than public health and EPI, patience in achieving a workable solution is a valuable commodity.

This chapter tried to leverage some lessons, including empirical and systemic analysis with a focus on multicausality that can be derived, from an extensive history of fighting disease in human populations and apply them to cybersecurity. If nations and individuals are to combat the challenges faced in cyberspace, it is going to be increasingly important to leverage multidisciplinary analysis to inform, guide, and push the field into the future. Not all solutions or analogies will be applicable or useful, some might even prove harmful, yet absent trial and error and intellectual discourse the state of the field will remain stagnant.

Notes

* The views expressed here are those of the author and do not reflect the official policy or position of the Department of the Army, Department of Defense, or the US Government.
1 Kenneth J. Rothman, *Epidemiology: An Introduction* [Kindle edition] (New York: Oxford University Press, 2012), 224.
2 Dorothy Porter, *Health, Civilization, and the State: A History of Public Health from Ancient to Modern Times* (London: Routledge, 1999), 15.
3 Rothman, *Epidemiology: An Introduction*, 288.
4 Ibid., 325; S. Declich and Anne O. Carter, "Public health surveillance: Historical origins, methods and evaluation," *Bulletin of the World Health Organization* 72/2 (1994): 286.
5 Rothman, *Epidemiology: An Introduction*, 407.
6 Ibid., 825; Thomas A. Glass et al., "Causal inference in public health," *Annual Review of Public Health* 34 (2013): 61–75.
7 Austin Bradford Hill, "The environment and disease: Association or causation?" *Proceedings of the Royal Society of Medicine* 58 (1965): 295–300.
8 Declich and Carter, "Public health surveillance," 286.
9 R. D. Parker and Csilla Farkas, "Modeling estimated risk for cyber attacks: Merging public health and cyber security," *Information Assurance and Security Letters* 2 (2011): 34.
10 Ibid.
11 K. Raska, "National and international surveillance of communicable diseases," *WHO Chronicle* 20 (1966): 316.
12 Donald A. Henderson, "Eradication: Lessons from the past," *Bulletin of the World Health Organization* 76 (1998): 17–21.
13 National Institute of Standards and Technology, *Framework for Improving Critical Infrastructure Cybersecurity* (Washington DC, 2014).
14 Shon Harris, *CISSP Certification Exam Guide* (New York: McGraw-Hill/Osborne, 2003), 154.
15 Parker and Farkas, "Modeling estimated risk for cyber attacks," 32.
16 Ibid.
17 Ibid., 33.
18 World Health Organization, *WHO – Recommended Standards for Surveillance of Selected Vaccine-Preventable Diseases* (Geneva, 2003), vii.
19 Declich and Carter, "Public health surveillance," 290–293.
20 Incidence rate is the ratio of cases from network live time or simply the time at risk for infection. See: Aaron F. Brantly, "Aesop's wolves: The deceptive appearance of espionage and attacks in cyberspace," *Intelligence and National Security* 31/5 (2015): 674–685.
21 World Health Organization, "Vector-Borne Diseases," February 2016, at www.who.int/mediacentre/factsheets/fs387/en/.
22 Julie L. Marble et al., "The human factor in cybersecurity: Robust & Intelligent Defense," in Sushil Jajodia et al. (eds), *Cyber Warfare* (New York: Springer International Publishing, 2015), 173–206.
23 World Health Organization, "Public Health Surveillance," at www.who.int/immunization/monitoring_surveillance/burden/vpd/en/; James W. Buehler et al., "Framework for Evaluating Public Health Surveillance Systems for Early Detection of Outbreaks: Recommendations from the CDC Working Group," at www.cdc.gov/mmwr/preview/mmwrhtml/rr5305a1.htm; Centers for Disease Control, *Surveillance Strategy: A Strategy for Improving the Centers for Disease Control and Prevention's Activities in Public Health Surveillance* (Atlanta, 2014).
24 Lucas Kello, "The meaning of the cyber revolution: Perils to theory and statecraft," *International Security* 38/1 (2013): 7–40.

25 Department of Defense, *Joint Publication 3–12: Cyberspace Operations* (Washington, DC, 2013).
26 David Mundie, "Unintentional Insider Threat and Social Engineering," *Software Engineering Institute* at http://blog.sei.cmu.edu/post.cfm/unintentional-insider-threat-social-engineering-090?wt.ac=hpBlog.
27 Daniel Kahneman, *Thinking, Fast and Slow* (New York: Farrar, Straus and Giroux, 2011).
28 Sam Machkovech, "Hacked French Network Exposed Its Own Passwords during TV Interview," *ArsTechnica*, at http://arstechnica.com/security/2015/04/hacked-french-network-exposed-its-own-passwords-during-tv-interview/.
29 Betsy McKay, Ana Campoy, and Dan Frosch, "CDC Chief Says 2nd Nurse with Ebola Should Not Have Flown," *Wall Street Journal*, October 15, 2014 at www.wsj.com/articles/ohio-officials-tracking-contacts-of-texsas-health-care-worker-with-ebola-1413396205.
30 Ellen Nakashima, "Cyber-intruder sparks response, debate" *Washington Post*, December 8, 2011, at www.washingtonpost.com/national/national-security/cyber-intruder-sparks-response-debate/2011/12/06/gIQAxLuFgO_story.html.
31 Here, system does not imply a single hardware-software system as is common in vernacular but rather indicates the concept of networking. Networking in a purely cyber context can be restrictive. System implies physical and virtual, human and technical.
32 George Rosen, *A History of Public Health* [Kindle edition] (New York: MD Publications, 1958), 624.
33 William H. Sewell and Vimal P. Shah, "Socioeconomic status, intelligence, and attainment of higher education," *Sociology of Education* 40/1 (1967): 3.
34 There is a lack of systematic research in this area. This statement is inferred from population, education and income surveys and serves as a hypothetical case example. At present, there is no study examining consumer use of antivirus, firewall use, basic digital hygiene, and socioeconomic status.
35 Rothman, *Epidemiology: An Introduction*, 407.
36 Shari Lawrence Pfleeger and Deanna D. Caputo, "Leveraging behavioral science to mitigate cyber security risk," *Computers & Security* 31/4 (2012): 597–611; Sean W. Smith, "Security and cognitive bias: Exploring the role of the mind," *IEEE Security and Privacy* 10/5 (2012): 75–78.
37 Jonathan Zittrain, *The Future of the Internet and How to Stop It* (New Haven: Yale University Press, 2008).
38 Gordon Kelly, "Report: 97% Of Mobile Malware Is on Android. This Is the Easy Way You Stay Safe," *Forbes*, March 24, 2014, at www.forbes.com/sites/gordon-kelly/2014/03/24/report-97-of-mobile-malware-is-on-android-this-is-the-easy-way-you-stay-safe/.
39 CERT, "2014 US State of Cybercrime Survey," *Software Engineering Institute* at https://resources.sei.cmu.edu/asset_files/Presentation/2014_017_001_298322.pdf.
40 Denise E. Zhang and James A. Lewis, *Cyber Threat Information Sharing: Recommendations for Congress and the Administration* (Washington, DC: Center for Strategic and International Studies, 2015).
41 Hareesh Khattri, Narasimha Kumar V. Mangipudi, and Salvador Mandujano, "HSDL: A security development lifecycle for hardware technologies," *Proceedings of the 2012 IEEE International Symposium on Hardware-Oriented Security and Trust*, 2012, 116–121.
42 Terence R. Flotte et al., "Phase 2 Clinical Trial of a Recombinant Adeno-Associated Viral Vector Expressing α(1)-Antitrypsin: Interim Results," *Human Gene Therapy* 22/10 (2011): 1239–1247; Debeep Mukhopadhyay and Rajat Subhra Chakraborty, *Hardware Security: Design, Threats, and Safeguards* (Boca Raton: CRC Press, 2015).
43 There are 8.5 million different species on earth, each with slightly different genetic patterns; in contrast, there will be in excess of 50 billion Internet-connected devices

each with slightly different preferences, software configurations, and use requirements by 2020. See: Dave Evans, "The Internet of Things," *Cisco*, at www.cisco.com/web/about/ac79/docs/innov/IoT_IBSG_0411FINAL.pdf.

44 Krzysztof Iniewski, *Embedded Systems: Hardware, Design, and Implementation* (Hoboken: John Wiley & Sons, Inc., 2013).

45 Russell Jones and Abhinav Rastogi, "Secure coding: Building security into the software development life cycle," *Information Systems Security* 13/5 (2004): 29–39; Bart De Win et al., "On the secure software development process: CLASP, SDL and touchpoints compared," *Information and Software Technology* 51/7 (2009): 1152–1171; Noopur Davis, "Secure Software Development Life Cycle Processes: A Technology Scouting Report," *Software Engineering Institute*, at http://oai.dtic.mil/oai/oai?verb=getRecord&metadataPrefix=html&identifier=ADA447047.

46 D. J. Clark and Kai A. Konrad, "Asymmetric conflict: Weakest link against best shot," *Journal of Conflict Resolution* 51 (2007): 457–469.

47 Robert O'Harrow, *Zero Day: The Threat in Cyberspace* (New York: Diversion Books, 2013).

48 Noopur Davis, "Secure Software Development Life Cycle Process," *Department of Homeland Security* at https://buildsecurityin.us-cert.gov/articles/knowledge/sdlc-process/secure-software-development-life-cycle-processes.

49 Michael Sikorski and Andrew Honig, *Practical Malware Analysis: The Hands-on Guide to Dissecting Malicious Software* (San Francisco: No Starch Press, 2012), xxi.

50 Within cyberspace, incidence rate is the ratio of cases from network live time or simply the time at risk for infection.

51 Prevalence is the proportion of cases of malware-infected assets present within a network at any given time (point prevalence) or over a period of time.

52 Unlike in biology, the case fatality rate of systems does not necessarily constitute the "killing" of a system, rather in cyberspace it reflects a spectrum of outcomes tailored to the functions of a system within the network that affects the confidentiality, integrity, or availability of assets.

53 Understanding the basic reproductive number of malware facilitates a dynamic understanding of how it interacts with the environment. The basic reproductive number, or R_o, is a measure of the infectiousness of a given type of pathogen or, in the case of cyberspace, malware.

54 See: Brantly, "Aesop's wolves," 674–685.

55 John Everett, "Integrated Cyber Analysis System (ICAS)," *DARPA*, at www.darpa.mil/program/integrated-cyber-analysis-system.

56 Department of Homeland Security, "Information Sharing and Analysis Organizations," at www.dhs.gov/isao.

8 The innovator's challenge

Can the US Army learn to out-hack those who attack us in cyberspace?

Ernest Y. Wong, Katherine R. Hutton, and Ryan F. Gagnon *

Ever since the origins of the Republic, the American people have demonstrated that they possess a strong speculative knack and a considerable amount of optimism that have motivated them to develop innovative solutions for resolving tough problems. From the first American colonists who had to make do with the limited resources at their disposal in order to survive, to astronauts who have boldly explored space with what was minimally necessary so that they could successfully break free of gravity, US people have a proud history of developing new concepts, processes, and material for getting the mission accomplished. Today, innovation has become a key buzzword in the US Army, and it is helping to shape the vision for the *Army of 2025 and Beyond*, as an agile organization that can achieve strategic advantage in a complex world.[1]

But does the US military have the capabilities and motivations needed to effectively protect vital national interests in cyberspace and meet the demands of the future security environment? Does the US military truly know how to foster innovations that can keep pace with the disruptive effects of cyberattacks in this critical domain of operations within the national security framework? The rapid growth of the Internet in a globally connected world has meant that the tools for operating in cyberspace are constantly changing. To make the situation even more problematic, there are those who believe the US military has turned into such an unwieldy bureaucratic structure that it will not be able to adapt itself into a force that is capable of winning tomorrow's wars. So, does the US military have the capacity to gain the strategic advantage necessary to effectively out-hack those who attack the nation in the cyber domain?

To address these perplexing issues, this chapter analyzes what innovation really means, and draws distinctions between four different types of innovation: disruptive, breakthrough, sustaining, and incremental. Despite considerable innovations that have taken place for cyber defense, new types of innovation will be necessary to effectively counter those taking place on the offensive side of cyber. Through an examination of disruptive innovations cyber adversaries have developed, this chapter provides insights into why the US military's focus on breakthrough innovations for cyber defense is failing. By encouraging the military to experiment with more disruptive defensive cyber innovations, US cyber forces have the potential to level the playing field between the offense and the defense in the cyber domain. Defensive and offensive cyber innovations will be more effective if they are used as part of a broader strategy. Here, the US should apply the lessons learned from recent counterinsurgency campaigns and treat malicious cyber actors as an asymmetric threat fighting for control of cyberspace.

Innovation, cyber defense, and cyber offense

Innovation is not a new concept to the US military, and neither is the need to innovate for effective operations in the cyber domain. Cardon, McHenry, and Cline define innovation with regards to military operations as "the implementation and integration of new concepts, processes, and material that enhance mission capability."[2] They promote the development of a military culture that welcomes innovative solutions for such areas where the United States "does not have a monopoly on the means to conduct cyberspace operations."[3] This chapter takes these ideas one step further and contends that the US military must harness the right types of innovation in order to prevail in cyberwarfare. Wong and Sambaluk segment innovation into four types: disruptive, breakthrough, sustaining, and incremental.[4] Each of these subsets within innovation is distinguished from the others by three key factors: whether the innovation targets existing markets or aims to benefit new and underserved markets; whether the innovation originates as a reactive response to a malicious cyber activity or is a proactive measure intended to shape the future into one's own favor; and whether the innovation is relatively simple to adopt or is technologically challenging to operationalize. Figure 8.1 provides a representation of disruptive, breakthrough, sustaining, and incremental innovations as quadrants on a graph that features these three factors. This innovation framework can help identify the types of innovation cyber adversaries are using and developing. These insights, in turn, will help advance the right mix of innovative solutions that will allow US military cyber forces to successfully defend against malicious cyber activity. In the following paragraphs, we explain each type of innovation and provide examples on the defensive and offensive side of cyber. According to the US DoD, defensive cyberspace operations "preserve the ability to utilize friendly cyberspace capabilities and protect data, networks, net-centric capabilities, and other designated systems," and offensive cyberspace operations "project power by the application of force in and through cyberspace."[5] From this perspective, defensive cyber innovation helps to preserve the ability to use cyberspace capabilities and offensive cyber innovation helps to project power in and through cyberspace.

Sustaining and incremental innovations, on the lower two quadrants of the framework, address existing market needs and often contribute the most to a company's balance sheet year after year. Sustaining innovations focus on improvements to a current product line or established service that either add greater efficiencies or provide for a modest adjustment that bumps up the appeal to an existing customer base. An example of a sustaining defensive cyber

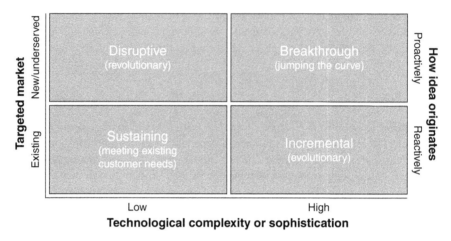

Figure 8.1 Wong and Sambaluk's innovation framework.[6]

innovation is the use of antivirus software, which provides baseline protection to computer systems and gradually improves over time to defend against new signatures and variants of malware as they are discovered so that existing customers will continue to subscribe to the service. A sustaining offensive cyber innovation occurs when cyber threats reuse malware exploits and recycle existing payloads that had previously worked on different networks and systems. Incremental innovations are evolutionary changes that usually occur when a company's product or process are challenged by a competitor and the company must evolve in order to survive in the marketplace. In the cyber domain, incremental innovations tend to occur when computer hackers and system defenders interact with one another and force the other side to respond in order to persevere. The creation of the US Computer Emergency Response Team (CERT) is an example of a defensive incremental innovation, formed in response to the Morris Worm, the first computer worm distributed via the Internet in 1988, resulting in a devastating wide-scale denial of service attack.[7] Today, the US-CERT continues to fulfill its mission of providing cybersecurity experts with a central point to coordinate responses to network emergencies. Software bugs and flaws in computer programming provide cyber threats with the ability to develop incremental offensive innovations. As soon as defenders are able to apply patches to close off discovered "back doors" and distribute hotfixes that remedy system errors, malicious users look for new software bugs, even flaws inside newly patched codes, to exploit. Over time, both sustaining and incremental innovations tend to generate gradual but modest improvements within existing systems, but they both typically originate as a reactive response to customers' needs or through the challenge of competitors and adversaries' actions.

Breakthrough and disruptive innovations, on the top two quadrants presented in Figure 8.1, have the capacity to create new structures and new lines of business. Since the markets for these types of innovation do not even exist, they are highly speculative, incur a great deal of risk, and are difficult to achieve. Yet, when successful, they have considerably greater potential to alter the status quo and change the environment. Breakthrough innovations are expensive, highly complex, and require long lead times to reach customers. An example of a breakthrough defensive cyber innovation currently being pursued is research into automated, scalable, machine-speed vulnerability detection and patching as articulated by the Defense Advanced Research Projects Agency (DARPA) Cyber Grand Challenge (CGC). In a ceremony announcing the CGC winners, DARPA Director Arati Prabhakar stated: "Our goal in cyber is to break past the reactive patch cycle we're living in today, and unleash the positive power and creative potential of the information revolution."[8] GCG Program Manager Mike Walker intimated at the market-changing potential of breakthrough innovations by saying, "Automation may someday overcome the structural advantages of network offense and give the defense a chance at a fair fight."[9] The Stuxnet virus serves as an example of an offensive breakthrough innovation, a first-of-its-kind digital weapon developed for the specific goal of physically destroying a key part of a nation's infrastructure.[10] With the release of Stuxnet, nation states began to realize that the market for computer attacks would no longer be confined to household computers and commercial systems. Disruptive innovations, on the other hand, embrace a different approach to product development by creatively leveraging available products and resources to target customers who typically fall on the low-cost fringe of mainstream markets. In 2006, the US space agency implemented a low-cost and relatively simple defensive disruptive cyber innovation when it instituted a policy and developed a system to block emails with attachments prior to space shuttle launches. This measure was implemented out of concerns that NASA systems would be hacked, and after the agency discovered that unknown foreign intruders had obtained plans for US space launch vehicles.[11] Nearly all offensive cyber innovations, to include most computer viruses, worms, Trojan horses, and other malware, originate in the disruptive realm. As a result, they tend to be relatively cheap to produce, are quicker to implement, and are inherently more flexible because they utilize assets that already exist.[12] Both breakthrough and disruptive innovations tend to be more proactive undertakings that are extremely risky endeavors but have considerably more potential to drastically transform the existing landscape and shift the balance of power in favor of those who possess the innovation.

Based on this innovation framework, it is possible to argue that cyber offense currently has significant structural advantages over cyber defense. Figure 8.2 illustrates how offensive cyber innovations typically originate in the disruptive, sustaining, and incremental quadrants with just a small portion coming out of the breakthrough quadrant. Cyber defense innovations, on the other hand, mostly emerge out of the breakthrough, incremental, and sustaining quadrants with only a scant amount arising from the disruptive space. The shortage of defensive cyber innovations originating as disruptive ideas helps to explain the difficulties US military cyber forces will have in trying to defend against cyber adversaries

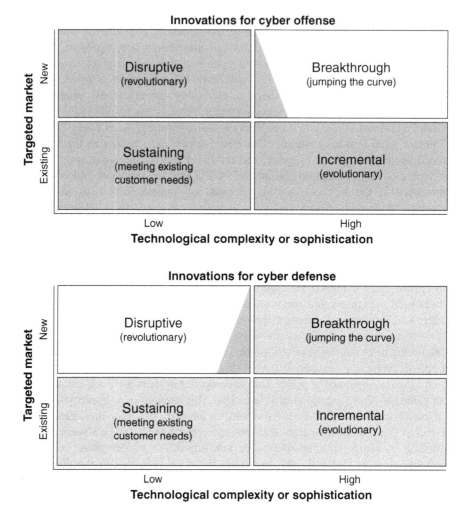

Figure 8.2 The preponderance of offensive and defensive cyber innovations.

with their arsenal of offensive tools that are cheaper and faster to create. Since breakthrough innovations typically originate as complex ideas that depend upon cutting-edge technologies, research into breakthrough defensive innovations normally involve long lead times for such defenses to reach markets. As a result, the wait for the implementation of new cyber defenses provides attackers with ample opportunities to reuse exploits and recycle malicious payload on to numerous targets. By conceding the disruptive space to malicious cyber actors, current US cyber defense strategy has led to a capabilities gap between attackers and defenders that has provided a decidedly structural advantage in favor of the offensive-minded cyber hacker. Defensive efforts based on breakthrough, incremental, and sustaining innovations are insufficient. To counter the advantages that are available to those conducting cyberattacks, the United States must pursue more disruptive defensive innovations.

Embracing the ~~defender's~~ innovator's challenge

The impact of disruptive innovation is not a new concept to the US military. History provides countless examples of battlefield victories built upon disruptive innovation in warfare. During the US War of Independence, revolutionists stymied the British regulars with guerrilla tactics, techniques, and procedures. World War II gave birth in the United States to the field of operations research after statistical analysis provided Allied Naval Forces with greater freedom of maneuver in the Atlantic Ocean—mathematicians found that when ships traveled together as convoys, their survival increased because German U-Boat captains greatly risked their own safety by initiating an attack on multiple vessels. Joint operations, as perfected in Desert Storm, brought the US Army, US Navy, and US Air Force capabilities together as part of the AirLand Battle Concept, which extended offensive action to the fullest extent possible, based on all available military assets. Military offensive operations were no longer limited by a focus on close battles where armies came into contact with one another; the operational reach of bomber and fighter aircraft permitted the United States to devote military resources to additional objectives well beyond the front lines of traditional warfare.[13] These historical examples demonstrate that the US military has the ability to be an innovative force, embracing the disruptive warfare paradigm. However, does the US military understand how to defend against disruption? In cyberwarfare, the operating environment can change at such a rapid pace that defenders can have a hard time keeping up. To be proactive in the cyber domain, the US military must embrace disruptive innovation for defense, as well as sustain its current competitive capabilities.

Figure 8.3 provides a risk-reward comparison using the innovation framework to help visualize the trade-offs for pursuing different types of innovation. Oftentimes, organizations that have produced a successful disruptive innovation at a point in time find themselves incapable of repeating the same feat afterwards—highlighting just how challenging it is to succeed in the disruptive space. Consistently developing successful disruptive solutions in-house is a rare phenomenon for any organization. Most companies have little incentive to speculate on disruptive projects because doing so is considerably riskier than choosing the more established sustaining or incremental activities. Even breakthrough proposals, just as risky as disruptive ones, traditionally attract a greater following because they possess the added benefits of having significantly larger budgets, larger staffs, greater command emphasis, and a more defined path toward promotion within a company.[14] In spite of the high potential for failure, disruptive innovation provides an opportunity to alter the status quo and level the playing field for cyber defense. This is a worthy pursuit given the adversaries' current systematic advantages in offensive cyber operations.[15]

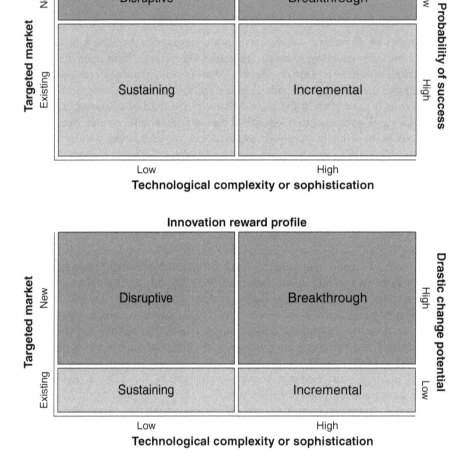

Figure 8.3 A risk-reward comparison for pursuing different types of innovation.

Companies such as Apple, Google, and Netflix have proven that they can suc-cessfully initiate disruptive innovations time after time.[16] These organizations have adopted at least one of the following four approaches, which helps explain their success in consistently generating disruptive solutions:

- cultivate an incubator within the parent organization that has the freedom to experiment on disruptive innovations
- purchase outright a proven successful disruptive solution, hire individuals who have succeeded as disruptive thinkers, or take over a successful disruptive firm

- form an alliance with other companies to pursue a common disruptive innovation for the well-being of the entire industry
- become an early adopter of promising experimentation.[17]

Market forces typically prevent many companies from succeeding in achieving disruptive success via the first three approaches. Even when organizations proclaim that they intend to vigorously pursue revolutionary business models and focus on radical transformations, oftentimes, they fail to account for entrenched cultural norms and established business practices that stymie efforts to cultivate long-term progress for their internal disruptive units. The pressure to meet short-term goals in resource-constrained environments places these units in competition for the means necessary to continue pursuing their disruptive efforts. Brown and Eisenhardt suggest adopting promising experimentation to foster disruptive innovations.[18] To increase the chances of favorable outcomes as an early adopter, they also recommend the monitoring, development, and creation of a portfolio of small, fast, and cheap experiments that help to provide a more dynamic strategy for the organization's future without consuming so many resources that put near-term organizational objectives and requirements at risk of failure. This approach gives businesses that do not have much experience with disruptive innovations the flexibility to continue focusing on their core competencies in sustaining, incremental, and even breakthrough solutions, whilst keeping abreast of the developments within industry-related groups that aim for disruptive solutions. Successful innovation requires a coherent strategy that balances different types of innovation and leverages all available resources to help reshape the future.

A cyber defense strategy employing lessons from counterinsurgency operations

The lessons learned from US counterinsurgency operations can provide a solid basis to develop a cyber defense strategy that leverages disruptive innovation. In spite of the difficulties associated with developing disruptive innovations, computer hackers seem to have no shortage of malware at their disposal and appear to have figured out how to consistently churn out disruptive exploits and payloads that put US military cyber forces, both literally and figuratively, on the defensive. In this context, it is fair to ask whether the US military has a fighting chance of developing a sound cyber defense strategy that can effectively combat against the incessant flow of disruptive threats. Military history, from the Revolutionary War to World War II and Operation Desert Storm, provides ample evidence that US forces can embrace disruptive innovations to gain significant advantage on the battlefield. Recent US operations against insurgent forces in the Middle East can provide the military with disruptive ways to think about combating cyber threats. This experience is particularly relevant since many of the cyber threats to the United States are asymmetric.

Having learned the difficult lessons of combat in Iraq and Afghanistan over the past decade and beyond, the US military retains considerable knowledge for how to prosecute a counterinsurgency (COIN) fight against asymmetric threats. The US military should apply some of the key lessons it has learned in executing COIN strategy, operations, and tactics that are appropriate for the defense of the cyber domain. Three key lessons stand out. First, the most efficacious time to counter an insurgency is at its infancy, when it has not yet had the time to mobilize popular support, gain the resources to continue the long fight, assemble its leadership, and organize itself with a coherent strategy.[19] Perhaps a number of adversaries with sufficient cyber resources have progressed beyond the infant stages in cyberwarfare, but can the US military influence and impact others still in the developmental phases of their cyber capabilities? Second, once an insurgency has progressed beyond its early stages and has taken advantage of the time needed to build strength and gain support, the counterinsurgent often has the disadvantage of having to come from behind and then must press the insurgent along as many logical lines of operation as possible in order to limit its freedom of action and deny its fighting forces sanctuary locations.[20] With regards to cyber proficient threats, can the US military overcome the significant advantages some adversaries already possess, gain enough intelligence to identify them, and then target them with not just traditional military responses, but legal, diplomatic, and economic options as well? Third, to win the hearts and minds of the local population in the counterinsurgency's favor, the counterinsurgent must quickly and effectively displace the insurgent from its advantageous position where it can score numerous victories without ever having to commit the totality of its limited resources.[21] Can the US military leverage existing capabilities and develop new ones that will effectively target, degrade, and neutralize cyber threats without restricting cyberspace to such an extent that only the United States and a privileged number of its allies gain the benefits of participation? By treating malicious cyber actors as asymmetric threats fighting for control of cyberspace, the US military will be better able to address these tough questions and challenge

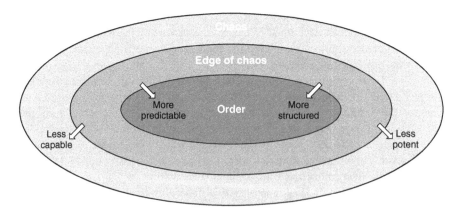

Figure 8.4 Dislodging cyber threats from the edge of chaos through a comprehensive COIN strategy.[22]

the conventional way of thinking of cyberwarfare as purely technical problems that require just technical solutions.

The US military has learned that in order to win in the long fight that constitutes COIN warfare, it must do everything possible to quickly dislodge an insurgency from its advantageous position where it holds considerably greater knowledge of the area and its people, blends in easily with the civilian population, has time to build strength and support, and can initiate attacks on counterinsurgent forces at the time and place of its choosing. Brown and Eisenhardt refer to this advantageous position as being at "the edge of chaos."[23] Figure 8.4 depicts the edge of chaos as the transition space between the chaos regime and the order regime and helps illustrate how the US military can apply this framework in the fight against cyber adversaries. The simultaneous combination of pushing an insurgency into chaos, by limiting its freedom and action and denying it of vital resources, and pulling an insurgency into order, by systematically fracturing its will to continue fighting through activities such as principled negotiations, structure the complementary goals of a comprehensive COIN strategy. By pushing the insurgents or cyber threat actors into chaos, US forces can make them less potent and less capable; by pulling them into order, US forces can make them more structured and more predictable. For instance, the US military can push known cyber threat actors into chaos by not only divulging their identities for traditional criminal prosecution, but also leveraging its own offensive innovations to attack them in new ways. To pull known cyber threat actors into order, the US military advocates adoption of international cyber norms and governance for all who want to operate freely, securely, and responsibly in cyberspace. Doing this does not require the US military to start from scratch; it can leverage a number of proposals already in the works, including the international legal structure proposed in the two Tallinn manuals,[24] Ridout's comprehensive recommendations for a cyber strategy,[25] and Mazanec's recommendations for the adoption of constraining norms for cyberwar and terrorism.[26] This push-and-pull cyber strategy leverages much from what the US military already knows about how to fight insurgencies, and the strategy provides the United States with disruptively innovative ways to construct a cyber defense strategy that will improve its chances of effectively protecting the cyber domain.

Conclusion

In 2010, the US Army Cyber Command was established with the task of conducting cyberspace operations in support of full spectrum operations to ensure US and allied forces have freedom of action in cyberspace and to deny the same to adversaries.[27] It was not until 2015 that the US Army established the Cyber branch as an occupational specialty where soldiers and officers focused on defense of the nation in cyberspace. With the recognition of cyber as a warfighting domain and a critical operational environment within the US national security framework, the development of the nation's cyber defensive strategy is still in its infancy. The ideas developed in this chapter aim to refine US strategy to better protect cyberspace against malicious cyber activities. By segmenting innovation into four distinct categories—disruptive, breakthrough, sustaining, and incremental—the United States can gain a fresh and powerful perspective on how best to transform its cyber military forces and resource them with the right mix of defensive and offensive cyber capabilities needed to prevail in the cyber-wars of tomorrow.

In spite of its inexperience and unproven record in defending the core of cyberspace, the US military has demonstrated time and time again that it can successfully adapt to new forms of warfare and emerge victorious. Decision makers should leverage the lessons of past wars and look to recent conflicts in Afghanistan and Iraq to employ COIN strategies to counter malicious cyber threats. Today, cyber adversaries are challenging the United States and testing its resolve with their disruptive arsenal of cyber weapons. However, by studying how cyber threats operate in this new warfighting domain, the US military can learn to harness new concepts, processes, and material to pursue victory. The US military has consistently distinguished itself as a formidable force that constantly studies, decisively acts against, and continually overwhelms its enemy in order to achieve victory. Even though cyberspace traditionally lends itself to the pursuit of cutting-edge breakthrough innovations for its defense, the US military must continue to study and embrace disruptive warfare principles espoused by Sun Tzu thousands of years ago:

> Now an army may be likened to water, for as flowing water avoids the heights and hastens to the lowlands, so an army avoids strengths and strikes weakness. And as water shapes its flow in accordance with the ground, so an army manages its victory in accordance with the situation of the enemy. And as water has no constant form, there are in war no constant conditions. Thus, one able to gain victory by modifying his tactics in accordance with the enemy situation may be said to be divine.[28]

By studying how cyberattacks occur and what innovative steps adversaries take to penetrate and exploit computer systems, the United States will be better able to grasp why its current processes for cyber defense are failing. More importantly, the United States will comprehend how to systematically advance the right mix of innovations for cyber defense that will prevail in this critically important domain within its national security framework.

Notes

* The authors would like to thank Colonel Andrew Hall, Director of the Army Cyber Institute (ACI), and Christopher Hartley, Deputy Director of the ACI, for their unwavering support. Their leadership and concerted efforts to engineer systematic ways to promote innovation and cyber awareness in the US Department of Defense and throughout our nation have been sources of encouragement and inspiration throughout the writing of this chapter. The views expressed in this chapter are those of the authors and do not reflect official policy of the US Military Academy, US Army, US DoD, or

the US Government. This work was authored as part of the contributors' official duties as members of the US Government and is, therefore, a work of the US Government. In accordance with 17 USC 105, no copyright protection is available for such works under US law.

1 Raymond T. Odierno and John M. McHugh. 2015. "The Army Vision: Strategic Advantage in a Complex World," United States Army, 6–9, at https://hbr.org/2015/12/what-is-disruptive-innovation.

2 Edward C. Cardon, David P. McHenry, and Christopher Cline, "The Relevance of Culture: Recognizing the Importance of Innovation in Cyberspace Operations," *Military Review* (July–August 2016): 34–39, at http://usacac.army.mil/CAC2/MilitaryReview/Archives/English/MilitaryReview_20160831_art009.pdf

3 Ibid., 36.

4 Ernest Y. Wong and Nicholas M. Sambaluk, "Disruptive Innovations to Help Protect against Future Threats," *Proceedings of the 2016 IEEE International Conference on Cyber Conflict* (Washington, DC: IEEE Xplore), October 21–23, 155–157.

5 US Department of Defense, Joint Publication 3–12 (R), Cyberspace Operations, February 5, 2013, II-2.

6 Wong and Sambaluk, "Disruptive Innovations to Help Protect against Future Threats," 156.

7 Bhavya Daya, "Network Security: History, Importance, and Future," University of Florida Department of Electrical and Computer Engineering, 2013, 4, at http://web.mit.edu/~bdaya/www/Network%20Security.pdf.

8 Defense Advanced Research Projects Agency, "DARPA Celebrates Cyber Grand Challenge Winners," DARPA News and Events, August 7, 2016, at www.darpa.mil/news-events/2016-08-05a.

9 Ibid.

10 Kim Zetter, "An Unprecedented Look at Stuxnet, The World's First Digital Weapon," *Wired*, November 3, 2014, at www.wired.com/2014/11/countdown-to-zero-day-stuxnet/.

11 Editor, "The history of cyber attacks—a timeline," *NATO Review*, at www.nato.int/docu/review/2013/cyber/timeline/EN/index.htm.

12 Clayton M. Christensen, Michael E. Raynor, and Rory McDonald, "What Is Disruptive Innovation?" *Harvard Business Review*, December 2015, 44–53, https://hbr.org/2015/12/what-is-disruptive-innovation.

13 John L. Romjue, "The Evolution of the Airland Battle Concept," *Air University Review* (May–June 1984), at www.au.af.mil/au/afri/aspj/airchronicles/aureview/1984/may-jun/romjue.html.

14 Joseph L. Bower and Clayton M. Christensen, "Disruptive technologies: Catching the wave," *Harvard Business Review* 73/1 (1995): 43–53.

15 Stewart A. Baker, "The Attribution Revolution: Raising the Costs for Hackers and Their Customers," Statement and testimony before the Senate Judiciary Committee's Subcommittee on Crime and Terrorism. May 8, 2013, 7, at www.judiciary.senate.gov/imo/media/doc/5-8-13BakerTestimony.pdf

16 Avi Dan, "The 25 Most Disruptive Brands of 2015," November 29, 2015, www.forbes.com/sites/avidan/2015/11/29/the-25-most-disruptive-brands-of-2015/#46bf1a762504

17 Shonda L. Brown and Kathleen M. Eisenhardt, *Competing on the Edge: Strategy and Structured Chaos* (Boston: Harvard Business School Press, 1998), 127–159.

18 Ernest Wong, "Is the US Military Ready to Win Tomorrow's Wars? What are Disruptive Innovations and Can They Help Us Win in Cyber Warfare?" presentation delivered at the 2016 Military Research Operations Society Symposium, June 20–23, 2016.

19 Ernest Y. Wong, "Leveraging science in the manoeuvrist approach to counterinsurgency operations," *The Land Warfare Papers* 80 (2010): 7.

20 US Department of the Army Headquarters and US Marine Corps Combat Development Command Headquarters, *Counterinsurgency, Army Field Manual 3–24, Marine Corps Warfighting Publication 3–33.5* (Washington, DC: DA and MCCDC, 2006) ix, 2-2, 4-3, 5-2 to 5-7.
21 Ibid., 1-16, 1-28, A-5, and B-1.
22 Wong, "Leveraging science in the manoeuvrist approach to counterinsurgency operations," 10. Figure adapted from David Kiersey, 2007, "The Edge of Chaos," at http://edgeoforder.org/eofchaos.html.
23 Brown and Eisenhardt, *Competing on the Edge*, 11–12.
24 NATO Cooperative Cyber Defense Centre of Excellence, "Tallinn Manual," at https://ccdcoe.org/tallinn-manual.html.
25 Tim Ridout, "Building a comprehensive strategy of cyber defense, deterrence, and resilience," *The Fletcher Forum of World Affairs* 40/2 (2016): 63–83.
26 Brian M. Mazanec, *The Evolution of Cyber War: International Norms for Emerging-Technology Weapons* (Lincoln, NE: University of Nebraska Press, 2015).
27 Army Cyber Command and Second Army, at www.arcyber.army.mil/Pages/Arcyber-Home.aspx
28 Sun Tzu, *The Art of War*, trans. by Samuel Griffith (New York: Oxford University Press, 1971), 101.

9 Evolving cyber intelligence

Stephen "Scuba" Gary and Randy Borum

"Cyber intelligence" seems to be one of the newest terms in the cybersecurity community, but different practitioners use it in very different ways.[1] If cyber intelligence is to advance as a discipline of practice and study, it will be necessary to have some shared understanding of the basic terms and concepts.[2] Although the word "cyber" can be somewhat ambiguous, the term "intelligence" is probably the greatest source of confusion. It is easy to equate intelligence with information and to use the terms interchangeably, but in practice they are quite different.[3] This chapter discusses the conceptual foundations and practical implications of defining cyber intelligence and describes how the field has been evolving so far and how it needs to evolve into the future.

Data, information, intelligence, and cyber intelligence

In the 1980s, there was a flurry of discourse in the field of Information Science about identifying the basic types or categories of content in the human mind.[4] Some consensus converged around four concepts: data, information, knowledge and wisdom (DIKW).[5] Sometimes "understanding" is considered a separate category between knowledge and wisdom. These units are described as being hierarchical, meaning each cumulatively builds upon the other. In fact, this particular stack is often called the DIKW hierarchy or just the "Information Hierarchy."[6] Systems theorist Russell Ackoff defined the elements of this construct in the following way:

- data: symbols with no inherent meaning
- information: data that have been given meaning; provides answers to "who," "what," "where," and "when" questions
- knowledge: application of data and information; answers "how" questions
- understanding: appreciation of "why"
- wisdom: evaluated understanding.[7]

In this hierarchy, information is defined in terms of data; knowledge is defined in terms of information, and wisdom is defined in terms of knowledge.[8] Analysis is the mechanism to get from data to information and from information to knowledge and understanding.

The word information is derived from the Latin *informare* (to inform), which means "give form to the mind." Functionally, information results from structure imposed on an indeterminate mass of words or symbols. Data becomes information when meaning is imposed and that meaning adds value. According to the *International Encyclopedia of Information and Library Science*, information holds a place in the spectrum between raw data and knowledge. "Seen in this way, information is an assemblage of data in a comprehensible form capable of communication and use; the essence of it is that a meaning has been attached to the raw facts."[9]

Intelligence is a higher-level concept—a hybrid of knowledge, understanding, and wisdom. Just as data becomes information when meaning is attached, when meaning is discerned within information, it can be used as intelligence. As intelligence expert Robert Clark suggests:

> intelligence in general can be thought of as the complex process of understanding meaning in available information. A typical goal of intelligence is to establish facts and then to develop precise, reliable, and valid inferences (hypotheses, estimations, conclusions, or predictions) for use in strategic decision making or operational planning.[10]

In that sense, intelligence is information in action, or in Michael Warner's words, "It is what people do with data and information that gives them the special quality we casually call intelligence."[11]

There are obvious differences between information and intelligence (see Table 9.1). Information is raw, unevaluated material, collected from everywhere. The accuracy, relevancy, and timeliness of information are questionable and it usually is not actionable. News is probably the best example of information, such as news on Chinese cyber espionage.[12] Intelligence, however, is analyzed and evaluated information, collected from trusted intelligence sources. Intelligence is accurate (or of considered accuracy), relevant, timely, and actionable.

The Mandiant (FireEye) report on one of the many Advanced Persistent Threats (APTs) in the world, *APT 1: Exposing One of China's Cyber Espionage Units*, is a good example of intelligence in the cyber domain. This report provided the who, what, when, where, why, and how, comprising the actionable

Table 9.1 Differences between information and intelligence

Information	Intelligence
Raw information	Analyzed information
Unevaluated	Evaluated
Collected from everywhere	Collected from trusted intelligence sources
Questionable accuracy, relevancy, and timeliness	Accurate, relevant, and timely
Usually not actionable	Actionable

intelligence necessary to identify if Chinese cyber units had compromised sensitive networks. The technical information provided in this report could be directly inserted into existing network security tools to block further infiltration. The Mandiant report also highlighted one of China's many cyber units, Unit 61398, focusing on its activities, infrastructure and personnel, and revealing that more than 20 APTs existed in China alone. With additional detailed descriptions of Unit 61398's mission, capabilities, and resources, the report demonstrated how this one unit has "systematically stolen hundreds of terabytes of data from at least 141 organizations."[13]

In 2014, the term "cyber intelligence" made its first appearance in the US National Intelligence Strategy, where it is listed as one of the intelligence community's core mission areas. That document defines cyber intelligence as:

> the collection, processing, analysis, and dissemination of information from all sources of intelligence on foreign actors' cyber programs, intentions, capabilities, research and development, tactics, and operational activities and indicators; their impact or potential effects on national security, information systems, infrastructure, and data; and network characterization, or insight into the components, structures, use, and vulnerabilities of foreign information systems.[14]

Cyber intelligence drives the success of network operations, in the same way that intelligence supports defenses, exploitations, and attacks in the physical world.

In the United States, cyber intelligence responsibilities are distributed across multiple governmental agencies and departments. The National Security Agency (NSA) and DoD via US Cyber Command, however, have led the nation's cyber operations: computer network defense (CND), computer network exploitation (CNE), and computer network attack. NSA spearheads America's signals intelligence operations, which includes CNE. The NSA's Information Assurance Directorate has primary responsibility for CND of sensitive US networks, especially military (.mil) networks. US Cyber Command, as a DoD entity, is reportedly in charge of offensive cyber operations (CNA). The US Department of Homeland Security (DHS) is charged with defending America's critical infrastructure, including emergency preparedness communications and process control systems, from cyber (and physical) threats. The hub of DHS' cyber intelligence efforts is its National Cybersecurity and Communications Integration Center (NCCIC), which operates 24/7 providing cyber situational awareness, as well as incident response and management. The NCCIC also coordinates information sharing with the Federal Bureau of Investigation (FBI), which uses technical and traditional investigative capabilities to fight cybercrime.[15]

In the cyber domain, data are abundant and information is common, but intelligence is sparser. As shown in Figure 9.1, five years ago, the term "cyber intelligence" was seldom used but in recent years the realization of the need for intelligence in cyberspace has accelerated the use of the term in the scholarly and professional literature.

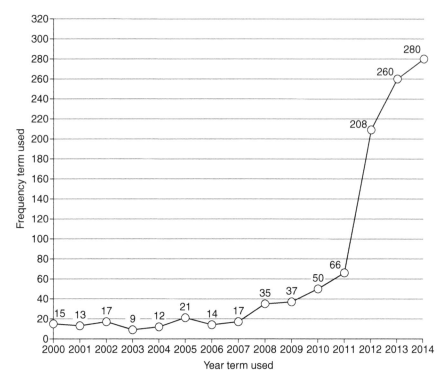

Figure 9.1 Frequency of "cyber intelligence" used in Google Scholar.

Cyber intelligence focuses primarily on the *source* of the threat, the person behind the keyboard or the cyber threat actor (CTA). As with other threat domains, a more thorough understanding of the adversary enables better anticipatory analysis, more accurate foresight, and more effective countermeasures. This is consistent with Sun Tzu's adage that:

> if you know your enemies and know yourself, you will not be imperiled in a hundred battles; if you do not know your enemies but do know yourself, you will win one and lose one; if you do not know your enemies nor yourself, you will be imperiled in every single battle.[16]

Although cyber intelligence, like other intelligence disciplines, follows the same basic process of direction, collection, analysis, production, and dissemination, in the cyber domain, information moves at light speed. As a result, the decision-making process must be faster than with traditional intelligence. Automation can augment, but not replace the function of trained analysts. There is no way to fully automate the entire cyber intelligence process.[17]

Inundated with messages about new "cyber intelligence" products, personnel in security operations centers (SOC) often say that their problem is not getting intelligence, but deciding what intelligence to use. That is an understandable sentiment, but it belies two deeper, hidden challenges. First, security personnel tend to be flooded with data, not with intelligence.[18] They have Computer Emergency Response Team feeds, Internet Protocol (IP) addresses, and artifacts that pour in with generic warning labels attached. That information has not been analyzed or assigned meaning in the context of that center's specific security mission. It remains as data.

Second, the accumulation of large, messy piles of data usually indicates that the operations center does not have an effective collection management (CM) plan. A basic tenet of intelligence is that, after the requirements have been established, it is necessary to create a CM plan to specify *which* information needs to be collected *when, from where, by whom*, and *how*.[19] All threat-related information is not created equal. The organization's cybersecurity personnel must assess and understand its own specific attack surface. It must then use the results of that assessment to systematically collect and prioritize the threat information that will be most relevant to the organization—as opposed to just compiling information about threats in general.[20]

The future of cyber intelligence lies in addressing those two challenges. To move forward, progress must be made in developing intelligence from data and in systematically collecting and analyzing cyber-related information and managing intelligence. Based on the Department of Defense Joint Publication 2–0, it is possible to envision the evolution of cyber intelligence (so far) as comprising three phases, which conveniently align with how intelligence is processed: one focused on data, one focused on information, and one focused on intelligence. As illustrated in Figure 9.2, in the Collection phase of intelligence, potential data

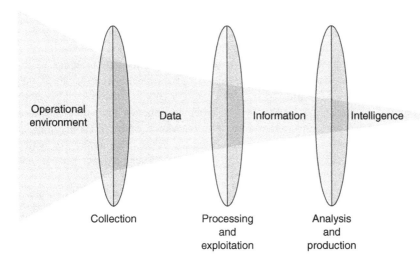

Operational environment   Data   Information   Intelligence

Collection   Processing and exploitation   Analysis and production

Figure 9.2 Relationship of data, information, and intelligence.[21]

are mined from the operational environment and queued for Processing and exploitation where those data are organized into information. The information is then processed and readied for the final stage of Analysis and production where it is analyzed and shaped into actionable intelligence and disseminated to decision makers. Over the past three decades, the field has consecutively focused on each of the three inflection points.

Evolutionary phases in the discipline of cyber intelligence

The field of cyber intelligence has evolved from the data focus of the 1980s to the emerging actionable intelligence focus of today. This evolution has kept pace with the threats and ensuing breaches that have facilitated new development. These changes have spanned across the tactical, operational, and strategic levels. Early efforts took a defensive posture and focused only on tactical-level intelligence. Over time, however, it became apparent that shifting the security posture from reactive to proactive would be necessary to mitigate the threat. Enacting that shift required a re-scoping of cybersecurity approaches, from a narrow focus on firewalls and antivirus software, to a comprehensive security approach, examining enterprise-specific threats in their full context. The information assurance mission pivoted from the impractical goal protecting the entire network to the prioritized protection of critical assets.

Throughout the cyber intelligence cycle, there have been global shifts from enterprise introspection to broader, context-driven threat characterization. Cyber intelligence collection and analysis widened its aperture beyond the network, seeking to better understand the threats and thereby improve situational awareness and decision making. Security operators sought not only to identify "cyber threats" but to identify evidence of the actor's targets, intentions, and capabilities. They began to more systematically analyze targets to understand why one was selected over another. Threat analysis drilled down to specific tactics, techniques, and procedures (TTPs), and technical analytics started to develop into more systematic indicators and warnings of future cyberattacks.

This overarching, outward-looking trend also paved a path for more widespread information sharing within and across cybersecurity sectors, which has probably been one of the more profound developments in proactive cybersecurity. Having a centralized repository for cyber intelligence that integrates and disseminates the intelligence accurately, with relevance, and in a timely way, is an important platform for the future of actionable cyber intelligence. To better understand cybersecurity trends, the chapter now examines the three phases that have marked the evolution of the cyber intelligence discipline.

Table 9.2 shows a detailed comparison of three phases in the development of cyber intelligence as a discipline of practice. For each timeframe, it first references four broad categories of cybersecurity posture (defense focus, mission, approach and information assurance focus), then describes the main elements of the intelligence cycle (collection, processing, analysis and dissemination), and highlights analytic dimensions for cyber intelligence

Table 9.2 Evolutionary phases in the discipline of cyber intelligence

	Phase I	Phase II	Phase III
Timeframe	1987–2004	2005–2014	2015 onwards
Cybersecurity focus	Data (tactical)	Information "intelligence" (operational and tactical)	Actionable intelligence (strategic, operational, and tactical)
Cybersecurity mission	[Reactively] Defend against all threats	Defend against known threats (known actors and "types" of attack)	Proactively defend against all threats (prevention of foreseeable attacks)
Cybersecurity approach	Technical focus, broad defense, bigger (fire)walls, antivirus (AV)	Focused defense, attribution, better/smarter (fire)walls	Comprehensive threat focus
Information assurance focus	Protect our network	Protect our information	Prioritize protection of our most valued assets (crown jewels)
Collection focus	Data for firewalls (hashes for AV filters)	Information for educating users, network logs, and packet information	Intelligence for making decisions (technical and non-technical [all-source] intelligence)
Processing focus	Internal traffic only	Internal traffic and select "intelligence" feeds	All traffic and all intelligence
Analysis focus	Analyze our network traffic only	Analyze our network's information and select "intelligence" feeds	Analyze and integrate all threat information
Dissemination focus	Disseminate internally	Disseminate to similar organizations	Disseminate to everyone
Adversary analysis	Undifferentiated hackers	Cyber threat actor types/categories	Cyber threat actors and their targets, intentions, TTPs, tools, and tech info
Target analysis	None/undifferentiated	Determine the target	Understand why that specific target
Intentions analysis	None/undifferentiated	Determine the intention	Understand the intention
Primary TTP/tool threats to network	Malware (virus, worm, Trojan), social engineering, DoS	Phishing, hacking, social engineering, DDoS	Zero-days, highly sophisticated and well-planned attacks using a variety of methods
Technical info analysis	Hashes	IP addresses	All technical information
Mechanism to thwart threat	Antivirus software, virus database, IDS	Cyber "intelligence" businesses, information/intelligence sharing, IPS	CTIIC, integrated intelligence, indication, and warning
Professional training	Primarily network engineers and IT professionals	Cross-training: IT professionals exposed to intelligence methodologies and intelligence Professionals exposed to technical training	Integrated training: blending both technical and analytic dimensions

products (target analysis, intention analysis, TTPs, technical information, and responses to thwart the threat). Finally, it contrasts the differences in how cyber intelligence professionals have been trained as the profession and discipline have evolved.

Phase I—before cyber intelligence: the data age

The Internet and everything connected to it were not designed with security in mind. In the late 1980s, as serious discussions of cybersecurity began to emerge, approaches were broad and focused on building walls and trying to defend against any and all threats, without even knowing what the threats were.[22] The information assurance focus was on protecting the network itself. Cyber defense was grounded in a reactive posture, responding and patching after an attack occurred or a known vulnerability was discovered. This resulted in a "cat and mouse" game in which CTAs continuously developed new exploits for each vulnerability, and defenders developed new countermeasures for each exploit. Through the 1990s, computer "viruses" were seen as the principal threat and antivirus software was created to identify viruses in the wild and block them at each possible node of entry.[23] This was typically implemented through the use of intrusion detection systems (IDSs), tools that monitor network traffic and system activities for malicious activity. Data concerning malicious indicators were "shared" through antivirus software updates, and therefore would defend only against known threats.[24]

A notable example of the threat during this phase was the "Internet Worm" also known as the "Morris Worm," named after its creator, Robert Tappan Morris. This was the most sophisticated worm to date because it could self-replicate, which not only led to infecting many different computers, but also to infecting the same computer multiple times. This forced the widespread need for antivirus software on every computer.[25]

During this period, the Collection phase of the intelligence cycle was centered on technical data, including hashes—algorithms that convert and compress variable data to a fixed length value for use in authentication. These data points were usually discerned after the malware was successful, and were then entered into malware database.[26] Security data were processed only from internal traffic, specific to the organization's own network, and sharing threat information was uncommon.[27] The analysis phase examined the network's traffic patterns, usually looking for abnormalities through network logs, but not knowing exactly what those deviations might mean. Dissemination of analytic or intelligence products was mostly internal or done only within organizations.

In the data age, threat analysis was unsophisticated. The adversary and the target analyses were both undifferentiated; the "cyber threat" was seen as a monolith. CTA analysis rarely examined the intentions or objectives of the attack. Adversary TTPs—including malware (e.g., virus, worm, Trojan), social engineering, and denial of service (DoS) attacks—were seldom analyzed in any depth. People working in cyber intelligence during this early phase were principally network engineers and information technology professionals with little, if any, background in intelligence collection or analytic methodologies.

Cyber intelligence in the data age was static. Over time, however, it became clear that threat data changed constantly and antivirus software, although still useful, could not keep pace or protect against "zero-day attacks," those attacks exploiting vulnerabilities unknown to the software developer. Moreover, by the mid-2000s, as industries realized that a risk accepted by one is a risk shared by all, it became clear that threat indicators needed to be shared, and perhaps more importantly, that it was also necessary to gather and disseminate information about the TTPs used to penetrate their networks. This required more than technical data; it required information.

Phase II—cyber intelligence in recent years: the information age

Since the mid-2000s, cybersecurity professionals have begun to more consistently add meaning and context to the threat data they collected and stored.[28] The currency of threat data evolved into the currency of threat information.[29] For the past ten years, the dominant cybersecurity posture has remained primarily defensive and reactive, but more focused, aiming not only to build bigger walls but ostensibly smarter walls with deeper packet inspection and more discriminating filters.[30] In practice, network defense strategies now not only use IDSs, but also Intrusion Prevention Systems (IPS), also known as Intrusion Detection and Prevention Systems. An IPS not only monitors the network and systems, but is also able to actively prevent or block intrusions that are detected.[31] Security operators are thus paying more attention to attribution, though their focus has remained on known threats, known actors, and known types of attacks.

The State Department breach in June 2006 is probably the best known attack to occur during this "Information" phase. The attack was attributed to North Korea and China, and today would be considered an APT attack, though it occurred before the APT designation was coined. The hackers primarily stole sensitive information and passwords, but also created "back doors" so that they could return at a later date; this is a main tactic of APTs.[32]

In recent years, the focus of information assurance in cyber defense has moved from the broad notion of protecting an entire network, to a more asset-based emphasis on protecting information. Thus, intelligence collection has centered on information for educating users, network logs, and packet information. IP addresses for "blacklisting" have dominated the technical data. Security data are processed both from internal traffic, network logs, and from select "intelligence" feeds.[33] Likewise, the analysis phase also incorporates—and sometimes integrates—internal network information with data from those feeds. Analytic products and threat data are now disseminated within and beyond the organization to other similar entities.

Threat analysis in the information age has leveled up in sophistication from the data era. CTA typologies and categories (e.g., state, criminal, hacktivist) remain basic but they have enhanced analysis of the adversary, allowing a more nuanced understanding of CTAs.[34] Rather than countering a monolith of cyber "bad guys," security professionals have started to consider the implications of different types of CTAs for a given organization's threat surface analysis.

Target analysis has also become slightly more refined. Security operators acknowledged that targets were selected and were differentiated, so that threats to a medical insurer might differ from those to a retail chain. Consequently, analysts began to explicitly consider CTA intentions and objectives and sought to identify them, at least for the broad categories of actors. Adversary TTPs have also evolved in the information age. Attacks are not only perpetrated through viruses, but also through more sophisticated targeting of human vulnerabilities, using tactics like phishing and social engineering, and techniques coordinating multiple attack vectors like distributed DoS.[35]

Information-sharing efforts are a boon to military and civilian users in the information age. Cyber threat information has become a valued commodity, spawning a cottage industry of threat intelligence services—provided by companies like FireEye, HP Intel, Crowdstrike, AlienVault, LookingGlass, etc.—as well as grassroots efforts to enhance information sharing within sectors. More than a decade ago, the owners and operators of critical infrastructure resources in specific sectors began to establish Information Sharing and Analysis Centers (ISACs). The ISAC Council website states that the goal of ISACs is "to provide users with accurate, actionable, and relevant information" to support their cyber defense, risk mitigation, and incident response. ISACs, a collection of trusted entities, flourished and gained traction within their respective sectors (approximately 27 at last count) including information technology, finance, healthcare, and supply chain.[36]

Private and public sectors, whether by, with or through ISACs, are sharing cyber threat information more than ever before, but too much *unanalyzed* information creates the same challenge as having too much data. Despite having more sector-specific information readily available, results from a recent 2015 survey by the Ponemon Institute suggest that most information technology leaders still lack confidence in their leaderships' ability to use that information effectively to protect their data and systems. Perhaps most troubling is the fact that among these IT leaders, a third (35 percent) relied on intuition for threat analysis, another third (32 percent) relied on "logical deductions" and only the remaining third (32 percent) used actual data or intelligence.[37]

In the current cybersecurity situation, there is no lack of cyber information, but often not the *analyzed* information—actionable intelligence—that is needed to inform critical decisions. Actionable cyber intelligence is integrated intelligence that is accurate, relevant, and timely in relation to the threat surface. It enables a cyber defense that is dynamic and adaptive to counter the rapidly evolving array of threats in the cyber domain. The military and government have long understood the need for actionable intelligence, even in cyberspace, but only recently have the public and private sectors realized the need for enhanced analytic capabilities.[38] The analytic function focuses on processing and exploiting data and information to provide actionable intelligence at the strategic, operational, and tactical levels.

In their framework for designing a security operations center, Schinagl and colleagues describe the intelligence function as:

> the kernel of the SOC ... [where the] competent and skilled analysts are located ..., exchanging information with internal and external parties, analyzing threat patterns and monitoring results, defining rules for event filtering and giving instructions to operational staff and security staff.[39]

In Phase II, cyber intelligence professionals are mainly cross-trained. In other words:

> people with a technical or computer science background and experience will pick up some intelligence concepts, terminology and tradecraft in the course of their work, just as individuals with a nontechnical intelligence analytic background will learn some cybersecurity concepts, terminology and technical skills.[40]

Systematically collecting information on the threat, analyzing and integrating that information, and producing actionable cyber intelligence are necessary prerequisites for moving toward a truly proactive cybersecurity posture. This proactive posture could emerge in the third phase of cyber intelligence's short history.

Phase III—the future of cyber intelligence: the age of actionable intelligence

In 2017, the third phase of the cyber intelligence evolution is emerging—the age of actionable intelligence. This advances the field beyond tactical-level actions and widens the strategic aperture of the intelligence picture. These new developments are enabling a shift to a proactive cybersecurity posture that defends against a full range of foreseeable attacks, not just those by known actors. Proactive, intelligence-driven cyber defense calls on cyber intelligence analysts to understand the intentions, capabilities, and activities of adversaries and intrusive competitors, and apply that understanding in a timely manner to inform enterprise decisions at all operational levels.

In the current era, cyber threats and attacks are all too common. Almost every day, news outlets report another breach, hack, compromise, or attack. One of the most recent high-profile incidents was the hack of the Democratic National Committee (DNC) in June 2016. The CTAs, attributed to two Russian hacker groups, were in the network for more than a year. The FBI warned the DNC, the State Department and the White House months before the breach that they were compromised.[41] This actionable cyber intelligence provided the necessary indications and warning, but the DNC did not take action until it was too late. This is a good example of how producing actionable cyber intelligence is necessary, but not sufficient to prevent a cyberattack. To be effective, actionable intelligence must be acted upon.

Security operators still stand watch on the perimeter, mindful of any vulnerabilities or early signs of intrusion, but with effective cyber intelligence, operations can also get "left of the hack," that is to say, CTAs of greatest concern are
identified and deterred before intruders get inside the network.[42] Beyond a hard-
ened perimeter defense, and enhanced intrusion detection and attribution, Phase
III efforts have a comprehensive threat focus. Prevention, through intelligence-
driven cybersecurity, requires an ability to assess the attack surface of a particular network or industry sector based on systematic collection and analysis of
technical (e.g., malicious code, malicious IP addresses, etc.) and nontechnical
threat data (e.g., CTA intentions, capabilities, activities, targets, etc.) and the
connections between them. For example, a CTA may typically use a certain
string of malicious code allowing that code to be linked to the CTA like a "fin-
gerprint." To stay ahead of the threats and zero-day exploits, inputting technical
threat data—however accurate and comprehensive—into firewall filters will not
be sufficient.

The hallmark of this third phase in the discipline's development, however, is
a new emphasis on intelligence integration. Intelligence integration differs from
intelligence or information sharing. Integrated intelligence articulates analyzed
findings from multiple sources and intelligence disciplines to compose a more
complete understanding of the threat environment and related requirements.[43]
From this perspective, integration adds value that is not present when single-
source intelligence is simply shared. Government and industry can provide cyber
intelligence based on their network activity, and companies can provide cyber
intelligence based on what they see on others' networks. Cyber intelligence must
be quickly pulled and received from these various organizations and integrated
to provide the actionable, timely and relevant cyber intelligence needed by
leadership to make strategic decisions and by cybersecurity personnel to protect
the networks.

Intelligence integration can move the field into the actionable intelligence
age.[44] Two recent events signal the emergence of a new era in cyber intelligence,
at least as it pertains to America's national intelligence mission. The first event
occurred on February 10, 2015, with the White House's announcement that the
Office of the Director of National Intelligence would create a new Cyber Threat
Intelligence Integration Center (CTIIC) to be led by the National Counterterrorism Center. According to the White House CTIIC Fact Sheet:

> the CTIIC will be a national intelligence center focused on "connecting the
> dots" regarding malicious foreign cyber threats to the nation and cyber inci-
> dents affecting US national interests, and providing all-source analysis of
> threats to US policymakers. The CTIIC will also assist relevant departments
> and agencies in their efforts to identify, investigate, and mitigate those
> threats.[45]

Having a centralized location for integrating and sharing this actionable cyber
intelligence can take the discipline to the next level.

The second watershed event occurred on March 6, 2015, when CIA Director John Brennan announced that the Agency was creating a new Directorate of Digital Innovation to focus on defending against cyber threats and exploiting advances in information and communication technologies.[46] This new Directorate, charged with setting and maintaining standards for digital tradecraft, will incorporate the Open Source Center and the Information Operations Center, an entity described as "a secret organization that handles missions including cyber-penetrations and sabotage and is now the second-largest center at the CIA."[47] US Director of National Intelligence James Clapper publicly endorsed the change, saying: "I see many advantages to this, but the one I want to highlight specifically is the impact this change will have in promoting integration."[48] Cyber intelligence integration is an essential foundation for securing cyberspace. The CTIIC and the CIA Directorate of Digital Innovation should bring the United States closer to accomplishing this monumental goal.

Along with movement toward greater integration, in Phase III, the information assurance focus is shifting from just protecting "information" to prioritized protection of the organization's most valued assets. This results from a greater focus at the strategic level and enhanced collaboration between technical security professionals and executive-level enterprise leaders. Intelligence collection is now focusing on both technical and nontechnical information that is pertinent to specific organizational and risk-related decisions. Security data are processed from all relevant sources, both inside and outside of the enterprise and network. Analysis focuses on integrating all-source information to produce intelligence products that can inform decisions at the strategic, operational, and tactical levels. The resulting actionable intelligence and products are disseminated and shared widely, even across business sectors.

Since the volume of all-source information is increasing and the state of information technologies is so advanced, it is tempting to believe, or at least to hope, that all collection and analysis can be automated—but analysts remain essential. The US DHS suggests that "automation frees humans to do what they do well—think, ask questions, and make judgments about complex situations."[49] Cyber threats are more than a technical challenge, and will require more than a technical solution. For example, in an automated system, a threat might be detected and the network automatically shuts down, but the threat could simply be a ruse to disrupt the network; a human could potentially have discerned the ruse and prevented an unnecessary stoppage.

Analysts always have been an integral part of network security: data analysts collect threat data, information analysts process and exploit the threat information, and now cyber intelligence analysts analyze and integrate the cyber intelligence from multiple sources and disciplines. Analytic capabilities are the bridge between information and integrated, actionable intelligence. In Phase III, the next generation of professionals in this domain will be trained in cyber intelligence as an integrated discipline, blending both technical and analytic dimensions.[50]

Adversary analysis in this era has become deeper and more enterprise-specific. Security operators are thinking beyond categories and typologies of

CTAs and exploring specific actors and crews that pose the greatest risk to their organizations, their targets, intentions, tools, artifacts, and TTPs. These developments in threat assessments have pushed analyses of targets and CTA intention to a new level of refinement. SOC personnel and analysts now not only try to identify the adversary's intent, but to understand it in a way that may reveal why the actors have chosen a specific target at a certain point in time. The enhanced sophistication of actionable intelligence is a necessary defensive counterweight to increasingly sophisticated and innovative attack methods, which enable more, and more effective, zero-day exploits and advanced, persistent threats. Some current threats, such as ransomware, did not even exist just a few years ago. In the future, CTAs may create new threats that defenders currently are unable to imagine, but with effective cyber intelligence it may be possible to foresee what future cyber threats will be before they arrive.

Not only are attack methods evolving, but the range of possible targets is also expanding. As the Internet of Things (IoT) proliferates, everything is becoming connected to the Internet, including items such as implanted medical devices, cars, and bridges. "From a cyber intelligence standpoint, the IoT provides a larger and more diverse set of targets for recruitment."[51] These "sensors" can sometimes be used for nefarious objectives, and this could, for instance, lead to sensory overload for the intelligence community. The IoT will provide the intelligence community with a wealth of new information that needs to be collected and analyzed to produce actionable cyber intelligence.

Conclusion

Over the past decade, "cyber intelligence" has become an increasingly popular term, but its broad use has also been confusing and misleading. Much of what is referred to as "threat intelligence" in the cyber domain is not processed intelligence, but raw data such as IP addresses and hashes. Technical data are only one component of cyber intelligence, and the data themselves only become useful when meaning is attached to them and they are applied in context. By distinguishing the characteristics of intelligence from those of data and information, it is possible to develop a clearer and more useful working definition, and to trace how the concept and the discipline have evolved over the past 30 years.

In the Internet's early years, security was focused mainly on building walls to keep out the hackers. Through the 1990s, the threat vector shifted to viruses, so threat intelligence mainly focused on data used to identify the signatures and indicators. That was the age of data. The mid-2000s ushered in the age of information, in which cybersecurity professionals began more consistently not only to collect and store threat data, but to add meaning and context to them. The focus was still principally technical, and aimed to enable "smarter walls" with deeper packet inspection, more discriminating filters, and "signatures" to be found in malware. We are now, arguably, entering the age of actionable intelligence.

The inclusion of "cyber intelligence" as a core mission area in the 2014 National Intelligence Strategy, the creation of the CTIIC, and emergence of the

CIA's new Directorate of Digital Innovation all signal the beginning of a new era in which the focus of cyber intelligence is on actionable intelligence, derived from multiple sources, agencies and disciplines, which includes actor-related information on intentions, capabilities, and activities, all integrated to address key issues at strategic, operational, and tactical levels, and disseminated widely among trusted partners in the private and public sectors.

Achieving cyber intelligence integration will be challenging, but it is essential. This actionable cyber intelligence will allow leaders to make informed decisions because they will have an advanced level of awareness and understanding of their cyber threats. One thing is certain: "as the technology world continues to evolve, one can expect the cyber intelligence discipline to keep pace."[52]

Notes

1 Randy Borum, John Felker, and Sean Kern, "Cyber intelligence operations: More than just 1s & 0s," *Proceedings of the Marine Safety and Security Council: The US Coast Guard Journal of Safety and Security at Sea* 71 (2014): 65–68.
2 Randall Dipert, "The essential features of an ontology for cyberwarfare," *Conflict and Cooperation in Cyberspace: The Challenge to National Security* (2013): 35–48; Leo Obrst, Penny Chase, and Richard Markeloff, "Developing an ontology of the cyber security domain," *STIDS* (2012): 49–56; Brian Ulicny et al., "Inference and Ontologies," in Alexander Kott, Cliff Wang, and Robert F. Erbacher (eds), *Cyber Defense and Situational Awareness* (New York: Springer, 2014), 167–199.
3 Michael Warner, "Wanted: A definition of 'intelligence'," *Studies in Intelligence* 46/3 (2002): 15–22.
4 Jennifer Rowley, "The wisdom hierarchy: Representations of the DIKW hierarchy," *Journal of Information Science* 33/2 (2007): 163–180.
5 Russell Ackoff, "From data to wisdom," *Journal of Applied Systems Analysis* 16/1 (1989): 3–9.
6 Rowley, "The wisdom hierarchy," 163–180; Chaim Zins, "Conceptual approaches for defining data, information, and knowledge," *Journal of the American Society for Information Science and Technology* 58/4 (2007): 479–493.
7 Ackoff, "From data to wisdom," 3–9.
8 Rowley, "The wisdom hierarchy," 163–180.
9 Tony Cawkell, "Information," in John Feather and Paul Sturges (eds), *International Encyclopedia of Information and Library Science* (New York: Routledge, 2003), 244.
10 Robert M. Clark, *Intelligence Analysis: A Target-Centric Approach* (Washington, DC: CQ Press, 2012), 13.
11 Warner, "Wanted: A definition of 'intelligence'," 17.
12 See, for example: Ellen Nakashima, "Researchers Identify Sophisticated Chinese Cyberespionage Group," *Washington Post*, October 28, 2014.
13 Mandiant, APT1. "Exposing One of China's Cyber Espionage Units," 2013, 3.
14 US Office of the Director of National Intelligence, *The National Intelligence Strategy of the United States of America*, (Washington, DC: 2014), at www.dni.gov/files/documents/2014_NIS_Publication.pdf.
15 Richard P. Quinn, *The FBI's Role in Cyber Security: Statement Before the House Homeland Security Committee, Subcommittee on Cyber Security, Infrastructure Protection, and Security Technologies* (Washington, DC: 2014), at www.fbi.gov/news/testimony/the-fbis-role-in-cyber-security.
16 Sun Tzu, *The Art of War*. Translated by Samuel B. Griffith. (New York: Oxford University, 1963), 65.

17 John Ferris, "Netcentric warfare, C4ISR and information operations: Towards a revolution in military intelligence?" *Intelligence and National Security* 19/2 (2004): 220.

18 Stef Schinagl, Keith Schoon, and Ronald Paans, "A Framework for Designing a Security Operations Centre (SOC)," *48th Hawaii International Conference on System Sciences (HICSS)*, 2015, 2253–2262.

19 Clark, *Intelligence Analysis: A Target-Centric Approach*.

20 Borum, Felker, and Kern, "Cyber intelligence operations," 65–68.

21 Department of Defense, *Joint Publication 2–0: Joint Intelligence* (Washington DC, 2013), I-2.

22 Michael Warner, "Cybersecurity: A pre-history," *Intelligence and National Security* 27/5 (2012): 781–799.

23 Frederick B. Cohen and Dr. Frederick Cohen. *A Short Course on Computer Viruses* (John Wiley & Sons, Inc., 1994).

24 Jeffrey O. Kephart et al., "Fighting computer viruses," *Scientific American* 277/5 (1997): 56–61.

25 Charles Schmidt and Tom Darby. "The What, Why, and How of the 1988 Internet Worm." *[Online]* (2001), at https://snowplow.org/tom/worm/worm.html.

26 Amon Ott, Simone Fischer-Hübner, and Morton Swimmer, "Approaches to Integrated Malware Detection and Avoidance," in *Proceedings of the 3rd Nordic Workshop on Secure IT Systems, Trondheim*, 1998.

27 Joan C. Hubbard and Karen A. Forcht, "Computer viruses: How companies can protect their systems," *Industrial Management & Data Systems* 98/1 (1998): 12–16.

28 Bronwyn Woods, Samuel J. Perl, and Brian Lindauer, "Data Mining for Efficient Collaborative Information Discovery," in *Proceedings of the 2nd ACM Workshop on Information Sharing and Collaborative Security*, 2015, 3–12; Justin M. Beaver, Ryan Kerekes, and Jim N. Treadwell, "An Information Fusion Framework for Threat Assessment," *12th International Conference on Information Fusion*, 2009, 1903–1910.

29 Oscar Serrano, Luc Dandurand, and Sarah Brown, "On the Design of a Cyber Security Data Sharing System," *Proceedings of the 2014 ACM Workshop on Information Sharing & Collaborative Security*, Scottsdale, AZ, 2014, 61–69.

30 Ido Dubrawsky, "Firewall evolution-deep packet inspection," *Security Focus* 29 (2003).

31 Xinyou Zhang, Chengzhong Li, and Wenbin Zheng, "Intrusion Prevention System Design," in *Proceedings of The Fourth International Conference on Computer and Information Technology*, IEEE, Seoul, 2004, 386–390.

32 "State Department Releases Details of Computer System Attacks," *Information Week*, July 13, 2006, at www.informationweek.com/state-department-releases-details-of-computer-system-attacks/d/d-id/1045112?

33 Tuomo Sipola, Antti Juvonen, and Joel Lehtonen, "Anomaly Detection from Network Logs Using Diffusion Maps," in Lazaros Iliadis and Chrisina Jayne (eds), *Engineering Applications of Neural Networks* (Germany: Springer, 2011), 172–181.

34 Timothy Shimeall and Jonathan Spring, *Introduction to Information Security: A Strategic-Based Approach* (Waltham, MA: Newnes, 2014).

35 Jason Milletary and CERT Coordination Center, "Technical Trends in Phishing Attacks," retrieved December 1 (2005): 3–3; Michael Workman, "Gaining access with social engineering: An empirical study of the threat," *Information Systems Security* 16/6 (2007): 315–331; Christopher Hadnagy, *Social Engineering: The Art of Human Hacking* (Hoboken, NJ: John Wiley & Sons, 2010); Jelena Mirkovic and Peter Reiher, "A taxonomy of DDoS attack and DDoS defense mechanisms," *ACM SIGCOMM Computer Communication Review* 34/2 (2004): 39–53.

36 Erwann Michel-Kerjan, "New challenges in critical infrastructures: A US perspective," *Journal of Contingencies and Crisis Management* 11/3 (2003): 132–141.

37 Ponemon Institute, LLC, *Intelligence Driven Cyber Defense* (Lockheed Martin, 2015).
38 Sarah Brown, Joep Gommers, and Oscar Serrano, "From Cyber Security Information Sharing to Threat Management," *Proceedings of the 2nd ACM Workshop on Information Sharing and Collaborative Security*, Denver, CO, 2015, 43–49.
39 Schinagl, Schoon, and Paans, "A Framework for Designing a Security Operations Centre (SOC)," 2258.
40 Randy Borum and Ronald Sanders, "Cyber Intelligence: Preparing Today's Talent for Tomorrow's Threats," Intelligence and National Security Alliance: Cyber Intelligence Task Force, 2015, 8.
41 Nigel Inkster, "Information warfare and the US presidential election," *Survival* 58/5 (2016): 23–32.
42 Randy Borum, "Getting 'left of the hack': Honing your cyber intelligence can thwart intruders." *InfoSecurity Professional* 3/6 (2014): 25–29.
43 Michael T. Flynn and Charles A. Flynn, "Integrating intelligence and information: Ten points for the commander," *Military Review* 92/1 (2012): 4.
44 Dariusz Korl, *Intelligence Integration in Distributed Knowledge Management* (London: IGI Global, 2008); Gregory Treverton, *The Next Steps in Reshaping Intelligence* (Santa Monica, CA: RAND Corporation, 2005).
45 US White House, *FACT SHEET: Cyber Threat Intelligence Integration Center*, (Washington, DC, 2015), at www.whitehouse.gov/the-press-office/2015/02/25/fact sheet-cyber-threat-intelligence-integration-center.
46 John Brennan, *Unclassified Version of March 6, 2015 Message to the Workforce from CIA Director John Brennan: Our Agency's Blueprint for the Future* (Langley: Central Intelligence Agency, 2015).
47 Greg Miller, "CIA plans major reorganization and a focus on digital espionage." *Washington Post*, March 6, 2015, at www.washingtonpost.com/world/national-security/cia-plans-major-reorganization-and-a-focus-on-digital-espionage/2015/03/06/87e94a1e-c2aa-11e4-9ec2-b418f57a4a99_story.html.
48 Ibid.
49 US Department of Homeland Security, *Enabling Distributed Security in Cyberspace – Building a Healthy and Resilient Cyber Ecosystem with Automated Collective Action* (Washington DC, 2011), at www.dhs.gov/xlibrary/assets/nppd-cyber-ecosystem-white-paper-03-23-2011.pdf.
50 Borum and Sanders, "Cyber Intelligence," 8.
51 Douglas Price, "A guide to cyber intelligence," *The Intelligencer* 21/1 (2014): 55.
52 Ibid.

10 Changing the game

Cyberspace and big data-driven national security intelligence

*Aaron F. Brantly**

Cyberspace and digital technologies writ large are profoundly affecting intelligence collection and analysis. The collection and analysis of intelligence is constantly evolving. Whether it was the machinations of Sun Tzu in the fifth century BCE, Kautilya in the third century BCE, George Washington during the Revolutionary War, the Office of Strategic Services during World War II or the combined 16 agencies of the US intelligence community (IC) today, each of these evolutions in intelligence has sought out information from both secret and open sources for the purpose of developing intelligence to aid decision makers.[1] The analysis below examines the data available to the intelligence community as it stands at the dawn of the age of the zettabyte.[2] The intelligence community is increasingly challenged by large volumes of data. Increasingly, data interact with, transit through, or are generated in cyberspace. This chapter serves as a developmental model for collection and analytical methodologies able to incorporate the spectrum of data from small to large into a robust and time-relevant intelligence process.[3]

We often hear the term "big data," but what does it mean and where is it effective for intelligence analysts and operators? This chapter argues that there are six broad typologies of large-scale data collection and that these typologies constitute multiple big data problems that filter into an IC that functions similarly to a big data computational analysis system. The IC's resources process data from various sources and synthesize that data to facilitate answers to both structured (directed) and unstructured queries from customers. Big data are growing in importance as more and more sensors and systems join cyberspace. As cyberspace becomes ubiquitous, it is incumbent on intelligence agencies to leverage and incorporate data to provide strategic and tactical insights for decision makers. Understanding the IC as a big data computational system helps to orient both the community and policymakers toward potential improvements in system design and function, enabling the development of more efficient and rigorous analytical products in support of national security.

What is big data and where does it come from?

Data are growing at near exponential rates as cyberspace expands to encompass more than 60 percent of the global population and tens of billions of

Internet-enabled devices. Simply put, data are big, nearly ubiquitous, and highly complex. To develop a model that incorporates big data into the broader intelligence collection and analysis processes it is necessary to identify what big data are. Big data maximize one or more of the following "Vs": volume, veracity, variety, velocity.[4] Each of these Vs services the goal of analyzing a fifth V: value. Value is representative of data significance and impact in solving complex problems. The Vs establish the attributes of data but do not indicate the sources of large-scale data and potential collection and analysis opportunities.[5] To develop rigorous theoretical foundations for the application of data to intelligence analysis it is helpful to survey what data are available and how that data comes to be. To understand the impact of data, this first section develops a framework for understanding the sources of data that can be leveraged across disciplines for analysis. By creating a framework of sources, intelligence analysts can establish connections between phenomena that were previously unknown and request additional collection sources to fill in potential gaps. This capability to connect the dots has never been more important than now, as dynamic and expanding cyber networks and the proliferation of digital sensors help in representing an increasingly complex reality.

How data come to be is an important theoretical question and one that determines implications and potential analytical applicability of data for intelligence analysts. Generally, data are human- or machine-generated or measured by a sensor, either internal to or external to cyberspace. Data can be sensed, generated, captured, created, compiled, transacted, experimental, or provoked.[6] Data within these categories can be either structured (highly organized) or unstructured (highly disorganized). Often, the lines between data types blur. However, data typically originate from:

1 extra-environmental sources (non-cyberspace/computer—meteorological, biological, geological, astronomical, etc.)
2 extra-human (non-cyberspace/computer-generated human activities—pre-digitized bibliographic materials and documents, recorded human behaviors, historical and non-historical data, archeological, cultural, etc.)
3 machine-generated environmental (data generated by cyberspace interactions absent direct control—network event logs, web server logs, etc.)
4 directed-environmental (data generated by directed component system interactions—Internet mapping, port scanning, etc.)
5 passive human-generated (data generated by passive human activities in cyberspace—web searches, online shopping, content consumption, etc.)
6 active human-generated (data generated through deliberate acts such as post or content generation, like buttons, etc.).

These categories attempt to distinguish between those sources external to cyberspace and computers and subsequently digitized for analytic purposes in items 1–2, and those sources internal to cyberspace or computers 3–6. Here, I artificially draw lines between different types of data to provide cognitive distinctions. In practice, these lines are often blurred as devices such as supervisory control and data acquisition systems automatically generate data. The origins of data from any automated system and do in fact have a point of origin found within their code or hardware configurations. Moreover, the line between passive and active human activities in cyberspace is blurry. A person's search behavior online or their general content consumption could be constitutive of active human data generation under certain circumstances. Figure 10.1 below illustrates a generalized radar plot assessing the origins of big data using four of the five "Vs" (volume, veracity, velocity, and variety). The chart is stylized and designed to visually represent the origins of data within the six data types identified above.

If the below data plot was broken down by specific types of data, it would look vastly different. Here, the aggregated attributes of extra-environmental data offer the highest volume, veracity, velocity, and variety. This should not come as a surprise as the natural environment is capable of continuously generating potential data points for analysis of various phenomena. Yet the ability to sense and subsequently operationalize the data associated with various phenomena remains limited compared to machine or human–machine interactions.

Much of the data generated by extra-environmental factors is constitutive of Measurement and Signature Intelligence (MASINT). MASINT is the scientific and technical intelligence obtained by quantitative and qualitative analysis of data and can include everything from radiologic signatures to chemical, biological, and geological sensors as well as hundreds of other measures.[7] Big data is not limited to conventionally sensed data and can include Imagery Intelligence

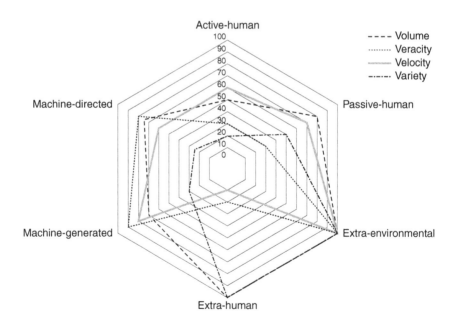

Figure 10.1 Assessing big data origins by attribute (general data origin-stylized).

(IMINT), Signals Intelligence (SIGINT), Human Intelligence (HUMINT), Open Source Intelligence (OSINT) and Cyber intelligence (CYBERINT). An example of big data IMINT would include the ARGUS-IS, a wide area persistent surveillance (WAPS) system with a 1.8 gigapixel video system capable of recording a 36-square mile radius.[8] The volume, veracity, and velocity of data generated by WAPS is constitutive of big data and requires special analytical methods and processing capabilities.

To provide a better understanding of various types of sensed data, Figure 10.2 is a word cloud representing 320 types of sensor able to collect a fraction of potential extra-environmental data generated every second outside of the cyber domain. It is the process of digitization that enables the processing and analysis of big data. The intent is twofold: first, the vast potential number of sources data should not be underestimated; second, big data are relative to the problem set to which they are applied. Just because a phenomenon can be studied thanks to big data does not mean that it helps in the development of substantive intelligence. Instead, it is the rigorous assessment of needs and the subsequent collection of data relevant to those needs that facilitates good intelligence.

The way data originates has profound consequences for subsequent analysis and implications. As an example, Google's "Flu Trends" project, designed to assess the location and magnitude of flu outbreaks, was considered ahead of its time and an exemplar of novel applications of big data.[9] However, subsequent analysis on the origin of the data indicated that the results were not as meaningful as originally thought, and the methodology for collecting data changed

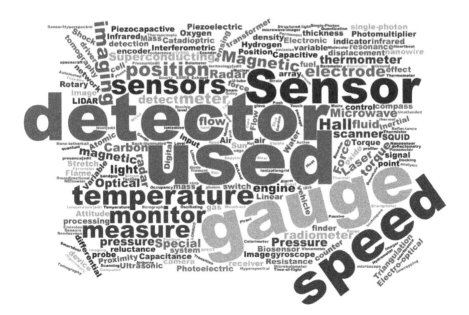

Figure 10.2 Visualizing 320 of the thousands of sensors capable of digitizing data.

multiple times mid-stream, thus introducing uncertainty and potential bias into the data.[10] Google's underlying search algorithm, the core of the analytic model, changed multiple times over the course of the study. Changing the underlying assumptions for the collection of data whilst the project was in progress introduced bias that could skew the findings. The same is true of many types of data analysis. Acquiring a robust understanding of the data, its strengths and weaknesses, is fundamental to the use of big data for intelligence.

Since data are representative of phenomena, the adequate assessment of that data is heavily dependent on how it was created or measured. Comprehension of data requires both an understanding of its creation and its operationalization into some measurable phenomena. The inaccurate representation of data introduces systemic bias into analysis found in later stages of the intelligence process. Although data generated through logs or similar machine-generated processes— which are commonplace in cybersecurity—appear to be less susceptible to this systemic bias, this is not entirely the case. Writing on the legal attributes of cyberspace, scholar Lawrence Lessig indicates that "code is law."[11] The way in which code is written inherently defines the parameters of machine-generated data. The choices of the hardware and software designers result in the creation of certain types of data. Understanding design choices greatly influences the resultant analysis of derived data.

Irrespective of its origin, all big data are processed within computers. An underlying knowledge of how these systems function, how they collect data, and when they err is crucially important when taking raw data and synthesizing it into intelligence products. Data misinterpretation can result in intelligence failures and have dire consequences. An example of misinterpretation of data by a machine occurred on October 5, 1960 when the Ballistic Missile Early Warning System (BMEWS) located at J-Site in northern Greenland identified a potential large volley of incoming intercontinental ballistic missiles, raising the alert level at the North American Aerospace Defense Command (NORAD).[12] The BMEWS data indicated the high probability of imminent nuclear attack; were it not for the quick actions of the deputy commander, Air Marshal Charles Roy Slemon (a Canadian), in confirming the incoming volley, NORAD would have prepared its weapons for an immediate retaliatory attack. Upon determining that the probability of attack was low due to Soviet Premier Nikita Krushchev being in New York at the time, Slemon asked J-Site for further confirmation.[13] At the time of the request, the technicians at J-Site should have been able to see incoming ballistic missiles overhead. Upon stepping outside, the technicians witnessed a large rising moon over Norway. Although its believed range was 3,000 miles, the BMEWS system had identified an object 238,900 miles away.

The BMEWS example offers a cautionary tale of digital data being interpreted falsely due to a failure to fully understand the capabilities of a collection system. Just as failures can occur in small data, for example when the US IC judged in 2002 that Iraq had continued its weapons of mass destruction programs,[14] they can occur with automated systems based on sensors and logs. Data, big and small, require veracity to be of value. In the incident above, blind trust in the veracity of a system absent additional intelligence, such as the location of Soviet leaders, might have resulted in a catastrophic intelligence failure. What processes are available to the IC to facilitate large-scale data analytics leading to efficient and meaningful synergies that enhance the accuracy and value of a given intelligence product? What tools exist within big data across the six data origin categories to enable automation of lower-level functions of sorting, processing, and reducing data to more effectively allocate limited analyst resources?

The IC is awash with information and the analyst is on the losing end of this data deluge.[15] Lessons from physical, social and computer sciences can be leveraged to streamline large volumes of diverse data across multiple complementary collection types. No single method obviates the fundamental need for human analysis, yet advanced data mining, crowd-sourced analytics, longitudinal statistical analysis of recurring phenomena working in tandem with small data collection from HUMINT, and directed SIGINT sources offer the possibility of making sense of a complex and ever-changing geopolitical environment.

How intelligence can and often does leverage big data

Big data is not a novel concept to intelligence agencies. Mark Lowenthal and Ronald Marks write that, in the wake of the 9/11 intelligence failures, the IC and Congress established robust efforts to sort through a mass of "big data."[16] Just as big data processing has been a challenge for numerous reasons, to include in-memory analysis,[17] database and storage issues, algorithms, data transport within and across network infrastructures, sample uncertainty quantification, parallel computation, data management, and many more.

Ample evidence of the IC's movement into rigorous big data analytics should not come as a surprise.[18] Recent National Security Agency (NSA) programs and research efforts are some of the more widely known manifestations of the trend toward incorporating big data into the intelligence process.[19] Some of the more interesting trends in the IC have focused on the visualization of large amounts of data to include biological systems analysis, network traffic flows, transnational network mapping, and more.[20] Other uses of big data include the storage and computational power of intelligence agencies to handle enormous volumes and velocities of data as well as attempt large computationally intensive activities against forms of data.[21] Even the CIA is actively recruiting individuals who are technically savvy and capable of organizing and interpreting big data.[22]

Media and academic accounts of IC uses of data often focus on the evolution of OSINT or what Sir David Omand, Jamie Bartlett, and Carl Miller call SOCMINT (Social Media Intelligence).[23] The value of SOCMINT and OSINT more generally cannot be understated, yet these sources are but small aspects of the broader data landscape available to the IC and are largely confined to what was referred to above as passive and active human-generated data in cyberspace. It is also necessary to consider fundamental issues regarding the origin and collection of SOCMINT and OSINT, as the veracity of this data is susceptible to a variety of internal and external biases capable of leading to inaccurate intelligence.[24] There are compelling accounts of state-based censorship and surveillance of individuals in cyberspace that make the development of unbiased content in many locations highly susceptible to self-censorship, government censorship, or other forms of content constraint that limit its meaning and value.[25] Understanding the constraints of where data comes from, how it is generated, and how it is collected can have profound implications for intelligence assessments. These constraints are particularly acute in the SOCMINT and OSINT collection types where vast amounts of data are collected from all types of sources, but also extend to other forms of collection.

Beyond SOCMINT and OSINT, some studies have proposed leveraging big data to solve specific IC-related issues across various domains to include cyberattack attribution, support for human decision making with automated algorithms and facilitating improved decision making and operational intelligence.[26] Diversifying the IC's approaches and applicability of large-scale data provides novel solutions to existing problems. Independent data collection, processing, storage and analysis methods can provide further solutions to reduce the aggregate stresses big data impose on the IC and increase the value of the resultant intelligence to the community.

Understanding the IC as a big data computational system

In many ways, the 16 agencies of the IC are an analogue structure comparable to modern supercomputers. Taken in aggregate, the IC comprises many functional lines of effort each attempting to derive intelligence from vast troves of specific data that are then (ideally) synthesized into a meaningful product for a decision maker. Although there are overlapping redundancies in certain aspects of the IC, the community operates in much the same way as a distributed computational system to facilitate analysis of complex phenomena. Within the subcomponents of this system, each agency is increasingly overwhelmed by the data within its purview and the aggregate system is, in turn, also stressed.

Functionally, aspects of the IC break down in much the same way as a distributed computational system such as Hadoop,[27] although some with notable differences in overlap and deliberate slowdown for human interaction prior to completed intelligence product. Whereas systems such as Hadoop are designed and implemented for maximum efficiency in processing large volumes of data and subsequently reducing that data, the IC necessarily interjects slowdowns into its analytic processes to provide analytic oversight that is unnecessary in purely machine-oriented tasks or automated tasks such as the Google search engine. The collection and analysis of intelligence is structured around different intelligence agencies, but numerous overlaps are built in to the US intelligence apparatus. SIGINT is largely rooted in the National Security Agency. SIGINT, IMINT, GEOINT, and MASINT, collected from orbital locations, originates at the National Reconnaissance Office which then conducts some analysis but also provides satellite-derived information to the NSA, DIA, NGA, and others for the development of intelligence. The National Geospatial Intelligence Agency (NGA) provides military commands with geospatial intelligence (GEOINT) and it also provides intelligence on various disasters and intelligence for events. The CIA is primarily focused on HUMINT, yet is also the primary general analytical agency under the Director of National Intelligence and, as such, it processes all sorts of data types. These and the other agencies overlap and work in tandem on various problem sets.

Why is it helpful to conceive of the IC as a big data computational system? The collection of information for the IC comes from multiple sources. These sources are encompassed in the broad categories identified earlier in the chapter, and comprise both sensed and generated data. These data are complex, non-uniform, and unstructured. The volume of data generated across the IC is immense. Due to the complex architecture of the IC, the data it deals with are often unwieldy and constrained by predefined rules in the form of legislation, executive policy constraints, and bureaucratic cultures.[28] When considering intelligence as a big data problem it is immediately apparent that the volume, variety, veracity, and velocity of data are extremely diverse. Rather than having each node process all available data and then reducing that data into a single analytic product, the IC serves to distribute the processing of information by data type. By processing information by data type, each individual node (intelligence agency) can then be tailored and specialized in the processing of specific data. Since the potential for analytic bias is embedded within single-source processing of data, particularly when taking account of organizational cultures and analytic methods by information type, the IC provides overlap of analysis as well as structured argumentation through methods such as analysis of competing hypotheses to minimize systemic biases.[29] Some nodes—the CIA, DIA, and the State Department's Bureau of Intelligence and Research—provide generalized analytic functions that serve to reduce (consolidate) findings whilst taking into account the analyses of other nodes. Moreover, the distribution of information across the nodes helps analysts to focus on consumer-specific needs. Intelligence analysis is not in service of a single client, but rather a diverse client set, ranging from civilian and military policymakers to operators. The overlapping structures with both embedded, focused, and generalized nodes offer clients multiple forms of query tailored to specific needs.

Conceiving of intelligence collection and analysis as a big data problem with fluid, dynamic and evolving data provides the decision maker with access points relevant to their needs yet encompassing information from other sources. Rather than focusing on intelligence as a single cycle, a process which has drawn a great deal of criticism, a modified version of the target-centric approach to intelligence proposed by Robert Clark that places the client at the center of a dynamic query process offers clear benefits.[30] As Clark notes, junior analysts often start by developing analysis based on initial guidance provided by a customer.[31] Yet, quite often, the customer's guidance is not fully formulated. The best way to conceive of guidance is as an initial query, much like the query a person enters into a web search engine such as Google or Bing. The general query is often lacking in specifics. Google and other search engines then leverage multiple other contextual pieces of information related to the individual providing the query as well as similar queries occurring both historically, in proximate temporal and spatial ranges to return tailored results. Moreover, search engines often consider individual query history and tailor the resultant search from an enormous volume of data to the needs of a given client.[32] The more specific the query request the more specific the return of data. In both instances, the results returned might provide the customer with information or context they did not realize they needed or wanted.

The above section served to establish the IC as a large computational entity able to facilitate answers to complex and simple queries. Just as Google handles and processes complicated queries of information, so too can the IC. Yet, both Google and the IC must have methods of collecting, storing and processing (sorting) data prior to query initiation. The next section focuses on establishing a method that informs query results through data triangulation.

Reducing data and generating intelligence

In recent years, there have been public calls for limitations on data storage predicated on the notions that the utility of data decreases over time and that the duration of data storage should be limited to protect privacy.[33] In understanding the applicability of data, the source of that data is extremely important and often impacts its temporal value. Large data sets often stress researchers and intelligence analysts. Yet, beyond the challenge of sorting and processing that data, there are rarely cries that data should not be collected. The collection of data plays a pivotal role in understanding diverse phenomena. The only instances when data collection constraints are wisely exercised are when there are reasonable ethical or moral constraints.[34] Whether a hard scientist or a social scientist, when conducting research, more data is generally better than less.[35] This assessment is predicated on both thoughtful and rigorous collection and proper subsequent analytical methods applied to large volumes of data. Big data does not obviate good science.[36]

What does the ideal relationship between data and intelligence look like? The question of the relationship between data and intelligence hints at how analysts and decision makers wish to see the world and hits at the heart of social scientific thought. Enough data absent robust theory can explain almost anything. Yet, poorly devised methods lead to spurious results and potentially negative outcomes. Therefore, the ideal relationship between data and intelligence necessarily depends upon the attributes of the query (i.e., the methods) and the customer querying. As the level of complexity of a given query increases, so too do the resources associated with answering that query. Hard problems such as forecasting future events require rigorous solutions originating in a solid grasp of epistemological foundations. If big data are captured and used absent an understanding of the data itself, then subsequent analysis and application of that data is fundamentally flawed. The same is true of small data from individual

HUMINT or similar sources. Understanding how we know what we know facilitates a more robust understanding of complex phenomena and enhances the ability of analysts to answer queries.

Generally, across the collection typologies discussed in this chapter, more data is better than less. Whilst more data is better than less it does not infer that all data must be immediately examined by a human analyst. Automated analysis of traffic in networks, known as anomaly-based intrusion detection systems, often functions on statistical models that leverage prior patterns to identify anomalies in current data.[37] The same general methods can be applied to multiple collection types. Automated image analysis can be used to determine changes in satellite or drone images.[38] Such analysis could identify changes in force positions over time, industrial developments, human movement patterns, and more. Data such as high-resolution reconnaissance imagery are often large, both at fixed temporal moments (the moment of collection) as well as longitudinally (sequential images over time). Failure to collect data over longitudinal periods minimizes the veracity of assessments in changes, whether they are human or environmental in origin. An example of such data would include imagery analysis of the development of the nuclear facility at Natanz by the Iranian government.[39]

SOCMINT collected over long durations can also help retroactively identify a single user through the historical study of account activity. As individual members of transnational terrorist organizations enhance their digital operational security and engage in a process referred to as "going dark," longitudinal analysis of SOCMINT can assist in asset identification by providing historical repositories of digital operational security mistakes that might inadvertently expose the location, network, equipment, or other details associated with a potential actor.[40] In this regard, the collection of large-scale SOCMINT (active human-generated data) stored indefinitely can provide small data clues as exhaust that can facilitate intelligence analysis. Alternatively, small data collected from extra-environmental human-generated data (HUMINT) can provide clues on where to place or establish a collection of extra-environmental (MASINT) sensors, directed-environmental data in cyberspace (CYBERINT) or any number of other collection venues.

Big data and small data work together. Just as a single piece of data, a user's location, facilitates a big data search to find a given Italian restaurant in Google, a small piece of contextual data can direct sensors or collection schema both internal and external to cyberspace to a given information set. Absent historical repositories of data from multiple sources, the probability of weak search results increases. Big data in intelligence does not function in the absence of small data, but rather in tandem with it. Often, big data can contain small data that are necessary to answer a customer's query. By collecting a diversity of data across the data typologies the probability of any given piece of small data being available for future queries increases. Yet, as big data advances and analytical methods of data mining, nonparametric analysis, and machine learning are enhanced, the core analytical functions of human analysts might evolve but will remain. First, human analysis facilitates and guides the customer query processes in a way that informs both the collection and analysis of information into subsequent intelligence products. Second, human analysis serves as a roadblock to coded biases as identified within the BMEWS example.

Combined, the distributed functional structure of the IC, from the collection of data across different data typologies through the overlapping analytical specialties, can and does function in aggregate as a big data system of systems. Approaching the IC as a big data computational system can provide a roadmap to enhance data sources both large and small and the analytic processes to provide efficient query responses in the form of robust intelligence products. As cyberspace and digital technologies expand, data will continue to challenge the IC; understanding that the big data challenge is evolving will establish the need for a flexible conceptual framework for collectors, analysts, and consumers of intelligence to adapt their practices. As cyberspace expands and the data available to the intelligence community grows, conventional intelligence models are going to be continuously inundated. Establishing the technical and organizational structures necessary to process and produce intelligence products will only grow in importance.

Notes

* The views expressed here are those of the author and do not reflect the official policy or position of the Department of the Army, Department of Defense, or the US Government.
1 Samuel B. Griffith, *Sun Tzu the Art of War: Translated and with an Introduction* (London: Oxford University Press, 1982); Kautalya and L. N. Rangarajan, *The Arthashastra* (New York: Penguin Books, 1992); Alexander Rose, *Washington's Spies: the Story of America's First Spy Ring* (New York: Bantam Books, 2007); Michael Warner, *The Rise and Fall of Intelligence: an International Security History* (Washington, DC: Georgetown University Press, 2014); Loch K. Johnson, *National Security Intelligence: Secret Operations in Defense of the Democracies* (Cambridge: Polity, 2012).
2 Three hundred trillion MP3s, two hundred billion DVDs. If every person living in the year 2000 had a 180 gigabyte hard drive filled completely with data, all the data on all those drives would occupy 1 zettabyte. See: The Hj03 Project, at www.hjo3.net/bytes. html; Cisco, "The Zettabyte Era—Trends and Analysis," May 29, 2013, at: www. cisco.com/c/en/us/solutions/collateral/service-provider/visual-networking-index-vni/VNI_Hyperconnectivity_WP.html.
3 Whilst this chapter focuses mostly on big data, it is important to recognize the need for understanding of information sources that do not qualify as big data.
4 Michael Schroeck et al., "Analytics: The Real-World Use of Big Data," IBM Institute for Business Value and Saïd Business School at the University of Oxford, October 2012.
5 IBM, "The Four V's of Big Data," at www.ibmbigdatahub.com/infographic/four-vs-big-data.
6 Michele Nemschoff, "7 Important Types of Big Data," February 26, 2014, at www.smartdatacollective.com/michelenemschoff/187751/7-important-types-big-data.
7 Loch K. Johnson, *Handbook of Intelligence Studies* (London: Routledge, 2010).
8 Jay Stanley, "Drone 'Nightmare Scenario' Now Has a Name: ARGUS," February 21, 2013, at www.aclu.org/blog/drone-nightmare-scenario-now-has-name-argus.

9   Google, "Flu Trends Data," at www.google.org/flutrends/about/.

10 David Lazer et al., "The parable of Google flu: Traps in big data analysis," *Science* 343 (2014): 1203–1205.

11 Lawrence Lessig, *Code and Other Laws of Cyberspace* (New York: Basic Books, 1999).

12 Annie Jacobsen, *Pentagon's Brain: An Uncensored History of DARPA, America's Top-Secret Military Research Agency* (New York: Little, Brown and Company, 2015), 85–89.

13 Ibid.

14 Peter Gill and Mark Phythian, *Intelligence in an Insecure World* (Cambridge, UK: Polity Press, 2006), 125–147; National Intelligence Council, Iraq's Continuing Programs for Weapons of Mass Destruction, October 2002, at http://nsarchive.gwu.edu/NSAEBB/NSAEBB129/nie.pdf.

15 Phil Nolan, "A curator approach to intelligence analysis," *International Journal of Intelligence and CounterIntelligence* 25/4 (2012): 786–794.

16 Mark M. Lowenthal and Ronald A. Marks, "Intelligence analysis: is it as good as it gets?" *International Journal of Intelligence and CounterIntelligence* 28/4 (2015): 662–665.

17 In-memory computing primarily relies on keeping data in a server's RAM as a means of processing at faster speeds. In-memory computing especially applies to processing problems that require extensive access to data—analytics, reporting or data warehousing, and big data applications.

18 Sean Gallagher, "What the NSA Can Do with 'Big Data'," November 6, 2013, at http://arstechnica.com/information-technology/2013/06/what-the-nsa-can-do-with-big-data/.

19 Paul Burkhardt, "An Overview of Big Data," *The Next Wave* 20/4 (2014): 4–10, at www.nsa.gov/research/tnw/tnw204/article1.shtml.

20 Randall Rohrer, Celeste Lyn Paul, and Bohdan Nebesh, "Visual Analytics for Big Data," *The Next Wave* 20/4 (2014): 41, at www.nsa.gov/resources/everyone/digital-media-center/publications/the-next-wave/assets/files/TNW-20-4.pdf.

21 James Bamford, "The NSA Is Building the Country's Biggest Spy Center (Watch What You Say)," *Wired*, March 15, 2012, at www.wired.com/2012/03/ff_nsadatacenter/.

22 Central Intelligence Agency, "Big Data Is a Big Deal at the CIA," April 30, 2013, at www.cia.gov/news-information/featured-story-archive/2012-featured-story-archive/big-data-at-the-cia.html

23 David Omand, Jamie Bartlett, and Carl Miller, "Introducing social media intelligence (SOCMINT)," *Intelligence and National Security* 27/6 (2012): 801–823.

24 Sauvik Das and Adam Kramer, "Self-Censorship on Facebook," in *Proceedings of the AAAI Conference on Weblogs and Social Media* (2013), 1–8, at www.aaai.org/ocs/index.php/ICWSM/ICWSM13/paper/viewFile/6093/6350.

25 Philip N. Howard and Muzammil M Hussain, *Democracy's Fourth Wave?: Digital Media and the Arab Spring* (Oxford; New York: Oxford University Press, 2013); Gary King, Jennifer Pan, and Margaret E. Roberts, "How censorship in China allows government criticism but silences collective expression," *American Political Science Review* 107/2 (2013): 326–343.

26 Aaron F. Brantly, "Aesop's wolves: The deceptive appearance of espionage and attacks in cyberspace," *Intelligence and National Security* 31/5 (2016): 674–685; TechAmerica Foundation, "Demystifying Big Data: A Practical Guide to Transforming the Business of Government," 2012, at http://breakinggov.com/documents/demystifying-big-data-a-practical-guide-to-transforming-the-bus/.

27 Hadoop is an open source software framework used for distributed storage and processing of very large data sets. It consists of computer clusters built from commodity hardware. All the modules in Hadoop are designed with a fundamental assumption that hardware failures are a common occurrence and should be automatically handled by the framework.

28 Examples of legislation would include the National Security Act of 1947 and the Intelligence Reform and Terrorism Prevention Act of 2004. Executive policy constraints include Executive Order 12333 and examples of bureaucratic cultures across federal agencies and departments is best examined by James Q. Wilson, *Bureaucracy: What Government Agencies Do and Why They Do It* (New York: Basic Books, 1989).

29 Richards J. Heuer, *Psychology of Intelligence Analysis* (Washington, DC: Center for the Study of Intelligence, 2010); Robert M. Clark, *Intelligence Analysis: A Target-Centric Approach* (Washington, DC: CQ Press, 2004).

30 Arthur S. Hulnick, "What's wrong with the intelligence cycle," *Intelligence and National Security* 21/6 (2006): 959–979.

31 Clark, *Intelligence Analysis*, 24.

32 Sergey Brin and Lawrence Page, "The Anatomy of a Large-Scale Hypertextual Web Search Engine," (1998), 1–20, at http://ilpubs.stanford.edu:8090/361/1/1998-8.pdf.

33 Joseph D. Mornin, "NSA metadata collection and the Fourth Amendment," *Berkeley Technology Law Journal* 29/4 (2014): 1–23.

34 Laurie A. Schintler and Rajendra Kulkarni, "Big data for policy analysis: The good, the bad, and the ugly," *Review of Policy Research* 31/4 (2014): 343–348.

35 Scott Ashworth, Christopher R Berry, and Ethan Bueno de Mesquita, "All else equal in theory and data (big or small)," *PS Political Science and Politics* 48/1 (2014): 89–94.

36 William Roberts Clark and Matt Golder, "Big data, causal inference, and formal theory: Contradictory trends in political science?" *PS Political Science and Politics* 48/1 (2014): 65–70.

37 Pedro Garcia-Teodoro et al., "Anomaly-based network intrusion detection: Techniques, systems and challenges," *Computers & Security* 28/1–2 (2009): 18–28.

38 Mourad Bouziani, Kalifa Goïta, and Dong-Chen He, "Automatic change detection of buildings in urban environment from very high spatial resolution images using existing geodatabase and prior knowledge," *ISPRS Journal of Photogrammetry and Remote Sensing*, October 2009, 1–11.

39 Kim Zetter, *Countdown to Zero Day: Stuxnet and the Launch of the World's First Digital Weapon* (New York: Broadway Books, 2014).

40 James B. Comey, "FBI—Going Dark: Are Technology, Privacy, and Public Safety on a Collision Course?" presented at the Brookings Institution, Washington, DC, October 16, 2014; Aaron F. Brantly and Muhammad al-`Ubaydi, "Extremist forums provide digital OPSEC training," *CTC Sentinel* 8/5 (2015), 10–14.

Part III

Organizing cybersecurity

11 Cybersecurity in the United States and the United Kingdom

The need for trust and cooperation

Kristan Stoddart

Cybersecurity is a growing issue and a significant challenge to the American and British intelligence communities. There are major areas of uncertainty lying ahead for both US and UK intelligence agencies in this field, including what the precise role of the state and its intelligence apparatus is in regard to cyber defense and cyber offense. In addition, state-based intelligence collaboration to fight cybercrime, particularly intrusions into systems leading to data theft, is complicated by the involvement of multiple actors, including non-state hackers and criminals, but also "patriotic hackers," and states themselves, including their intelligence agencies. Another challenge is how to satisfy public concerns regarding the oversight and regulation of intelligence practices in the wake of the furor that followed revelations about mass data collection and surveillance programs directed by the US National Security Agency (NSA).[1] With these challenges in mind, this chapter seeks to answer three relatively simple and inter-related questions. First, what threats are the US and UK intelligence communities facing in the field of cybersecurity? Second, what are the US and UK governments doing to combat these threats? Third, how are their actions being seen by other states and by civil society? Answering these questions will demonstrate the difficulties the United States and the United Kingdom are facing and some of the limitations of their efforts to map, mitigate, and deter hostile threats to government, private industry, individual computer systems, and cloud services. It will be argued that cyber deterrence needs to be built on agreed red lines between nation states by upholding the rule of law within and between states in areas of cybercrime and cyberespionage. In addition, with around 80 percent of critical national infrastructure owned and operated privately, civil society and private industry have to be fully engaged in this security process for US and UK government cybersecurity policies to be successful. In sum, the future of cybersecurity lies in greater cooperation between governments, industry, and civil society.

Threats and threat actors

Western societies are now confronting diverse and complex cyber threats on an unprecedented scale. As Iain Lobban, Director of the UK's Government Communications Headquarters (GCHQ), made clear in 2012: "Every day, all around the world, thousands of IT systems are compromised. Some are attacked purely for the kudos of doing so, others for political motives, but most commonly they are attacked to steal money or commercial secrets." Lobban further recognized the importance of the Internet to business and the risks its pervasiveness carries.[2] These threats and trends are not exclusive to the United Kingdom.

Recent evidence suggests that cybersecurity risks to the private sector are growing faster than companies' ability to secure their data and systems from a wide variety of hostile actors.[3] The reasons for cyberattacks remain multifarious, but Verizon's 2014 data breach investigations report lists among them the long-standing problem posed by espionage.[4] This encompasses espionage from states and private companies, as well as lone wolves. There are currently 70 billion cyber events a month. Of these, 250,000 attacks are noteworthy with 60 to 70 of them meriting considered attention. This volume of attacks is too large to deal with without sufficient infrastructure and increased investment in skilled personnel, and cannot be tackled by governments acting alone.[5]

These threats are fueled by both low entry points to the Internet and growing levels of technical knowledge in a spectrum encompassing multiplying threat actors. Cyber threat actors range from amateur "script kiddies" and online collectives such as the hacktivist group Anonymous, through to highly sophisticated and well-resourced Advanced Persistent Threats (APTs) associated with nation states. Criminals have also sought to monetarize cybercrime and sell expertise, information about specific vulnerabilities, or personal information through encrypted forums such as those found on the dark net. Cyber threats emanate from individuals and groups who are often well organized and "based in hard-to-reach jurisdictions."[6] They can also come, sometimes simultaneously, from industrial competitors and foreign intelligence services or simply hackers or hacktivists who draw on political or ideological rationales.[7] They can originate abroad or domestically, in other organizations, or come from an insider working within the target organization.[8] The so-called insider threat poses significant problems to all businesses, as it does to government organizations, despite security vetting procedures. As the *Financial Times* reported, "MI5, the British internal security service, has been warning UK corporations that foreign intelligence services are attempting to install agents in British companies in order to obtain access to business information on their computer systems."[9] James R. Clapper, the former US Director of National Intelligence, gave similar warnings in his latest worldwide threat assessment to the US Senate's Armed Services Committee.[10]

Cyber threats are often complex and have included theft of intellectual property, theft of commercially sensitive data, unauthorized access to sensitive government information, the disruption of government and industry services, and the exploitation of information security weaknesses through the targeting of partners, subsidiaries, and supply chains, both foreign and domestic. These threats come in several guises, varying in magnitude and tempo and might be basic or sophisticated, but one of the most concerning aspects of these cyber threats is that they are often successful. In a study produced by the cybersecurity firm

Mandiant (FireEye), which analyzed real-world data taken from over 1,216 organizations in 63 countries and over 20 major industries, "attackers got through organizations' cyber 'Maginot Line' at least 97 percent of the time. They compromised more than 1,100 critical systems spanning a wide gamut of geographies and industries." Twenty-five percent of the organizations experienced events that were believed to be consistent with techniques associated with actors deemed to be APTs, and with 75 percent having their command, control and communications (C^3) breached, data was potentially being actively leached.[11] According to the report, "this suggests that thousands upon thousands of organizations around the world may be breached and not even know it."[12] The company's findings are worrying and the answer provided by public and private organizations has so far remained inadequate. Mandiant cautioned against the "Maginot Line" mentality:

> Constructed at a massive cost to the French government in the run-up to World War II, the 940-mile line proved futile in the face of a new style of warfare. The Maginot Line didn't fail, exactly. In fact, it held up superbly against several direct assaults. But Germany, employing new weapons and a lightning-fast blitzkrieg attack style, simply sidestepped the line and invaded through Belgium. The IT security industry faces a similar predicament. Organizations spend more than $67 billion on IT security. Yet attackers routinely breach those defenses with clever, fast-moving attacks that bypass traditional tools. Like the Maginot Line, the prevailing defense-in-depth security model was conceived to defend against yesterday's threats. As applied today, it leaves organizations all but defenseless against determined attackers.[13]

Though government and industry might be able to defeat a vast majority of known attacks by "embedding basic information security practices" within their workforce, processes and technologies,[14] they have been slow to adapt. Legacy systems, hardware which has been around since at least the 1980s when the Internet was in its infancy and computer security was not considered an issue, present many weak spots. From the 208,184 malware downloads tested in the "Maginot Line" report, 124,289 were found to be unique variants leading the authors to believe "many of them were custom made for a particular attack."[15] Cyber threats are often tailor-made and therefore they vary. A large number of attacks may also remain unknown, further complicating appropriate defense and responses. For Mandiant (FireEye), industry responses are insufficient to defend against today's rapidly evolving threats. The company's "Maginot Line" report concludes that the current "defense-in-depth" model is deeply flawed. Cyberattackers are often stealthy, or at least seek to cover their digital tracks. This is often an area where the intelligence communities will step in.

US government cybersecurity initiatives

US vulnerability to cyberattack was recognized as far back as 1997 in a report by the President's Commission on Critical Infrastructure Protection and in a number of subsequent exercises.[16] In 2003, the administration of President George W. Bush established a Computer Emergency Response Team (US-CERT) under the Department of Homeland Security (DHS). Within DHS, this is a branch of the Office of Cybersecurity and Communications (CS&C) and National Cybersecurity and Communications Integration Center.[17] US-CERT's remit is to lead "efforts to improve the nation's cybersecurity posture, coordinate cyber information sharing, and proactively manage cyber risks to the Nation whilst protecting the constitutional rights of Americans."[18]

Responsibility for cybersecurity is also vested in the Federal Bureau of Investigation (FBI), and the Department of Defense. This includes US Cyber Command, which coordinates activities with the NSA, alongside the Department of State and Department of Commerce, which take the lead on international negotiations and the development of cybersecurity standards.[19] The long-standing National Institute of Standards and Technology within the Department of Commerce promotes risk reduction and raises awareness of cybersecurity issues for owner-operators in the private sector.[20] An additional federal-level program is administered by the National Cyber Response Coordination Group, a joint enterprise between the Department of Defense and the Department of Justice, to coordinate the 13 federal agencies under their authority in the event of a major national cyber incident.[21]

The United States introduced the Cyber Security Awareness Act in 2011 with the three senators who sponsored the bill, noting:

> [W]e as a nation remain woefully unaware of the risks that cyber attacks pose to our economy, our national security, and our privacy. This problem is caused in large part by the fact that cyber threat information ordinarily is classified when it is gathered by the government or held as proprietary when collected by a company that has been attacked. As a result, Americans do not have an appropriate sense of the threats that they face as individual Internet users, the damage inflicted on our businesses and the jobs they create, or the scale of the attacks undertaken by foreign agents against American interests.[22]

As a result of mounting public concern about cyber threats, President Obama signed Presidential Policy Directive 20 (PPD-20) in October 2012 to set the parameters for defensive and offensive cyber operations conducted by the US government. PPD-20 helped formulate new rules of engagement and strengthened US Cyber Command and the military branches it oversees.[23] A year later, the signing of Executive Order 13636, entitled "Improving Critical Infrastructure Cybersecurity," sought to promote further voluntary "sharing of actionable threat information and warnings between the private sector and the US government and to spread industry-led cybersecurity standards and best practices to the most vulnerable critical infrastructure companies and assets."

Major cyber incidents, including a major leak of confidential data from the film studio Sony Pictures in November 2014 and the subsequent hacking of sensitive government personnel data concerning 21.5 million employees (from the Office of Personnel Management), highlighted the existence of significant vulnerabilities within government as well as private industry.[24] Cybersecurity clearly became a top priority for the Obama administration as evidenced in the President's 2015 State of the Union Address in which he declared that:

> No foreign nation, no hacker, should be able to shut down our networks, steal our trade secrets, or invade the privacy of American families, especially our kids. We are making sure our government integrates intelligence to combat cyber threats, just as we have done to combat terrorism.[25]

The president's remarks were later echoed by Philip D. Quade, Chief of NSA Cyber Task Force, who emphasized the importance of cyber resilience as a key business and social issue:

> America's national security and economic prosperity are increasingly dependent upon critical communications infrastructures that are at risk from a variety of hazards, including cyberattacks. These infrastructures are the backbone of our nation's economy, security, and health and requires a unified whole-of-nation, whole-of-community effort to maintain secure, functioning, and resilient critical infrastructures. Safeguarding the physical and cyber aspects of critical infrastructures is a national priority that requires information sharing and partnerships at all levels of government and industry. While the majority of our nation's critical infrastructure is privately owned and operated, both the government and the private sector have a shared interest to prevent and reduce the risks of disruptions to critical infrastructures. The need to prepare for all types of events shifts the focus from asset protection to one of overarching system resilience.[26]

Achieving cyber resilience across the public–private divide is a complex matter. Private industry finds the legislative proposals on the table "burdensome" and unnecessarily intrusive, whilst the US federal government sees merit in this approach to combat valid national security concerns.[27]

Legislative proposals include the Cybersecurity Information Sharing Act (CISA), which was first introduced in 2014.[28] CISA could improve cybersecurity information sharing to counter state, sub-state, and non-state cyber espionage and cybercrime, but also allow government organizations to target legitimate activities with attendant consequences for civil liberties, privacy, and the right to free speech. For its critics, CISA threatens to establish a surveillance state as it can be used not only to mitigate, prevent, or deter shared cybersecurity threats, but also collect every individual's digital footprints nationally and, potentially, globally. The data behind these footprints can help to identify persons of interest, be they suspected terrorists or criminals, and help determine their pattern of life through their communications, social groups, and their website visits. This data could then be shared by the US government with its partners and allies. One of the main concerns at this level is that this data could be used to target political dissidents in various countries. Industry giants like Microsoft, Google, Apple and Facebook cite concerns that civil liberties and privacy will be infringed by CISA as it legally mandates private companies to share their metadata with the US government—even if the arrangements are voluntary.[29]

For others, particularly those in the intelligence and security communities, CISA does not go far enough.[30] Joel Brenner, a senior cybersecurity advisor at the NSA, argues:

> Our nation is being turned inside out electronically and we seem helpless to stop it. The Russians have broken into a White House network and JPMorgan Chase. The Chinese have stolen blueprints, manufacturing processes, clinical trial results and other proprietary data from more than 140 companies and have utterly penetrated major media. The Iranians attack our banks, our electric grid is assaulted with frightening frequency and North Korea has brought Sony to its knees. Meanwhile, credit card data from big retailers such as Target and Home Depot are for sale electronically by the boatload. Infrastructure is at risk. Last month, attackers disrupted production at a German steel plant and damaged its blast furnaces, using only cyber methods.
>
>   The fact that network attacks are getting worse, even after vast sums have been invested in defense, should tell us something fundamental about the deeply flawed nature of our networks. Unfortunately, the measures just announced by President Barack Obama do not address these flaws. He's right that better information-sharing between the private sector and the government is overdue; Congress should finally pass legislation to make it possible. But it would not address underlying weaknesses in the Internet. Stiffer sentences for cyber crime may be useful, but they would not make our infrastructure harder to attack or our communications more secure. His proposal for a uniform breach-notification law would simplify companies' legal compliance, but it would do nothing to prevent breaches.[31]

The US government and private sectors have clearly struggled to determine their cybersecurity roles and effectively confront rising cyber threats to national security. Within this context of cyber insecurity, the controversies surrounding the NSA bulk collection of metadata have further complicated the government's room for maneuver in cyberspace.

Public concerns about government surveillance in cyberspace

Among other operations, the NSA has government-mandated responsibilities to gather signals intelligence on states and target individuals based abroad.[32] In early June 2013, the *Washington Post* and *Guardian* newspapers ran stories simultaneously on each side of the Atlantic, exposing a top-secret intelligence gathering operation run by the NSA and codenamed PRISM. With much of the world's electronic communications routed through the United States and the United Kingdom, along with their partners in the "Five Eyes" community (Australia, Canada, and New Zealand), it was reported that both the FBI and GCHQ also had access to the intelligence gathered from PRISM. The data gathered by the US intelligence community through PRISM was reportedly extracted from "the central servers of nine leading US Internet companies"—Microsoft, Yahoo, Google, Facebook, PalTalk, AOL, Skype, YouTube, and Apple. The "audio and video chats, photographs, emails, documents, and connection logs" that were accessed enabled analysts to track foreign targets.[33] These data sources were shared with the British services via GCHQ under the codename TEMPORA through long-standing US–UK intelligence agreements.[34]

Part of the public furor over PRISM followed the disclosure that the US telecommunications company Verizon had been required to pass NSA metadata of the calls it handled both at the domestic and international levels, if either the recipient or destination originated in the United States.[35] In practice, such a request would make domestic, as well as international, surveillance possible.[36] The volume of the data being collected and analyzed through PRISM is eye watering, and these kinds of big data sets can be extremely useful in tracking and tracing targets and their social networks. As the *New York Times* reported, "separate streams of data are integrated into large databases—matching, for example, time and location data from cellphones with credit card purposes or E-Zpass use—intelligence analysts are given a mosaic of a person's life" with only four data points needed from the time and location of a phone call needed to correctly identify a caller 95 percent of the time.[37] These data can be used alongside social media intelligence and other elements of open source intelligence to produce a pattern of life for a person of interest and those they are connected to.

In the aftermath of the 9/11 attacks, the administration of George W. Bush tasked the NSA with gathering large amounts of metadata from worldwide communications.[38] According to General Keith B. Alexander, the Commander of US Cyber Command and former Director of the NSA, "together with other intelligence, [these measures] have protected the US and our allies from terrorist threats around the globe ... over fifty times since 9/11 ... in over twenty countries around the world."[39] Alexander added, "I believe we have achieved this security and relative safety in a way that does not compromise the privacy and civil liberties of our citizens ... [and] are critical to the intelligence community's efforts to connect the dots."[40] Representative Mike Rogers (R-AL), the Chairman of the US House Permanent Select Committee on Intelligence, noted during Alexander's appearance before the Committee in the wake of the PRISM disclosures, that the activities undertaken for this program "are legal, court-approved and are subject to an extensive oversight regime" authorized under Section 702 of the Foreign Intelligence Surveillance Act, which was first passed in 1978.[41]

Both Admiral Alexander and Representative Rogers are acutely aware of the balance between the protection of civil liberties and democratic values whilst guarding national security. According to them, PRISM and the wider efforts of the IC have prevented another 9/11 whilst maintaining checks through the political oversight from the House and Senate intelligence committees and judicial review by the Foreign Intelligence Surveillance Court.

Despite the government's reassurance, public opinion has remained concerned about government activities in this area.[42] At the same House intelligence committee hearing, Representative Rogers continued:

> One of the frustrating parts about being a member of this Committee is sitting at the intersection of classified intelligence programs and transparent democracy as representatives of the American people. The public trusts the government to protect the country from another 9/11 type attack, but that trust can start to wane when they are faced with inaccuracies, half truths and outright lies about the way intelligence programs are being run.[43]

For Edward Snowden, the former NSA contractor whose leaks revealed PRISM, that trust has broken down, meaning "the government has granted itself power it is not entitled to. There is no public oversight. The result is people like myself have the latitude to go further than they are allowed to."[44] A number of foreign governments, many of whom are allied to the United States, became uncomfortable with US surveillance activities following the Snowden releases. For example, German Justice Minister, Sabine Leutheusser-Schnarrenberger, publicly articulated her government's concerns when she stated in *Der Spiegel*:

> The suspicion of excessive surveillance of communication is so alarming that it cannot be ignored. For that reason, openness and clarification by the US administration itself should be paramount at this point…. The global Internet has become indispensable for a competitive economy, the sharing of information and the strengthening of human rights in authoritarian countries. But our trust in these technologies threatens to be lost in the face of comprehensive surveillance activities. […] America has been a different country since the horrible terrorist attacks of September 11, 2001. The relationship between freedom and security has shifted, to the detriment of freedom, especially as a result of the Patriot Act…. We should remember that the strength of the liberal constitutional state lies in the trust of its citizens.[45]

German opposition Social Democrat leader, Thomas Oppermann, went further in pointing to the alleged use of PRISM by Britain's GCHQ, when he argued "The accusations make it sound as if George Orwell's surveillance society has become reality in Great Britain."[46] In a country steeped in the memory of state surveillance of its own citizens, first by the Nazis and then in East Germany by the Stasi, PRISM has powerful resonance.

In the face of criticism, the British government has been quick and steadfast in defending the US–UK intelligence-sharing arrangement, whilst refusing to go into any details regarding PRISM. Following discussions with then US Secretary of State John Kerry, then British Foreign Secretary William Hague stated "that's something the citizens of both our countries should have confidence in, in particular that that relationship is based on a framework of law in both countries, a law that is vigorously upheld."[47] The remaining "Five Eyes" partners (Canada, Australia and New Zealand) have been more muted in condemning PRISM, with a spokesperson for the Communications Security Establishment Canada (CSEC) declaring that CSEC does not access PRISM.[48] Instead CSEC uses an indigenous, and equally controversial, intelligence program to gather metadata.[49] A similarly controversial program was being proposed in Australia but was shelved by the government ahead of the 2013 election which saw Kevin Rudd replace Julia Gillard.[50] The Gillard government refused to divulge whether Australian intelligence agencies were receiving information gathered via PRISM because such a disclosure would threaten intelligence sources and methods, as well as "risk of serious complications in our relations with our neighbours."[51]

Whatever the rights and wrongs of PRISM, as intelligence historian Rhodri Jeffreys-Jones argues, what is needed is "an intelligence arrangement we can trust."[52] There needs to be a public debate about the extent of metadata collection and analysis by Western intelligence agencies, and how these processes can enhance security and satisfy privacy and civil liberties concerns within and between modern democracies. There are two major questions which the global surveillance disclosures pose for the United States, its intelligence partners in the "Five Eyes" community, and indeed for all liberal democracies. First, at what point does the right to privacy, freedom, and civil liberties outweigh the protection of national security? Second, in the nebulous and largely secret world in which these legally mandated intelligence agencies operate, does democratic oversight go far enough in holding these practices to account?

In the United Kingdom, the debate on how to balance the security of the nation with the rights of free speech and privacy, and the needs of private industry has also been intense. This issue has been particularly acute at the domestic level in legislative proposals—including the 2016 Investigatory Powers Act (widely referred to as the "Snoopers Charter")—requiring Internet service providers to log user data which might then be subject to government oversight.[53] Legislating domestic surveillance in the information age is a difficult balancing act and has provoked fierce debate between those wishing to protect national security and those wishing to guard against government intrusion into their personal and professional lives. In this context, the 2015 United Kingdom Strategic Defence and Security Review (SDSR) emphasized the growing number of state and non-state actors capable of deploying cyber tools and technology to target critical national infrastructure and threaten national security.[54] The SDSR further points out:

New forms of communication empower individuals and groups to communicate rapidly. But encrypted communications, often provided by global companies operating outside the United Kingdom, will continue to be used by terrorists and organised crime groups. The relationship between individual privacy and national security is increasingly challenging, and increasingly important to get right. For security reasons, Western states will want access within a narrow set of tightly prescribed circumstances to travel, financial and communications data held by other states and by the private sector. Conversely, the proliferation of cyber capabilities will make it ever harder to protect the information and well-being of private individuals, corporations and states.[55]

The United States and United Kingdom are heavily networked and data dependent and clearly concerned with state-level and asymmetric threats. Damage or disruption to their governments, militaries, and critical infrastructure are recognized threats, which explains why both nations have invested heavily in their cyber intelligence capabilities and publicly defended their activities.

Institutionalizing cyber intelligence and security in the United Kingdom

In the last few years, the UK government has strived to institutionalize its cyber-security capabilities. The 2009 Cyber Security Strategy led to the formation of the multi-agency Cyber Security Operations Centre (CSOC) hosted by GCHQ.[56] CSOC monitored developments in cyberspace, analyzed trends, ensured coherent dissemination of information on cyber threats across the government and private sectors, and coordinated technical response to cyber incidents.[57] CSOC was directed by the Office of Cyber Security and Information Assurance (OCSIA), which advised the British Cabinet Office and National Security Council by providing strategic direction and coordination for government in the field of cybersecurity and information assurance.[58] CSOC and OCSIA's roles and responsibilities are now being absorbed into the United Kingdom's National Cyber Security Centre (NCSC), based in London.

The 2011 National Cyber Security Strategy furthered the UK government efforts to mitigate cyber threats and emphasized four main objectives:

1   The United Kingdom to tackle cyber crime and be one of the most secure places in the world to do business in cyberspace.
2   The United Kingdom to be more resilient to cyber attacks and better able to protect our interests in cyberspace.
3   The United Kingdom to have helped share an open, stable and vibrant cyber-space which the UK public can use safely and that supports open societies.
4   The United Kingdom to have the cross-cutting knowledge, skills and capability it needs to underpin all our cybersecurity objectives.[59]

To fulfill these objectives, the UK government has multiplied its efforts to build bridges across the public and private sectors to improve situational awareness and responses to cyber threats.

Until the formation of NCSC in October 2016, efforts to combat cybersecurity threats were previously overseen in the United Kingdom by a national Computer Emergency Response Team (CERT-UK) established in 2014. CERT-UK is one of over 100 similar centers set up by national governments around the world.[60] It was designed to "work closely with industry, government and academia to enhance UK cyber resilience."[61] To keep up to date with the multiplying cyber threats the United Kingdom is facing, CERT-UK worked with a number of public and private agencies. These included the Communications-Electronics Security Group (CESG) within GCHQ, which provided assistance on the security of communications and electronic data to industry and academia.[62] The Cyber Security Information Sharing Partnership, part of CERT-UK, was a joint initiative to share information between the government and industry and increase situational awareness of cyber threats to UK business, which counts 1,700 member organizations.[63]

CERT-UK should not be confused with GovCERT, the UK Government Computer Emergency Response Team which operated under CESG and provided warnings, alerts, and assistance to public-sector organizations to reduce and respond to computer security incidents. GovCERT gathered data from all available sources to monitor the general cyber threat level 24 hours a day, seven days a week.[64] Within GCHQ, a Centre for Cyber Assessment, established in April 2013, brought together government departments, agencies, and law enforcement bodies to provide all-source intelligence-driven reports to government customers including "top industry bodies and companies."[65] All these structures have provided an important set of platforms to maintain dialogue between government, regulators, and industry.

The 2015 SDSR expressed the government's intent to be more open in sharing information on cyber threats in partnership with the private sector.[66] Importantly, given the large number of organizations dealing with cybersecurity, the review announced the establishment of the NCSC under the leadership of GCHQ. NCSC is designed to "manage our future operational response to cyber incidents, ensuring that we can protect the United Kingdom against serious attacks and minimise their impact."[67] The NCSC will act as a one-stop shop against cyber threats to the United Kingdom. The 2015 SDSR also increased funding for the security and intelligence services by £2.5 billion, with half of this figure dedicated to counterterrorism. It will permit the recruitment of 1,900 additional staff to "respond to, and deter those behind, the increasing international terrorist, cyber and other global threats."[68] The review earmarked £1.9 billion for cybersecurity from 2016–2020, and was a precursor to the second five-year National Cyber Security Strategy launched in November 2016.[69] The bulk of this funding is expected to go to GCHQ which remains the dominant agency for UK cybersecurity.[70] As British Chancellor, George Osborne, unequivocally stated in November 2015, "GCHQ is rightly known as equal to the best in the world. And I am clear that the answer to the question 'who does cyber?' for the British government is to very large degree GCHQ."[71]

Outside of GCHQ, the United Kingdom's other intelligence agencies also have a role in cybersecurity in the form of data collection and analysis by the

Security Service, the Secret Intelligence Service (SIS is the British foreign intelligence agency), and Defence Intelligence.[72] In 2013, the Ministry of Defence issued a *Cyber Primer* in which it noted that cyberspace was a crucial source of information that can be exploited to improve situational awareness and conduct intelligence preparation of the battlespace.[73] Civilian intelligence agencies have also been increasingly involved in cyberspace. The Security Service is primarily responsible for combating domestic and international terrorism and counter espionage, counter proliferation, and protective security.[74] Andrew Parker, the Director General of the Security Service (MI5), stated in a public interview in September 2015 that his agency needs the authority to "navigate the Internet" and to able to use data sets to "join the dots" to counter heightened terrorist threats emanating from Islamic State and elsewhere. This means being able to access their Internet-based communications on social media and on other software platforms before their plots come to fruition. In his entreaty, Parker made a case that private companies such as Facebook have an ethical responsibility to approach the UK government to tackle terrorism and crime where they hold and carry that information.[75] Alex Younger, the head of SIS, similarly argued that "using data appropriately and proportionately offers us a priceless opportunity to be even more deliberate and targeted in what we do and thus be better at protecting our agents and this country." He went on to caution:

> That is good news. The bad news is that the same technology in opposition hands, an opposition often unconstrained by consideration of ethics and law, allows them to see what we are doing and put our people and agents at risk.[76]

Finding the right balance

Modern intelligence and law enforcement agencies all face similar problems when dealing with terrorism. How can they legally access Internet-based communications whilst also safeguarding legitimate free speech and possessing mass surveillance capabilities? These issues are complex and raise a series of ethical questions which are compounded by the pace of technological change and the growing use of encryption. Some of the questions and challenges posed by encryption and for Internet-based mass surveillance have been referred to by James B. Comey, the Director of the FBI, as potentially leaving them "going dark." Comey, in an October 2014 speech to the Brookings Institution, presented some of the main challenges technology poses for the intelligence and security services. He reasoned:

> Technology has forever changed the world we live in. We're online, in one way or another, all day long. Our phones and computers have become reflections of our personalities, our interests, and our identities. They hold much that is important to us. And with that comes a desire to protect our privacy and our data…. Unfortunately, the law hasn't kept pace with technology, and this disconnect has created a significant public safety problem.

We call it "Going Dark...." We face two overlapping challenges. The first concerns real-time court-ordered interception of what we call "data in motion," such as phone calls, email, and live chat sessions. The second challenge concerns court-ordered access to data stored on our devices, such as email, text messages, photos, and videos—or what we call "data at rest." And both real-time communication and stored data are increasingly encrypted ... those conspiring to harm us ... use the same devices, the same networks, and the same apps to make plans, to target victims, and to cover up what they're doing. And that makes it tough for us to keep up ... even with lawful authority, we may not be able to access the evidence and the information we need. Current law governing the interception of communications requires telecommunication carriers and broadband providers to build interception capabilities into their networks for court-ordered surveillance. But that law, the Communications Assistance for Law Enforcement Act, or CALEA, was enacted 20 years ago—a lifetime in the Internet age. And it doesn't cover new means of communication.[77]

Comey also added during his speech that "Perhaps it's time to suggest that the post-Snowden pendulum has swung too far in one direction—in a direction of fear and mistrust. It is time to have open and honest debates about liberty and security."[78] This debate regarding the balance needed between liberty and security also remains active in the United Kingdom.

Much of the work conducted by government agencies to fight cyber threats is classified and therefore oversight is provided by the United Kingdom's parliamentary oversight body, the Intelligence and Security Committee (ISC). The ISC frequently addresses issues regarding the trade-off between security and liberty in cyberspace. In deliberating the Draft Investigatory Powers Bill (now the Investigatory Powers Act) the ISC noted in February 2016 that:

> privacy protections should form the backbone of the draft legislation, around which the exceptional powers are then built. Whilst recent terrorist attacks have shown the importance of the work the Agencies do in protecting us, this cannot be used as an excuse to ignore such important underlying principles or unnecessarily override them.[79]

The ISC also raised privacy concerns regarding the use of bulk personal data sets in identifying persons of interest and their social connections as they "contain personal information about a large number of individuals, the majority of whom will not be of any interest to the Agencies."[80] GCHQ's access to these personal data sets under the proposed legislation was also questioned. Indeed, the ISC asked:

> Given the background to the draft Bill and the public concern over the allegations made by Edward Snowden in 2013, it is surprising that the protection of people's privacy—which is enshrined in other legislation—does not feature more prominently.[81]

Defining cyber red lines

The key cyber issue confronted by governments around the world today is to better determine the scope of their activities in cyberspace. The NSA and GCHQ have offensive cyber capabilities against both state and non-state actors, but where does the balance between cyber defense and cyber offense lie? This is not a straightforward calculation and is further exacerbated by the speed, range, sophistication, and diversity of attacks confronting Western (and many other) countries. The range of passive and active measures undertaken by governments has not only to contend with well-resourced and sophisticated attacks at the highest (state-based) level, but also lower-level threats. Distributed Denial of Service attacks, for example, have been used by hacktivist groups such as Anonymous, but also by states including in a Russian attack against Estonia in 2007.[82]

Given the ever-growing importance of cyberspace, it is worth wondering whether there is a point where a cyberattack will lead to calls for a kinetic or military response. Under international law, cyberattacks would have to lead to violent "real-world" deeds before such a response can be contemplated.[83] In this vein, a number of former policymakers have called for an international treaty under the United Nations to mitigate or penalize cyberattacks by nation states or individuals and groups within states.[84] As Mazanec and Ridout demonstrate in this volume, at present, there are few clear and unambiguous norms, rules, and regulations in cyberspace and the legal and governance frameworks currently in place are contested.[85] This global-level issue of governance has become increasingly pressing in recent years.[86]

Within this rapidly evolving context it is clear that the US and UK governments are faced with a series of mounting difficulties, both at national and international levels, in attempting to manage an ever-growing and deepening number of cyber threats. The range of these threats is broadening, promoted both by the expansion and low entry costs of computer technology, and the advent of the Internet of Things. A variety of agencies in the United States and United Kingdom defend against cyber threats, but the global scale of these threats suggests an international alliance will be necessary to secure cyberspace for all. As Estonian Defense Minister, Jaak Aaviksoo, asked after the Russian cyberattacks on his country in 2007:

> Do we have a proper legal code that defines the cyberattacks in detail— where does cybercrime stop and terrorism or war begin? Should NATO, for example, safeguard and defend not only its communications and information systems but also some national critical physical infrastructures? And what to make of collective defense in case of cyberwar against one of the allies?[87]

This line of reasoning helped initiate the establishment of the NATO Cooperative Cyber Defence Centre of Excellence and the subsequent publication of the

Tallinn Manual on the International Law Applicable to Cyber Warfare, but, so far, this set of issues remains unresolved. Providing for a common cyber defense remains a complex issue for alliances like NATO, national governments, and intelligence communities.[88] As the title of this edited volume suggests, the national interest remains dominant in conceptualizing cyber threats even though these threats, and some of the actors behind them, span national jurisdictions. The fact that cyber threats might emanate from state actors adds a layer of complexity to the political efforts to establish a stronger international regime for cyberspace. Effective government action is further complicated by the problems that exist in attributing the identity and the motivations of attackers in cyberspace.[89] Understanding threats is only a start, and targeting threat actors through legal, diplomatic, or even kinetic remedies poses further challenges. The difficulty in finding appropriate responses to cyber threats was evident during the 2016 US presidential elections by alleged Russian hacking and information operations which sought to favor then Republican candidate Donald Trump.[90]

Conclusion: the need for cooperation

Cooperation between governments, the public and private sectors and civil society, will be needed to mount more effective cyber defenses. The British Ministry of Defence's *Cyber Primer* unequivocally recognizes that one of the main challenges for managing cybersecurity is the coexistence and overlap of "civilian and military information infrastructures, whether national, coalition or international."[91] Well aware of these challenges, the US and UK governments have actively sought to institutionalize cooperation between government agencies and industry to improve situational awareness. Governments have also sought to reinforce deterrence through denial thanks to the cyber offensive capabilities provided by their signals intelligence agencies. Whilst offensive cyber capabilities might successfully hit hostile countries, deterrence and offensive actions against organizations like the Islamic State and Al Qaeda seem more complicated.

Efforts to increase transparency, trust, and cooperation have been relatively evident bilaterally, but they have remained more problematic at the multilateral level. In the future, effective cybersecurity will require diplomatic building blocks to establish red lines and rules for state behavior in cyberspace.[92] This political effort might be limited by the agenda pursued by states like Russia and China whose behavior in cyberspace has widely been perceived by Western countries to be aggressive. Other major powers might not want to develop an international governance framework limiting their activities in cyberspace. Yet significant economic interest might eventually warrant more trust and cooperation in cyberspace. For the United Kingdom, increased transparency, trust, and cooperation are certainly important for trade relations, such as the series of £30 billion agreements Britain has entered into with China which includes deals on the United Kingdom's next-generation civil nuclear power plants, so that these do not provide gateways into strategic influence over computer-controlled UK critical national infrastructure.[93] With China and Russia's intelligence agencies both accused of mapping the electricity grids in the United States and installing software traps which could be used to damage or disrupt their critical infrastructure, government concern has been growing, despite assurances.[94]

The United States has established breach-reporting procedures with Germany, Italy and France, and cybersecurity issues are under active discussion through the "London Cyber Process" which calls for responsible state-based behavior in cyberspace, including not attacking critical national infrastructure.[95] With the United States planning to sign separate treaties with Russia and China to establish rules regarding cybersecurity breaches, governance is clearly an issue that is rising on the international political agenda.[96] Still, much more needs to be done in terms of multilateral cooperation to establish trust and confidence-building measures between all the major actors evolving in cyberspace.

With publicly discussed fears of a cyber Pearl Harbor, or even a statewide "cybergeddon" scenario, it is important to debate the roles and responsibilities of the intelligence communities in an increasingly interconnected and globalized world.[97] Many experts believe cyberspace should not be used as a battleground with states acting as both targets and attackers.[98] This poses a conundrum for international law, and is now a more visible issue due to the global surveillance disclosures. The United States, United Kingdom, and their allies require coordinated intelligence sharing on a global scale to inform cyber national security. Political impetus is also necessary to implement a series of state-based confidence-building measures that will need further development rooted in diplomacy and international law.[99] In this context, again, intelligence will be essential for governments to trust but verify other countries' cyber activities.

Notes

1 It is alleged PRISM stands for Planning Tool for Resource Integration, Synchronization, and Management. Benjamin Dreyfuss and Emily Dreyfuss, "What is the NSA's PRISM program? (FAQ)," *CNET*, June 7, 2013, at www.cnet.com/uk/news/what-is-the-nsas-prism-program-faq/.
2 UK Communications-Electronics Security Group, *Cyber Security Guidance for Business* (London, 2015).
3 David Chinn, James Kaplan, and Allen Weinberg, "Risk and Responsibility in a Hyperconnected World: Implications for Enterprises," *McKinsey & Company*, January 2014, at www.mckinsey.com/insights/business_technology/risk_and_responsibility_in_a_hyperconnected_world_implications_for_enterprises.
4 Editor, "2014 Verizon Data Breach Investigations Report," *Verizon Communications*, at www.verizonenterprise.com/DBIR/2014/reports/rp_Verizon-DBIR-2014_en_xg.pdf.
5 Comments made under Chatham House Rules at Chatham House Conference: Cyber Security Building Resilience Reducing Risk Chatham House, London (May 19–20, 2014), at www.chathamhouse.org/Cyber14#.
6 Misha Glenny, *DarkMarket: How Hackers Became the New Mafia* (London: Vintage, 2012); Jamie Bartlett, *The Dark Net Inside the Digital Underworld* (London: Random House, 2014).

7 On "hacktivism," see: Jonathan Diamond, "Early Patriotic Hacking," in Jason Healey (ed.), *A Fierce Domain: Conflict in Cyberspace 1986–2002* (Vienna: CSSA/Atlantic Council, 2013), 136–151.

8 UK Communications-Electronics Security Group, *Cyber Security Guidance for Business*.

9 Tom Groenfeldt, "Insiders Pose a Serious Threat to Corporate Information," *Forbes*, May 8, 2014, at www.forbes.com/sites/tomgroenfeldt/2014/05/08/insiders-pose-a-serious-threat-to-corporate-information/#3300cd5c1c0d.

10 James Clapper, *Statement for the Record, Worldwide Threat Assessment of the US Intelligence Community, Senate Armed Services Committee* (February 9, 2016), 1–4, at www.dni.gov/files/documents/SASC_Unclassified_2016_ATA_SFR_FINAL.pdf.

11 Editor, "FireEye Advanced Threat Report: 2013," *FireEye*, at www2.fireeye.com/rs/fireye/images/fireeye-advanced-threat-report-2013.pdf.

12 FireEye and Mandiant, "Cybersecurity's Maginot Line: A Real-World Assessment of the Defense-in-Depth Model," 18, at www2.fireeye.com/rs/fireye/images/fireeye-real-world-assessment.pdf.

13 Ibid.

14 UK Communications-Electronics Security Group, *Cyber Security Guidance for Business*.

15 FireEye and Mandiant, "Cybersecurity's Maginot Line," 3.

16 US Congressional Research Service, *Critical Infrastructure: Control Systems and the Terrorist Threat*, Dana A. Shea (Washington, DC, February 21, 2003); Michael Warner, "Cyber-security: A pre-history," *Intelligence and National Security* 27/5 (2012), 781–799; Myriam Dunn Cavelty, *Cyber-Security and Threat Politics: US Efforts to Secure the Information Age* (London: Routledge, 2008); Healey, *A Fierce Domain*, 14–88.

17 In October 2010, a Memorandum of Understanding between the DHS and DoD was signed to increase interdepartmental collaboration; United Nations Institute for Disarmament Research, *The Cyber Index International Security Trends and Realities*, James Andrew Lewis and Götz Neuneck (Geneva, 2013), 53, at www.unidir.org/files/publications/pdfs/cyber-index-2013-en-463.pdf.

18 United States Computer Emergency Readiness Team, "About Us," *Department of Homeland Security*, at www.us-cert.gov/about-us.

19 Lewis and Neuneck, *The Cyber Index International Security Trends and Realities*, 52–54.

20 Their latest guidance can be found at: US National Institute of Science and Technology, *Update on the Cybersecurity Framework* (Gaithersburg, 2014), at www.nist.gov/cyberframework/upload/NIST-Cybersecurity-Framework-update-073114.pdf.

21 Lewis and Neuneck, *The Cyber Index International Security Trends and Realities*, 52–54; US National Institute of Science and Technology, *Update on the Cybersecurity Framework*.

22 US Senate, "Senators Introduce Legislation to Promote Public Awareness of Cyber Security," (Washington, DC, 2013), at www.whitehouse.senate.gov/news/release/senators-introduce-legislation-to-promote-public-awareness-of-cyber-security.

23 Lewis and Neuneck, *The Cyber Index International Security Trends and Realities*, 52–54; Glenn Greenwald and Ewen MacAskill, "Obama Tells Intelligence Chiefs to Draw Up Cyber Target List Full Document Text," *Guardian*, June 7, 2013, 1.

24 US White House, *Foreign Policy—Cyber Security* (Washington, DC, 2013), at www.whitehouse.gov/issues/foreign-policy/cybersecurity; Dominic Rushe and Spencer Ackerman, "Obama Plans For Cybersecurity Aim 'To Make Internet Safer Place'," *Guardian*, January 20, 2015, at www.theguardian.com/us-news/2015/jan/20/obama-cybersecurity-state-of-the-union-address-speech; Michael D. Shear, "Obama to Announce Cybersecurity Plans in State of the Union Preview," *New York Times*, January 11, 2015, at www.nytimes.com/2015/01/11/us/politics/obama-to-announce-cybersecurity-plans-in-state-of-the-union-preview.html?_r=0.

25 Julianne Pepitone, "SOTU: Will Obama's Cybersecurity Proposals Actually Protect You?" *NBC News*, January 21, 2015, at www.nbcnews.com/storyline/2015-state-of-the-union/sotu-will-obamas-cybersecurity-proposals-actually-protect-you-n289826.

26 US National Security Agency, "In Discussion with Philip Quade, Chief of NSA Cyber Task Force," October 9, 2015, at www.nsa.gov/news-features/news-stories/2015/in-discussion-with-philip-quade.shtml; Kelly Jackson Higgins, "Former Director of NSA and CIA Says US Cybersecurity Policy MIA," *Information Week Dark Reading*, January 13, 2016, at www.darkreading.com/attacks-breaches/former-director-of-nsa-and-cia-says-us-cybersecurity-policy-mia/d/d-id/1323888.

27 Jody Westby, "The Government Shouldn't Be Lecturing Private Sector On Cybersecurity," *Forbes*, June 15, 2015, at www.forbes.com/sites/jodywestby/2015/06/15/the-government-shouldnt-be-lecturing-the-private-sector-on-cybersecurity/#45c2d9df38d6; Andrew Nolan, "Cybersecurity and Information Sharing: Legal Challenges and Solutions," Congressional Research Service, March 16, 2015; Steve Rosenbush, "Former NSA Chief Mike McConnell Says Culture, Not Tech, Is Key to Cyber Defense," *Wall Street Journal*, June 20, 2014, at http://blogs.wsj.com/cio/2014/06/20/former-nsa-chief-mike-mcconnell-says-culture-not-tech-is-key-to-cyber-defense/.

28 United States Congress, S.754—Cybersecurity Information Sharing Act of 2015, (Washington, DC, 2015), at www.congress.gov/bill/114th-congress/senate-bill/754.

29 Aime Stepanovich, "Bursting the Biggest Myth of CISA—That the Program is Voluntary," *Wired*, August 19, 2015, at www.wired.com/2015/08/access-cisa-myth-of-voluntary-info-sharing/.

30 Jessica L. Beyer, "The Cybersecurity Information Sharing Act (CISA)," *Jackson School of International Studies*, at https://jsis.washington.edu/news/the-cybersecurity-information-sharing-act-cisa/.

31 Joel Brenner, "How Obama Fell Short on Cybersecurity Under the President's Proposals, We'll Remain America the Vulnerable," *Politico*, January 21, 2015, at www.politico.com/magazine/story/2015/01/state-of-the-union-cybersecurity-obama-114411.html#ixzz3PjrwwEnf.

32 Part of the controversy regarding PRISM is that the NSA has the capacity to monitor domestic traffic. See: James Bamford, "Edward Snowden: The Untold Story," *Wired*, August 2014, at www.wired.com/2014/08/edward-snowden/.

33 Barton Gellman and Laura Poitras, "US, British Intelligence Mining Data from Nine US Internet Companies in Broad Secret Program," *Washington Post*, June 7, 2013, at www.washingtonpost.com/investigations/us-intelligence-mining-data-from-nine-us-internet-companies-in-broad-secret-program/2013/06/06/3a0c0da8-cebf-11e2-8845-d970ccb04497_story.html.

34 US National Security Agency, *UKUSA Agreement Release 1940–1956* (Fort Meade, Maryland, 2010), at www.nsa.gov/public_info/declass/ukusa.shtml.

35 Editor, "US Confirms Verizon Phone Records Collection," *BBC News*, June 6, 2013, at www.bbc.co.uk/news/world-us-canada-22793851.

36 Andrew Clement, "NSA Surveillance: Exploring the Geographies of Internet Interception," in *iConference Proceedings* (2014), at www.ideals.illinois.edu/bitstream/handle/2142/47305/119_ready.pdf?sequence=2.

37 James Risen and Eric Lichtblau, "How the US Uses Technology to Mine More Data More Quickly," *New York Times*, June 9, 2013, A1; Yves-Alexandre de Montjoye et al., "Unique in the crowd: The privacy bounds of human mobility," *Scientific Reports* 3 (2013).

38 James Risen and Eric Lichtblau, "Bush Lets US Spy on Callers Without Courts," *New York Times*, December 17, 2005, A22; US Privacy and Civil Liberties Oversight Board, *Report on the Surveillance Program Operated Pursuant to Sec 702 of the Foreign Intelligence Surveillance Act*, (Washington, DC, 2014).

39 Keith Alexander, "Statement to the NSA/CSS Workforce," June 25, 2013, at www.nsa.gov/public_info/speeches_testimonies/25jun13_dir.shtml.

40 Ibid.
41 US House of Representatives, Permanent Select Committee on Intelligence, *How Disclosed NSA Programs Protect Americans, and Why Disclosure Aids Our Adversaries* (Washington, DC, 2013).
42 George Gao, "What Americans Think About NSA Surveillance, National Security and Privacy," Pew Research Center, May 29, 2015, at www.pewresearch.org/fact-tank/2015/05/29/what-Americans-think-about-nsa-surveillance-national-security-and-privacy/.
43 US House of Representatives, Permanent Select Committee on Intelligence, *How Disclosed NSA Programs Protect Americans, and Why Disclosure Aids Our Adversaries.*
44 Glen Greenwald, "Edward Snowden: The Whistleblower Behind the NSA Surveillance Revelation," *Guardian*, June 11, 2013, at www.guardian.co.uk/world/2013/jun/09/edward-snowden-nsa-whistleblower-surveillance.
45 Sabine Leutheusser-Schnarrenberger, "US Prism Scandal: 'Security Is Not an End in Itself'," *Spiegel Online International*, June 11, 2013, at www.spiegel.de/international/world/minister-leutheusser-schnarrenberger-criticizes-us-over-prism-scandal-a-905001.html.
46 Michael Nienaber, "German Minister Seeks Answers from UK Over Spying 'Catastrophe'," *Reuters UK*, June 22, 2013, at http://uk.reuters.com/article/2013/06/22/usa-security-britain-germany-idUKL5N0EY09Y20130622.
47 Editor, "Intelligence Sharing Lawful, Hague Says after US Talks," *BBC News*, at www.bbc.co.uk/news/uk-politics-22883340.
48 David Ljunggren, "UPDATE 2-Canada Says Not Receiving Information from US Spying Program," *Reuters UK*, June 11, 2013, at http://uk.reuters.com/article/usa-security-canada-idUKL2N0EM1SZ20130611.
49 Canadian Broadcasting Corporation, "What We Know About CSEC, Canada's Eavesdropping Agency," *The Huffington Post Canada*, at www.huffingtonpost.ca/2013/06/14/what-do-we-know-about-can_n_3440432.html.
50 Ben Grubb, "Government Shelves Controversial Data Retention Scheme," *Sydney Morning Herald*, at www.smh.com.au/technology/technology-news/government-shelves-controversial-data-retention-scheme-20130624-2oskq.html.
51 David Wroe, "Government Refuses to Say if it Receives PRISM Data," *Sydney Morning Herald*, June 12, 2013, at www.smh.com.au/opinion/political-news/government-refuses-to-say-if-it-receives-prism-data-20130612-2o3ot.html. See also: David Fisher, "Key: No GCSB Legal Loophole," *New Zealand Herald*, June 11, 2013, at www.nzherald.co.nz/nz/news/article.cfm?c_id=1&objectid=10889696. New Zealand Prime Minister, John Key, publicly denied New Zealand national law had been circumvented by access to PRISM but did say "We do exchange—and it's well known—information with our partners. We do that. How they gather that information and whether they use techniques or systems like Prism I can't comment on that."
52 Rhodri Jeffreys-Jones, "A Critique of the Surveillance Flap," *E-International Relations*, June 30, 2013, at www.e-ir.info/2013/06/30/a-critique-of-the-surveillance-flap/.
53 UK Parliament, Investigatory Powers Act 2016, at www.legislation.gov.uk/ukpga/2016/25/contents/enacted; Editor, "Net Firms Condemn Revival of 'Snoopers' Charter," *BBC News*, January 25, 2015, at www.bbc.co.uk/news/technology-30952592; Patrick Tucker, "Why Obama's Cybersecurity Plan May Not Make Americans Safer," *Atlantic*, January 23, 2015, at www.theatlantic.com/technology/archive/2015/01/why-obamas-cybersecurity-plan-may-not-make-average-Americans-safer/384733/.
54 UK Prime Minister, *National Security Strategy and Strategic Defence and Security Review 2015 A Secure and Prosperous United Kingdom* (London, UK, 2015), 6.
55 Ibid, 19.
56 Despite the contrary acronym, this group is still known as CESG and dates back to 1919. Editor, "CESG: The Information Security Arm of GCHQ," at www.cesg.gov.uk/articles/cesg-information-security-arm-gchq.

57 UK Cabinet Office, *Cyber Security Strategy of the United Kingdom: Safety, Security and Resilience in Cyber Space* (London, UK, 2009).

58 UK Government, "Office of Cyber Security and Information Assurance," at www.gov.uk/government/groups/office-of-cyber-security-and-information-assurance; Shaun Harvey, "Unglamorous Awakenings: How the UK Developed Its Approach to Cyber," in Jason Healey (ed.), *A Fierce Domain: Conflict in Cyberspace 1986–2002* (Vienna: CSSA/Atlantic Council, 2013), 261–262; Kristan Stoddart, "UK cyber security and critical national infrastructure protection," *International Affairs* 92/5 (2016): 1079–1105.

59 Computer Emergency Readiness Team United Kingdom, "Homepage," at www.cert.gov.uk/; Thomas Rid, *Cyber War Will Not Take Place* (London: Hurst, 2013), 112.

60 CERT, "List of National CSIRTs," at www.cert.org/incident-management/national-csirts/national-csirts.cfm?

61 Computer Emergency Readiness Team United Kingdom, "Homepage," at www.cert.gov.uk/.

62 United Kingdom Government, "CESG: The Information Security Arm of GCHQ," at www.cesg.gov.uk/articles/cesg-information-security-arm-gchq.

63 UK Cabinet Office, *The UK Cyber Security Strategy Report on Progress and Forward Plans December 2014* (London, UK, 2014), 5.

64 United Kingdom Government, "GovCERTUK," at www.cesg.gov.uk/articles/govcertuk.

65 The existence of the CCA was only made public in June 2015 specifically to encourage these dialogues and partnerships. Editor, "Foreign Secretary Highlights the Work of the Centre for Cyber Assessment," at www.gchq.gov.uk/press_and_media/news_and_features/Pages/Centre-for-Cyber-Assessment.aspx.

66 UK Prime Minister, *National Security Strategy and Strategic Defence and Security Review 2015 A Secure and Prosperous United Kingdom*, 40–41.

67 Ibid., 41.

68 UK Prime Minister, *National Security Strategy and Strategic Defence and Security Review 2015 A Secure and Prosperous United Kingdom*, 24.

69 UK Cabinet Office, *National Cyber Security Strategy 2016 to 2021*, at www.gov.uk/government/publications/national-cyber-security-strategy-2016-to-2021.

70 UK Prime Minister, *National Security Strategy and Strategic Defence and Security Review 2015 A Secure and Prosperous United Kingdom*, 40; Evan Lawson, "The Joint Forces Command and the 2015 SDSR: Too Soon to Tell," *Royal United Services Institute*, at https://rusi.org/commentary/joint-forces-command-and-2015-sdsr-too-soon-tell.

71 UK Cabinet Office, "Chancellor's Speech to GCHQ on Cyber Security," at www.gov.uk/government/speeches/chancellors-speech-to-gchq-on-cyber-security.

72 UK Ministry of Defence, *Cyber Primer* (London, UK, 2013), 1–17. The Defence Intelligence Staff use all-source intelligence provided to them by the other agencies, open source, and diplomatic sources to analyze foreign military threats to the UK. It is part of the MoD and funded by it. For more information, see: Brian Jones, *Failing Intelligence: The True Story of How We Were Fooled into Going to War in Iraq* (London: Biteback Publishing, 2010), 3–11. On SIS: Editor, "Homepage," *Security Intelligence Service MI6*, at www.sis.gov.uk/about-us/what-we-do.html.

73 UK Ministry of Defence, *Cyber Primer*, 1–25/1–26; Ibid., *Cyber Primer*, Second Edition, July 2016, at www.gov.uk/government/uploads/system/uploads/attachment_data/file/549291/20160720-Cyber_Primer_ed_2_secured.pdf.

74 Security Service MI5, "What We Do," at www.mi5.gov.uk/home/about-us/what-we-do/major-areas-of-work.html.

75 Editor, "MI5 Director General Andrew Parker on Terrorism," *BBC Radio 4*, September 17, 2015, at www.bbc.co.uk/programmes/p032qcgm.

76 Gordon Corera, "Plaque Unveiled for First MI6 Chief Mansfield Cumming," *BBC News*, March 31, 2015, at www.bbc.co.uk/news/uk-32126061.

77 James B. Comey, "Speech at the Brookings Institution on October 16, 2014," at www. fbi.gov/news/speeches/going-dark-are-technology-privacy-and-public-safety-on-a-collision-course.

78 Ibid.

79 UK Intelligence and Security Committee of Parliament, *Report on the Draft Investigatory Powers Bill*, 3, at https://sites.google.com/a/independent.gov.uk/isc/files/20160209_ISC_Rpt_IPBill%28web%29.pdf?attredirects=1.

80 Ibid., 6.

81 Ibid., 9–11.

82 On Stuxnet, see: Peter W. Singer and Allan Friedman, *Cybersecurity and Cyberwar: What Everyone Needs to Know* (New York: Oxford University Press, 2014), 158–159.

83 Rid, *Cyber War Will Not Take Place*, 11–34.

84 Richard A. Clarke and Robert K. Knake, *Cyber War: The Next Threat to National Security and What to Do About It* (London: ECCO Press, 2010), 220–228, 235–242, 268–269; David Omand, *Securing the State* (London: Hurst, 2010), 11, 66–72, 80–84.

85 Paul Walker, "Law of the Horse to Law of the Submarine: The Future of State Behaviour in Cyberspace," in M. Maybaum, A.-M. Osula, and L. Lindström (eds), *2015 7th International Conference on Cyber Conflict: Architectures in Cyberspace* (Tallinn: NATO CCD COE Publications, 2015), 93–104.

86 Gordon Corera, "NSA Warns of Growing Danger of Cyber-Attack by Nation States," *BBC News*, October 27, 2015, at www.bbc.co.uk/news/world-us-canada-34641382.

87 Jaak Aaviksoo, "Cyber Defense—The Unnoticed Third World War," Estonian Ministry of Defence, May 8, 2008, at www.kaitseministeerium.ee/en/news/defence-minister-jaak-aaviksoo-cyber-defense-unnoticed-third-world-war.

88 Michael N. Schmitt (ed.), *Tallinn Manual on the International Law Applicable to Cyber Warfare* (Cambridge: Cambridge University Press, 2013); Ibid., "The law of cyber warfare: Quo vadis?" *Stanford Law & Policy Review* 25 (2014), 269–300; Timothy Farnsworth, "China and Russia Submit Cyber Proposal," *Arms Control Association*, November 2, 2011, at www.armscontrol.org/act/2011_11/China_and_Russia_Submit_Cyber_Proposal.

89 Misha Glenny, *DarkMarket: How Hackers Became the New Mafia* (London: Vintage, 2012); Misha Glenny, *DarkMarket Cyberthieves Cybercops and You* (London: Bodley Head, 2011); Doug Drinkwater, "London Police Chief Admits Cyber-Crime Failings," *SC Magazine UK*, April 15, 2015, at www.scmagazineuk.com/london-police-chief-admits-cyber-crime-failings/article/409167/.

90 Barbara Starr et al., "Intel Analysis Shows Putin Approved Election Hacking," *CNN*, December 15, 2016, at http://edition.cnn.com/2016/12/15/politics/russian-hacking-vladimir-putin-donald-trump/index.html.

91 UK Ministry of Defence, *Cyber Primer*, 1–23.

92 Corera, "NSA Warns of Growing Danger of Cyber-Attack by Nation States."

93 Editor, "Hammond Rejects Security Fears Over China Investment'," *BBC News*, October 20, 2015, at www.bbc.co.uk/news/uk-politics-34582673.

94 Siobhan Gorman, "Electricity Grid in US Penetrated by Spies," *Wall Street Journal*, April 8, 2009, A1; Kamal Ahmed, "China Admits Our Reputation is on the Line Over Nuclear Security," *BBC News*, at www.bbc.co.uk/news/business-34595677.

95 For the current state of play: Jones Day et al., "Europe Proposes New Laws and Regulations on Cybersecurity," *Lexology*, January 2, 2014, at www.lexology.com/library/detail.aspx?g=1f872876-3d23-44e7-a8f1-92a9be8d080b; Editor, "Managing Cyber Risks in Interconnected World," *PWC*, September 30, 2014, at www.pwc.com/gx/en/consulting-services/information-security-survey/assets/the-global-state-of-information-security-survey-2015.pdf; Editor, "Cyber Incident Reporting in the EU: An Overview of Security Articles in EU Legislation," *European Network and Information Security Agency*, August 2012.

96 Graham Burton, "Russia and China to Sign Cyber-Security Treaty in November," *Computing*, October 26, 2014, at www.computing.co.uk/ctg/news/2377766/russia-and-china-to-sign-cyber-security-treaty-in-november.

97 Clarke and Knake, *Cyber War*; Elisabeth B. Miller and Thom Shanker, "Panetta Warns of Dire Threat of Cyberattack on US," *New York Times*, October 12, 2012, A1.

98 Views expressed at CyCon 2015, Tallinn, Estonia, May 27–28, 2015, under Chatham House Rules. See also: 7th International Conference on Cyber Conflict: *Proceedings* (2015), at https://ccdcoe.org/multimedia/7th-international-conference-cyber-conflict-proceedings-2015.html.

99 Conference: Cyber Security Building Resilience Reducing Risk, Chatham House, London, May 19–20, 2014; Council of Europe, *Details of Treaty No. 185: Convention on Cybercrime* (Budapest, Hungary, 2001), 6; Council of Europe, "Action against Cybercrime," at www.coe.int/t/DGHL/cooperation/economiccrime/cybercrime/default_en.asp; Michael A. Vatis, "The Council of Europe Convention on Cyber-crime," in *Proceedings of a Workshop on Deterring Cyberattacks: Informing Strategies and Developing Options for US Policy* (2010), at www.nap.edu/catalog/12997/proceedings-of-a-workshop-on-deterring-cyberattacks-informing-strategies-and; UK Ministry of Defence, *Cyber Primer*.

12 From information to cybersecurity

Bridging the public–private divide

Damien Van Puyvelde

In the last decade, contractors have played a significant role in the US national security effort.[1] Today, close to a million contractors hold a security clearance, which grants them access to sensitive government information.[2] The risks these cleared contractors pose to government information security have become more apparent in recent years but they have not been examined in detail. The government itself recognized in the mid-2000s that, despite its efforts to maintain control over contractors, outsourcing services increases risks "by reducing control over access to systems and information."[3] In 2013, the unauthorized disclosure of sensitive government information orchestrated by former National Security Agency (NSA) contractor Edward Snowden shed light on the risks that contractors with a need to know can pose to government information security.[4] Some commentators found that the Snowden leaks exposed "cracks" in the contractor system.[5] In 2016, media reports alleged that Harold Martin, an NSA contractor working on offensive cyberwarfare programs, had been taking home classified material for 16 years.[6] Recognizing these concerns, this chapter explores the risks contractors have posed to the security of sensitive government information throughout history. A particular emphasis is put on the nature of these risks, their possible evolution, and the government's efforts to mitigate them in cyberspace.

Two concepts lie at the core of this chapter: information security and cybersecurity. US law defines information security as "protecting information and information systems from unauthorized access, use, disclosure, disruption, modification, or destruction."[7] Information security relies on three core components: confidentiality, integrity, and availability. Confidentiality prevents sensitive information from reaching the wrong hands; integrity guarantees that information remains accurate and trustworthy, and availability ensures that only authorized parties are able to access the information. Since anything that occurs in cyberspace involves information and information systems, cybersecurity can be considered as a component of information security. There are significant overlaps between information and cybersecurity and the two terms are often used interchangeably. However, information security concerns are broader than cybersecurity concerns because they encompass the confidentiality, integrity, and availability of information beyond cyberspace. For example, trusted employees can share paper copies of sensitive documents or discuss their content with outsiders. In the last decade, cybersecurity concerns have dominated public discussions about information security. This raises important questions regarding the evolving nature of compromises to national security and the need for public–private collaboration to maintain information security in cyberspace.

From a methodological point of view, the dearth of publicly available information on compromises to US national security is a significant hurdle that is worth mentioning. When compromises are made public, reports often conspicuously lack substantive detail regarding the intrusion, such as the number of systems and computers that have been compromised and the nature of the intrusion.[8] Understandably, instances and details regarding intrusions often remain unreported because of their sensitive nature, liability concerns, and the weaknesses they point out.[9] This state of affairs complicates and limits the representativeness of research in this domain but it does not make it impossible.

The chapter first considers the historical threats and concerns relating to contractors and information security. Contractors have played a significant role in the development of the US national security effort, and as such they have benefited from and helped secure access to sensitive government information. This historical role helps explain why contractors have been involved in a series of information security breaches throughout history. However, publicly available evidence suggests that most of the compromises to US national security have originated with government employees. The fact that more government employees have accessed sensitive government information throughout the years can explain this situation.

The second section of the chapter seeks to explain compromises to US national security. Much of the discussions about compromises have focused on individual motivations to compromise national security. Yet the vulnerability of communications systems has also posed technical risks to information security. The spread of computer networks since the 1960s and the ubiquity of cyberspace in the contemporary world has increased the risk of technical vulnerabilities. The private sector has played a visible role in this context, providing a pool of expertise to the government when public officials sought new IT solutions to gather, process, store, analyze, and disseminate sensitive information. Cross-sector collaboration has provided a number of opportunities for the government to augment its national security effort, but it also poses risks to national security.[10]

An examination of recent government cybersecurity breaches caused by contractors shows that the nature of compromises in cyberspace has not fundamentally changed. Individual behavior and technical vulnerabilities remain two key factors to explain compromises. However, the prominent place of the industry in cyberspace generates issues of public–private coordination, which deserve more attention as the government seeks to mitigate cyber threats. Whilst the government has taken a series of measures to foster public–private coordination on cyber threats, further efforts are necessary to align incentives and create a climate of trust between the public and private sectors.

Contractors as historical partners and sources of compromise

The historically close bonds between the US national security apparatus and the private sector have long bred the possibility that hostile organizations could target contractors to collect sensitive government information. Throughout the nineteenth and in the first half of the twentieth century, the Pinkerton Agency provided a number of security services to the US government. Pinkerton agents conducted espionage and counterespionage for George B. McClellan, the commander of the Union's Army of the Potomac during the Civil War (1861–1865), tracked American support to Cuban rebels after the War, and helped in setting up one of the first federal criminal databases.[11] Prior to the First World War, the Pinkerton Agency also served a host of foreign governments such as Britain, France, Russia, Canada, and Germany, which posed problems of reliability that discredited the company.[12] Since Pinkerton and his men served other governments to make a profit, could they be trusted with sensitive government information? The different incentives followed by government officials and private actors became increasingly evident as the public administration paradigm emerged in the early twentieth century. The government claimed ownership over its information and Congress passed a series of laws which made it a crime to share sensitive government information with the enemy.[13]

Concerns about national security secrets evolved with the advent of new technologies. During the Second World War, the ability of the Allies to maintain communications security and break in to the communications of the Axis played a significant role in their victory.[14] In the early 1940s, Bell Laboratory provided secure teletypewriter communications systems to the US Army and Navy, and subsequently discovered the existence of compromising radio and acoustic emissions, which could have allowed the enemy to gather American secrets. Following this discovery, the laboratory developed technical counter-surveillance measures to mitigate these vulnerabilities.[15] This example shows how technical systems developed by government contractors could already create information security vulnerabilities for the government at the time.

The establishment of the US national security state in 1947,[16] and its expansion during the Cold War, provided new opportunities for the private sector to capture government contracts. As intelligence became increasingly technical, the industry provided a source of technological innovation and expertise that became essential to US national security. For instance, American companies played a crucial role in the research and development of new reconnaissance platforms such as the CORONA satellites.[17] As they expanded their contribution to the national security effort, contractors became a more visible target of infiltration.[18] As former CIA officer Robert Wallace puts it, "with more Americans working in national security disciplines having more access, more often, to more information than ever before, the pool of potential spies is multiplied."[19]

US authorities have long been aware of the risks posed by contractors who need to know sensitive government information, and established a number of structures to liaise with the industry. In 1953, a National Security Council decision established the Communications Security Board bringing government and industry partners together to discuss and oversee communications security issues.[20] In the late 1960s, the Advanced Research Projects Agency within the Department of Defense (DoD) established a task force to study "the risks introduced by the widespread use of resource-sharing information systems and to make recommendations to improve their security."[21] In subsequent years, these recommendations were codified by various government organizations including the National Institute of Standards and Technology (NIST), a government technology agency that works with the private sector to develop standards of conduct, including information security standards. More than a decade later, a 1976 National Security Council decision expressed continuing concern about "possible damage to the national security and the economy from continuing Soviet intercept of critical non-government communications, including government defense contractors and certain other key institutions in the private sector." The decision highlighted the president's decision to extend communications security "to government defense contractors dealing in classified or sensitive information."[22]

Concerns about the ability of the private sector to maintain the security of government information were widely publicized a few years later with the release of Robert Lindsey's book *The Falcon and the Snowman: A True Story of Friendship and Espionage* and its subsequent adaptation into a movie by John Schlesinger.[23] The fact-inspired story followed Christopher Boyce, a disillusioned employee working for an intelligence contractor, TRW, who decided to use his post in a secure communication facility to spy for the Soviet Union. When Boyce was arrested for espionage in the late 1970s, TRW became infamous for its lax security protocols.[24] This raised questions about the implementation of government-mandated information security standards in the industry. The release of the Mitrokhin archive, the collection of notes secretly made by Vasili Mitrokhin during his career as KGB archivist, confirmed that the government's concerns were justified. Documents in the archive show that the Soviet Union successfully intercepted fax communications from major defense companies working on sensitive government contracts such as Boeing, General Dynamics, Grumman, IBM, and Lockheed.[25] KGB residencies in the United States also ran a series of agents who were working for leading American defense contractors such as McDonnell Douglas and TRW.[26] All these cases suggest that penetrating the US national security state through its contractors is a traditional method of infiltration used by hostile organizations.

Though US authorities have been aware of the vulnerability posed by contractors for decades, there has been little effort to systematically consider the extent of their involvement in compromises to national security. An examination of the data compiled by the Defense Personnel and Security Research Center (PERSEREC) shows that contractors have been at the origin of 10–15 percent of the publicly known compromises to national security. PERSEREC published two main reports on compromises to US national security. The first report reviews compromises to national security from 1947 to 2001 and only considers Americans as a source of compromise. In this report, 10 percent of the breaches originate with contractors. The second report covers the period from 1975 to 2008 and includes both Americans and non-American sources of compromise. In this report, 15 percent of the compromises originate with contractors.[27] These percentages reveal the historical significance of the risk posed by contractors, but they are indicative at best. The PERSEREC databases are incomplete since they are based on publicly known compromises. More contractors have probably been involved in compromises that have remained secret or have gone unnoticed. Nevertheless, some basic conclusions can be drawn from these data. First, contractors have been involved in a significant amount of compromises to national security (at least 27 cases from 1963 to 2008). Second, the involvement of the private sector in compromises to national security has been relatively stable throughout the years, as shown in Figure 12.1. The trends shown in this figure also suggest that compromises originating with government officials have grown faster than those originating with contractors.

Explaining compromises to national security

Research in the area of security studies on compromises to national security has largely focused on insiders and their motivations to compromise the secrets of the organization they work for. Kate Randal, an insider threat analyst at the FBI, considers that information security threats are essentially "a people-centric

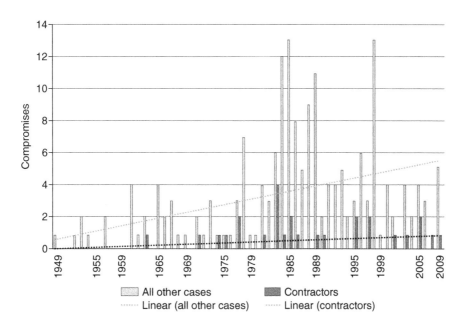

Figure 12.1 Compromises to US national security, 1949–2008.

problem" that needs to be approached in a multidisciplinary way by combining technical, contextual, and psychosocial information.[28] Much of the research into compromises to national security, including PERSEREC reports used to develop Figure 12.1, focuses on individuals.[29] At an individual level, the psychosocial motives behind espionage and other compromises to national security are often presented thanks to the acronym MICE, which stands for money, ideology, compromise, and ego. From this perspective, insiders compromise government secrets to make money, to serve an ideology, to respond to blackmail, and to satisfy their ego.[30]

The use of computer systems to process, analyze, and disseminate sensitive information creates technical vulnerabilities, both at the level of the hardware and the software, that should also be taken into account in discussions about information security. Government and private-sector experts started discussing these vulnerabilities publicly in the late 1960s.[31] Computer systems have provided tremendous opportunities for government and private-sector organizations to improve the national security effort, for example by facilitating the processing of increasingly large numbers of logistical and operational data. However, they have also created vulnerabilities across the public–private divide.[32] As computerized networks spread throughout the 1980s, the expansion of the US national security apparatus into cyberspace provided new opportunities for hostile actors to compromise government secrets. In 1986, system administrator Clifford Stoll noticed an accounting discrepancy on a computer system at Lawrence Berkeley National Laboratory. Subsequent investigations revealed that a group of West German hackers run by the KGB had penetrated sensitive systems connecting computers at the laboratory and the MITRE Corporation to access the Advanced Research Projects Agency Network/Military Network, and infiltrate dozens of computers at the Pentagon as well as at various defense contractors. The story hit the headlines when Stoll published a book recounting the story of the investigation in 1989.[33] This attack demonstrated the ability of cyber threats to spread across networks and reinforced the need for cooperation between the individuals and organizations using these networks.

In recent decades, information security threats targeting the US government and contractors' systems have become increasingly sophisticated, effective, and numerous.[34] The risks posed by contractors have also become more common as the industry became a key source of IT innovation. For instance, the government has outsourced the design, implementation, and maintenance of its IT systems needs to foreign countries, thus offering significant opportunities to potential adversaries to learn about US systems.[35] To be sure, the importance of individuals as sources of compromise has not disappeared in the cyber era. As a group of experts notes, all "cyber activity is ultimately the result of human motivation, behavior, and intent."[36] Foreign agents have, for example, established technology companies in the United States and "served as subcontractors on US defense contractors to obtain access to technology."[37] The leaks orchestrated by Edward Snowden, who used his insider position to access and disclose vast amounts of classified information, is another case in point. Snowden used his position as system administrator to access sensitive information he did not need to know, thus exposing information security vulnerabilities in the NSA classified networks. Snowden's actions can also be explained through the lens of individual motivations. The former contractor claims his leaks served the public debate (ideological motive), but commentators have noted his actions put his ideas above the national interest (ego).[38]

The conceptual divide between insider and outsider threats can help distinguish between different types of threats that have been presented so far. Multiple rationales can explain insiders' compromise to national security, be they government officials or private contractors. Understanding the motivations driving insiders' threats to information security is important to develop appropriate countermeasures that can help identify and deter possible threats. Compromises can also be related to technical vulnerabilities originating in the public or private sector, and allowing outsiders to compromise sensitive government information. In such cases, motives matter less than the vulnerabilities that are exploited. The next section examines recent cases in which contractors compromised cyber national security to further expand this construct.

Compromises targeting contractors in cyberspace

This section examines three cases of cyber compromise that originated with contractors. These cases have been selected for convenience, because sufficient information was available about them in the public domain to illustrate some of the issues associated with contractors' information security in cyberspace.[39] In 2007, Unisys Corporation intentionally concealed a large cyber intrusion attributed to foreign hackers. The company had been contracted in 2002 by the Department of Homeland Security (DHS) to provide network and information technology security for the Transportation Security Administration (TSA). When this initial contract ended, DHS awarded a $750 million follow-on contract to the company in 2005.[40] Unisys subsequently failed to install and manage intrusion detection systems on the TSA networks and this, some commentators note, left them vulnerable to cyberattacks.[41] From June through October 2006, Unisys experienced a security breach that occurred at an unclassified level and compromised both TSA and DHS network systems. More than 150 computers were infiltrated and unknown amounts of sensitive government information were transferred to a Chinese language website.[42] The hackers reportedly cracked the password of a network administrator at Unisys and gained access to modify system files on hundreds of computers on the DHS networks. An initial congressional investigation into the breach blamed Unisys for its negligence, and its attempt to hide security gaps and mislead DHS officials about the source of the attacks. However, the media reported that senior DHS officials also failed to recognize the situation's gravity when they were first informed of the breach.[43] The Unisys case shows how contractors can provide a gateway for hostile actors to access government networks and gather information from the outside. The possibility that Unisys concealed part of the breach from its government sponsor suggests that the incentives of the public and the private sectors were misaligned. Whilst public authorities need to be made aware of any information security breaches to protect sensitive government information, contractors may prefer to conceal them to safeguard their reputation and maintain their competitiveness. This case highlights the need to consider organizational incentives to coordinate cybersecurity across the public–private divide.

In another case, Operation Shady RAT (an acronym for remote access tool), one single actor, widely assumed to be China, constituted an advanced persistent threat (APT) to various international victims from mid-2006 to 2011. After gaining control of one of the servers used in this operation, the company McAfee was able to analyze and reveal its scope to the public. The attacker behind Shady RAT relied on spear-phishing techniques, the sending of emails with attachments to the employees of various public and private organizations. These attachments contained exploit codes that compromised the recipients' computers allowing the attacker to install software, monitor their activities, and access their data. McAfee's analysis identified 71 compromised parties across a range of sectors in 14 countries. The strategy pursued by the attacker targeted both government agencies and contractors to get access to their information. At least 49 of the victims were located in the United States, and included 12 defense contractors, half a dozen companies working in sensitive sectors such as satellite communications, network security, information services and electronics, and a dozen government organizations at the federal, state, and local levels.[44] Whilst the details of the compromises and the specific entities that were targeted have not been disclosed, it is reasonable to assume that sensitive government information was compromised. Shady RAT shows how cyberattacks, particularly spear-phishing, can trick insiders into giving access to their computer and give hostile outsiders access to their network. In this case, insiders were apparently tricked into giving access to their computers and networks. This case is interesting because it shows how cyberattacks can rely on both technical and human vulnerabilities to compromise sensitive government information. The use of spear-phishing also suggests that human compromises are not always motivated by money, ideology, compromise, or ego, but can sometimes be caused by negligence.

More recently, in June 2015, the Office of Personnel Management (OPM) revealed that a cyber intrusion within its information technology systems had compromised unencrypted databases containing the personal information of millions of former and current federal employees. In the following month, this breach was estimated to have compromised the personal information of about 21.5 million individuals who had applied for a security clearance. This information is particularly sensitive because it contains personal information about the lives of millions of workers who have or have had access to sensitive government information. Hostile actors could use this information to identify, compromise, and recruit employees who know some of the government's secrets. The hackers behind this breach reportedly targeted an individual contractor employed through KeyPoint Government Solutions via a phishing attack to compromise his or her security credentials and gain access to OPM's systems.[45] This breach gave the attacker, widely assumed to be tied to China, access to a vast amount of sensitive information through a single entry point, thus revealing the devastating threat posed by spear-phishing and poor information security practices.[46] In October 2015, the US government began notifying OPM breach victims by providing them with identity theft services valued at a total of $133 million.[47]

These three cases show the extent of the damage that cyberattacks targeting government contractors can cause. They can also help refine the conceptual model developed above. In all three cases, a hostile actor targeted one or more individuals to gain entry into secured networks. The cases of Shady RAT and the OPM hack both relied on spear-phishing, capitalizing on the gullibility or negligence of insiders. In these two cases, no evidence suggests that the insiders had specific motivations to compromise information security. In the Unisys case, the hacker relied on external means to crack a password and infiltrate sensitive networks. The Unisys case also emphasizes issues of coordination with the private sector. This introduces an organizational dimension that is often overlooked in the study of compromises to national security, but crucial to the development of appropriate and timely responses to compromises.

Organizing information security across the public–private divide

The threats posed by compromises to the US government and its contractors have pushed the government to react. Since the 1990s, a long list of government strategies, reports, and decisions have emphasized the need to coordinate public and private efforts to maintain information security.[48] These documents leave no doubt that government officials are well aware that contractors—that develop, operate, and own a vast majority of US critical technologies and infrastructures—need to protect their information. Federal agencies are required to protect and maintain the confidentiality, integrity, and availability of their information and information systems, even when these systems are used by the private sector.[49] The government has used its authority to ensure contractors' compliance with mandated security standards. The Information Security Oversight Office, for instance, has "the authority to conduct on-site reviews of the implementation of the National Industrial Security Program by each agency, contractor, licensee, and grantee that has access to or stores classified information and to require of each cooperation."[50] In 2013, the Defense Federal Acquisition Regulation Supplement was amended to include a clause requiring DoD contractors to rapidly report cyber incidents within 72 hours of discovery and communicate the extent of the compromise to the government.[51] The 2014 Intelligence Authorization Act requires the Director of National Intelligence (DNI) to develop procedures for intelligence contractors to report "penetrations" of intelligence community (IC) networks and information systems, give government officials access to equipment and information necessary to conduct investigations, and establishes procedures to prohibit the dissemination of information about the breach.[52] The Act also enjoined the DNI to develop security planning standards for IC networks in consultation with the industry, including a requirement that contractors develop insider threat detection capabilities. The Cybersecurity Act of 2015 mandates the establishment of procedures to facilitate timely sharing of cyber threat indicators between federal and non-federal entities. The Act also provides protection from liability to the industry for the monitoring and sharing of cyber threat indicators of defensive measures.[53] This is a clear signal that the government understands the need to take into account private-sector incentives to remove obstacles to cooperation.

In recent decades, the government has also established a number of forums to share information on cyber threats and coordinate cybersecurity efforts across the public–private divide but paid little attention to the private-sector incentives to invest resources in these platforms. In 1998, President Clinton signed a Presidential Decision Directive encouraging the development of Information Sharing and Analysis Centers (ISAC) that could facilitate the protection of critical infrastructure and key resources through information sharing. These centers can serve as a mechanism to gather, analyze, sanitize and disseminate private-sector information to the industry and the government, and for the government to share threat information with the industry.[54] The government's efforts in this domain accelerated significantly following the launch of the Comprehensive National Cybersecurity Initiative in 2008.[55] That year, the DoD established the Defense Industrial Base Collaborative Information Sharing Environment for the government to share cybersecurity products with select companies, and these companies to share anonymous intrusion reports with the DoD.[56] In 2009, representatives from NIST, the DoD and the IC set up a joint task force to "produce a unified information security framework for the federal government" encompassing both national security and non-national security systems.[57] The same year, DHS opened the National Cybersecurity and Communications Integration Center (NCCIC), which brings together 13 federal departments and agencies and 16 private-sector entities, and collaborates with over 100 private-sector organizations. The center analyzes and shares information on cyber threats, and coordinates responses, mitigation, and recovery efforts.[58] The NCCIC serves as the national response center during major cyber or communications incidents, helping to coordinate the efforts of multiple partners. Within the NCCIC, the Cyber Information Sharing and Collaboration Program seeks to establish a community of trust between the federal government and the critical infrastructure industry.[59] Another DHS initiative, the Enhanced Cybersecurity Services program, allows the government to share sensitive cyber threat information with accredited commercial service providers.[60] In 2015, President Obama signed an executive order to encourage companies and industries to set up Information Sharing and Analysis Organizations (ISAO). ISAOs can be used to develop a common set of voluntary standards regulating security procedures and privacy protection across the public–private divide.[61] The government has made significant efforts to raise awareness and improve public–private coordination in the field of cybersecurity, but the success of these efforts remains debated. New structures and procedures cannot guarantee public and private partners will remain committed to the improvement of information and cybersecurity.

Aligning public and private incentives

Despite the government's efforts to foster coordination across the public–private divide, problems have subsisted. Regulations requiring contractors to report cyberattacks and other security breaches have sometimes appeared to have little effect on their behavior.[62] The reluctance of Unisys to communicate the breach it experienced in 2006 to DHS is a case in point. More recently, the Defense Security Service found that, between 2009 and 2011, only 10 percent of cleared defense contractors reported cybersecurity breaches to their government sponsor in a given year.[63] Evidence also suggests that government contractors have underinvested in information security. In 2013, a report by the Intelligence and National Security Alliance found that a significant number of private companies working on government programs lacked a formal insider threat mitigation program.[64] The public discourse on cybersecurity has repeatedly highlighted the need for public–private partnerships and this suggests that, thus far, partnerships have remained elusive. In a recent review of national cybersecurity strategies, Madeline Carr found that public–private relations have been characterized by disjuncture about the roles, responsibilities, and authority of each partner.[65]

Multiple factors can explain the lack of communication between the government and the private sector. In some cases, cleared contractors may legitimately not have realized their systems came under attack. Contractors might also be aware of a compromise but prefer not to report it to government because of the absence of clear requirements or a misunderstanding of communication procedures.[66] However, given the government's regulatory and outreach efforts it is unlikely that a contractor would simply not know about its obligation to report breaches to its government sponsor. The most concerning case by far is when contractors decide not to report a compromise for fear it may impact on their reputation, benefit competitors, undermine their profit, and lead to legal pursuits.[67] In such cases, the shortfalls of cross-sector collaboration can be explained by the divergence of incentives between the government and the industry.

Whilst companies have an interest in maintaining their security and avoiding data breaches, the need for cybersecurity can contradict their profit incentive. Maintaining demanding security standards increases costs in research and development, operations and maintenance, and administration.[68] From a business perspective, profit is more important than security. Madeline Carr notes that private-sector owners accept responsibility for cybersecurity "as far as the cost of dealing with an outage promises to cost more than preventing it."[69] Companies also have an incentive to underreport or even conceal data breaches to maintain a good reputation and remain competitive. Government knowledge of their vulnerabilities could impact on their performance review and decrease their chances of getting future contracts. Furthermore, the model followed by many companies is based on obtaining and selling information, not sharing it. Business incentives contrast with the government's, which is more concerned about the public interest in cybersecurity than financial and reputational costs.[70] The government's national security responsibilities create stronger incentives for public officials to seek collaboration from the industry.[71]

Most of the government's efforts to foster cross-sector collaboration on information and cybersecurity issues have relied on regulations and voluntary platforms to share information and coordinate policies. These measures are unlikely to yield significant results as long as private incentives are not aligned with the government's. If companies are not convinced that cooperating with the government and sharing sensitive information about security breaches will serve them, they will continue to seek regulatory loopholes or even disregard their obligations. This is problematic, because the government needs committed private partners. With more than a million contractors eligible for access to classified information, maintaining control over private-sector uses of sensitive government information is a tremendous task.[72] The government cannot reasonably be expected to track compliance with all of its requirements and needs support from the industry.[73]

Repeated interactions are essential to improve trust between public and private partners and improve contractors' commitment to cyber national security. Scholars of social trust emphasize the importance of "shared identity and solidarity, such as common values, group membership, and the feeling of working towards common goals," in building trust.[74] This approach is in line with discussion about public–private partnerships, which have become a mainstay of the public discourse on cybersecurity.[75] Partnerships suppose a high level of trust corresponding to a mutual belief in the positive gains of collaboration. Focusing on the development of social capital, in addition to external guarantees to cooperative behavior such as regulatory requirements, has the potential to reorient private-sector calculations and improve partnerships.[76] In the Netherlands, for example, cross-sector collaboration on cybersecurity has developed through the organization of periodic conferences where public and private actors sit down together and discuss the challenges they confront.[77] Events like the White House Summit on Cybersecurity and Consumer Protection of 2015 provide multiple opportunities for public and private-sector leaders to engage in formal and informal forms of dialogue. These interactions should not be limited to senior executives, but also involve mid- and entry-level professionals. Multiplying opportunities for shared training and education is another way to foster cross-sector interactions whilst improving cybersecurity skills across the board.[78] Education also provides opportunities to disseminate the latest knowledge and drive collaboration through evidence. Recent research conducted by the Ponemon Institute, for instance, shows that sharing threat intelligence could thwart 39 percent of cyberattacks.[79] Over the long term, dialogue and interactions have the potential to foster a culture of collaboration that is essential to protect the nation's information systems.

Conclusion

This chapter has explored issues of information and cybersecurity across the public–private divide. The long history of cross-sector collaboration on sensitive national security programs has made the private sector a constant source of compromise. The chapter reviewed a series of compromises originating with contractors to better understand their sources, and concluded that compromises are not fundamentally different across the public–private divide. Individuals, whether they are government officials or contractors, sometimes decide to leak sensitive government information. In such cases, money, ideology, compromise, and ego best explain their behavior. They can also inadvertently give access to sensitive information, for example when they fall victim to a spear-phishing scam. Technical vulnerabilities can also allow external actors to infiltrate government systems and gain access to sensitive information. As the government shares sensitive information with its contractors, it needs to coordinate its efforts to mitigate these threats with the private sector. This organizational dimension has become increasingly important in recent decades and the government has passed a number of laws and regulations to require and foster information sharing with its private partners. However, effective cross-sector collaboration cannot be forced upon the industry. The social dimension of public–private partnerships is equally important. Frequent interactions and shared training have the potential to develop a culture of collaboration that will improve information and cybersecurity across the public–private divide.

Notes

1 See, for example: Peter W. Singer, *Corporate Warriors: The Rise of the Privatized Military Industry* (New York: Cornell University Press, 2003); Deborah Avant, *The Market for Force. The Consequences of Privatizing Security* (Cambridge: Cambridge University Press, 2005); Glenn Voelz, "Contractors and intelligence: The private sector in the intelligence community," *International Journal of Intelligence and CounterIntelligence* 22/4 (2007): 588–591; Tim Shorrock, *Spies for Hire. The Secret World of Intelligence Outsourcing* (New York: Simon & Schuster, 2008).
2 Office of the Director of National Intelligence, National Counterintelligence and Security Center, 2015 Report on Security Clearance Determinations, June 28, 2016, 5.
3 National Science and Technology Council, Federal Plan for Cyber Security and Information Assurance Research and Development, Report by the Interagency Working Group on Cyber Security and Information Assurance, April 2006, 8; Government Accountability Office, Information Security: Improving Oversight of Access to Federal systems and Data by Contractors Can Reduce Risk, Report to Congressional Requesters, April 2005, 2; Government Accountability Office, Information Security. Weaknesses Continue Amid New Federal Efforts to Implement Requirements, October 2011, 32.
4 Kimberly Dozier and Stephen Braun, "Edward Snowden Leaks Lead To Pentagon Change, Top Official Says," *Huffington Post*, February 4, 2014.
5 Philip Ewing and Tony Romm, "Edward Snowden Leak Exposes Cracks in Contractor System," *Politico*, June 9, 2013, at www.politico.com/story/2013/06/edward-snowden-leak-contractor-92472_Page2.html.
6 Scott Shane, Matt Apuzzo, and Jo Becker, "Hacking Tools Among Data Stolen From US," *New York Times*, October 20, 2016, A1.

7   US Code, Chapter 44, § 3542—Definitions (2016).
8   Dmitri Alperovitch, Revealed: Operation Shady RAT Version 1.1, 2011, 2.
9   John Esterbrook, "Many Hack Attacks Go Unreported," *CBS News*, April 7, 2002 at www.cbsnews.com/news/many-hack-attacks-go-unreported/.
10   Barry M. Leiner et al., "The Past and Future History of the Internet," *Communications of the ACM* 40/2 (1997): 102–108; Martin Libicki, *Conquest in Cyberspace: National Security and Information Warfare* (Cambridge: Cambridge University Press, 2007); Joel Brenner, *America the Vulnerable: Inside the New Threat Matrix of Digital Espionage, Crime, and Warfare* (London: Penguin, 2011).
11   Frank Morn, *The Eye That Never Sleeps: A History of the Pinkerton National Detective Agency* (Bloomington, IN: Indiana University Press, 1982), 63; James MacKay, *Allan Pinkerton: The Eye Who Never Slept* (Edinburgh: Mainstream Publishing Company, 1996), 11, 71–72, 78, 149–153, 183; Bruce Durie (ed.), *The Pinkerton Casebook* (Edinburgh: Mercat Press, 2007), 1, 36, 176.
12   Rhodri Jeffrey-Jones, *American Espionage* (New York: The Free Press, 1977), 3, 16–21, 26, 37, 55.
13   US Congress, Defense Secret Act, 62nd Congress, 1st sess., March 3, 1911; Ibid., Espionage Act, 65th Congress, 1st sess., June 15, 1917; Ibid., Sedition Act, 65th Congress, 2nd sess., May 16, 1918.
14   Harry Hinsley, *British Intelligence in the Second World War. Abridged Version* (New York: Cambridge University Press, 1993).
15   National Security Agency, "TEMPEST: A Signal Problem," *Cryptologic Spectrum* 2/3 (1972): 27.
16   US Congress, National Security Act, 80th Congress, 1st sess., July 26, 1947, Titles I and II.
17   Kevin C. Ruffner, *CORONA: America's First Satellite Program* (Washington, DC: Center for the Study of Intelligence, 1995), 37.
18   Matthew M. Aid, "All glory is fleeting: Sigint and the fight against international terrorism," *Intelligence and National Security* 18/4 (2003): 72–120; Ayse Ceyhan, "Technologization of security: Management of uncertainty and risk in the age of biometrics," *Surveillance & Society* 5/2 (2008): 102–123.
19   Robert Wallace, "A Time for Counterespionage," in Jennifer E. Sims and Burton Gerber (eds), *Vaults, Mirrors, and Masks: Rediscovering US Counterintelligence* (Washington: Georgetown University Press, 2009), 115.
20   National Security Council, Decision 168, Communications Security, October 20, 1953.
21   Evan E. Anderson and Joobin Choobineh, "Enterprise information security strategies," *Computers & Security* 27 (2008): 23; Willis H. Ware, Security Controls for Computer Systems: Report of Defense Science Board Task Force on Computer Security, RAND Report R-609-1, Reissued October 1979, xi.
22   Brent Scowcroft, National Security Council, National Security Decision Memorandum 338, Further Improvements In Telecommunications Security (TS), September 1, 1976, 1.
23   Robert Lindsey, *The Falcon and the Snowman: A True Story of Friendship and Espionage* (New York: Simon & Schuster, 1979); Gabriel Katzka and John Schlesinger (Producers), John Schlesinger (Director), *The Falcon and the Snowman* (1985).
24   Michael J. Sulick, *American Spies. Espionage against the United States from the Cold War to the Present* (Washington, DC: Georgetown University Press, 2013), 62–63.
25   Christopher Andrew and Vasili Mitrokhin, *The Mitrokhin Archive. The KGB in Europe and the West* (London: Allen Lane, 1999), 454.
26   Ibid., 280–281.
27   Katherine L. Herbig and Martin F. Wiskoff, Espionage Against the United States by American Citizens 1947–2001, Technical Report 02–5, July 2002; Defense Personnel Security Research Center, Espionage and Other Compromises to National Security 1975–2008, November 2, 2009.

28 Editor, "RSA 2013: FBI offers lessons learned on insider threat detection," at http://searchsecurity.techtarget.com/news/2240179082/RSA-2013-FBI-offers-lessons-learned-on-insider-threat-detection.

29 Theodore R. Sarbin, "Computer Crime: A Peopleware Problem," Proceedings of a conference held October 25, 1993, (Monterrey, CA: Defense Personnel Security Research Center); Center for the Study of Intelligence, *Of Moles and Molehunters: A Review of Counterintelligence Literature, 1977–92*, October 1993; Frank J. Rafalko (ed.), *A Counterintelligence Reader: American Revolution into the New Millenium, Volume Four* (Washington, DC: National Counterintelligence Center, 2004); Stephen R. Band et al., "Comparing Insider IT Sabotage and Espionage: A Model-Based Analysis," December 2006, vii, 4 (Pittsburgh, PA: Software Engineering Institute, Carnegie Mellon University).

30 Stan A. Taylor and Daniel Snow, "Cold war spies: Why they spied and how they got caught," *Intelligence and National Security* 12/2 (1997): 101–125; Randy Burkett, "An alternative framework for agent recruitment: From MICE to RASCLS," *Studies in Intelligence* 57/1 (2013): 7–17.

31 Michael Warner, "Cybersecurity: A pre-history," *Intelligence and National Security* 27/5 (2012): 783–785.

32 Corey D. Schou and Kenneth J. Trimmer, "Information assurance and security," *Journal of Organizational and End User Computing* 16/3 (2004): ii; Intelligence and National Security Alliance, Cyber Intelligence. Setting the landscape for an emerging discipline, Conference held in Monterrey, CA, September 2011, 7, at www.insaonline.org/CMDownload.aspx?ContentKey=0a8910f4-a937-4ed3-b50b-9ac6db3ab692&ContentItemKey=8f63849c-1511-46d3-9abe-6a98b7576da2; Evan E. Anderson and Joobin Choobineh, "Enterprise information security strategies," *Computers & Security* 27 (2008): 22.

33 Clifford Stoll, *The Cuckoo's Egg: Tracking a Spy Through the Maze of Computer Espionage* (New York: Simon & Schuster, 1989); Wayne Madsen, "Intelligence agency threats to computer security," *International Journal of Intelligence and CounterIntelligence* 6/4 (1993): 415–418.

34 Government Accountability Office, Information Assurance. National Partnership Offers Benefits, but Faces Considerable Challenges, Report to the Honorable William Lacy Clay, House of Representatives, March 2006, 1. On the rising number of cyber threats, see: Department of Homeland Security, US-CERT Year in Review. United States Computer Emergency Readiness Team, CY 2012, 6; Verizon, 2014 Data Breach Investigations Report, 38.

35 Intelligence and National Security Alliance, Cyber Intelligence. Setting the landscape for an emerging discipline, September 2011, 6.

36 Intelligence and National Security Alliance, Operational Cyber Intelligence, October 2014, 5.

37 National Science and Technology Council, Federal Plan for Cyber Security and Information Assurance Research and Development, Report by the Interagency Working Group on Cyber Security and Information Assurance, April 2006, 8–9.

38 On the Snowden affair, see: Loch K. Johnson et. al, "An *INS* Special Forum: Implications of the Snowden Leaks," *Intelligence and National Security* 29/6 (2014): 793–810; US House of Representatives, (U) Review of Unauthorized Disclosures of Former National Security Agency Contractor Edward Snowden, September 15, 2016.

39 One case, in which a Department of Defense contractor was compromised of 24,000 files, was left aside because of the paucity of publicly available information. For more information, see: Thom Shanker and Elisabeth Bumiller, "After Suffering Damaging Cyberattack, the Pentagon Takes Defensive Action," *New York Times*, July 14, 2011, A6; Jeremy White, "Government Hacked: 24,000 Files Stolen in Worst Pentagon Cyber Attack," *International Business Times*, July 14, 2011.

40 Robert Block, "Unisys Denies Coverup of Security Breaches," *Wall Street Journal*, September 25, 2007, A15.
41 Jason Mick, "Unysis Blamed for China-Connected Homeland Security Hacks," *DailyTech*, September 26, 2007, at www.dailytech.com/Unisys+Blamed+for+China Connected+Homeland+Security+Hacks/article9043.htm.
42 Block, "Unisys Denies Coverup of Security Breaches."
43 Ellen Nakashima and Brian Krebs, "Contractor Blamed in DHS Data Breaches," *Washington Post*, September 24, 2007, A1.
44 Alperovitch, *Revealed: Operation Shady RAT Version 1.1*, 3–9.
45 Kristin Finklea et al., Cyber Intrusion into US Office of Personnel Management: in Brief, Congressional Research Service Report, July 17, 2015, 1.
46 Brendan, I. Koerner, "Inside the Cyberattack that Shocked the US Government," *Wired*, October 23, 2016.
47 Joe Davidson, "Months after government hack, 21.5 million people are formally being advised, and offered help," *Washington Post*, October 2, 2015, A19.
48 White House, Presidential Decision Directive/NSC-63, Critical Infrastructure Protection, May 22, 1998; Ibid., Defending America's Cyberspace. National Plan for Information Systems Protection, 2000; General Accounting Office, Information Security: Serious and Widespread Weaknesses Persist at Federal Agencies, September 6, 2000; White House, Executive Order 13231. Critical Infrastructure in the Information Age, October 16, 2001; General Accounting Office, Critical Infrastructure Protection. Federal Efforts Require a More Coordinated and Comprehensive Approach for Protecting Information Systems, July 2002, 20–21; White House, National Strategy to Secure Cyberspace, February 2003, ix; Government Accountability Office, Industrial Security. DoD Cannot Ensure Its Oversight of Contractors under Foreign Influence Is Sufficient, July 15, 2005, 1; White House, National Security Presidential Directive 54/Homeland Security Presidential Directive 23, January 9, 2008, 7; Ibid., Cyberspace Policy Review, May 8, 2009; Ibid.; Presidential Policy Directive 8 on National Preparedness, March 30, 2011; Ibid., Executive Order 13587—Structural Reforms to Improve the Security of Classified Networks and the Responsible Sharing and Safeguarding of Classified Information, October 7, 2011.
49 Government Accountability Office, Information Security. Weaknesses Continue Amid New Federal Efforts to Implement Requirements, 38; US Congress, Federal Information Security Management Act (FISMA), 107th Congress, 2nd sess., December 17, 2002; Federal Acquisition Regulation 52.239-1, Privacy or Security Safeguards.
50 White House, Executive Order 12829, January 6, 1993.
51 Department of Defense, Defense Federal Acquisition Regulation Supplement. Clause 252.204-7012. Safeguarding Unclassified Controlled Technical Information, November 18, 2013.
52 US Congress, Intelligence Authorization Act for Fiscal Year 2014, 113th Congress, 2nd sess., June 11, 2014, Sec. 325.
53 US Congress, Consolidated Appropriations Act, 2016, Division N-Cybersecurity Act of 2016, 114th Congress, 1st sess., December 15, 2015.
54 White House, Presidential Decision Directive/NSC-63.
55 White House, National Security Presidential Directive 54/Homeland Security Presidential Directive 23, January 8, 2008.
56 Rachel Nyswander Thomas, *Securing Cyberspace Through Public-Private Partnership. A Comparative Analysis of Partnership Models* (Washington, DC: Center for Strategic and International Studies, 2013).
57 Government Accountability Office, Progress Made on Harmonizing Policies and Guidance for National Security and Non-National Security Systems, Report to the Chairwoman, Subcommittee on Government Management, Organization, and Procurement, Committee on Oversight and Government Reform, House of Representatives, GAO-10-916, September 2010, 13.

58 National Cybersecurity and Communications Integration Center, at www.dhs.gov/national-cybersecurity-and-communications-integration-center; Intelligence and National Security Alliance, Strategic Cyber Intelligence, March 2014, 6.

59 Department of Homeland Security, "Cyber Information Sharing and Collaboration Program (CISCP)," at www.dhs.gov/ciscp.

60 Department of Homeland Security, "Enhanced Cybersecurity Services (ECS)," at www.dhs.gov/enhanced-cybersecurity-services; Scott E. Jasper, "US cyber threat intelligence sharing frameworks," *International Journal of Intelligence and Counter-Intelligence* 30/1 (2017): 59.

61 Executive Office of the President, Executive Order Promoting Private Sector Cyber-security Information Sharing, February 13, 2015.

62 White House, Executive Order 12829—Intelligence and National Security Alliance, A preliminary examination of insider threat programs in the US private sector, September 2013, 8.

63 Office of the National Counterintelligence Executive, Foreign Spies Stealing US Economic Secrets in Cyberspace: Report to Congress on Foreign Economic Collection and Industrial Espionage, 2009–2011, October 2011, A-1.

64 Intelligence and National Security Alliance, A preliminary examination of insider threat programs in the US private sector, 1,5.

65 Madeline Carr, "Public-private partnerships in national cyber-security strategies," *International Affairs* 92/1 (2016): 44.

66 US Senate, Committee on Armed Services, Inquiry into Cyber Intrusions Affecting US Transportation Command Contractors, 113th Congress, 2nd sess., September 17, 2014, 17–20.

67 Shorrock, *Spies for Hire*, 309, 323; Government Accountability Office, Critical Infrastructure Protection: Key Private and Public Cyber Expectations need to be Consistently Addressed, July 15, 2010, 22.

68 J. Todd Hamill, Richard F. Deckro, and Jack M. Kloeber Jr., "Evaluating information assurance strategies," *Decision Support Systems* 39 (2005): 464; Anderson and Choobineh, "Enterprise information security strategies," 23.

69 Carr, "Public-private partnerships in national cyber-security strategies," 57.

70 Ibid., 55.

71 Daniel Javorsek II et al., "A formal risk-effectiveness analysis proposal for the compartmentalized intelligence security structure," *International Journal of Intelligence and CounterIntelligence* 28/4 (2015): 736.

72 Secrecy News, Security-Cleared Population Rises to 5.1 Million, March 24, 2014, at http://fas.org/2014/03/security-cleared; Office of the Director of National Intelligence, 2013 Report on Security Clearance Determinations, 4.

73 See, for example: Government Accountability Office, Industrial Security. DoD Cannot Ensure Its Oversight of Contractors under Foreign Influence Is Sufficient, Report to the Committee on Armed Services, US Senate, July 2005; Government Accountability Office, Information Security. Weaknesses Continue Amid New Federal Efforts to Implement Requirements, 32; White House, Office of Management and Budget, Suitability and Security Processes Review Report to the President, February 2014, 4.

74 Vincent Charles Keating and Erla Thrandardottir, "NGOs, trust, and the accountability agenda," *The British Journal of Politics and International Relations* 19/1 (2016): 140–141.

75 See, for example: White House, Office of the Press Secretary, "Remarks by the President at the Cybersecurity and Consumer Protection Summit," February 13, 2015.

76 Keating and Thrandardottir, "NGOs, trust, and the accountability agenda," 143.

77 Max Manley, "Cyberspace's dynamic duo: Forging a cybersecurity public-private partnership," *Journal of Strategic Security* 8/3 (2015): 94.

78 W. Victor Maconachy et al., "A Model for Information Assurance: An Integrated Approach," *Proceedings of the 2001 IEEE Workshop on Information Assurance and Security, US Military Academy, West Point, June 5–6, 2001*, IEEE, 30, at http://it210. groups.et.byu.net/theitbok_files/msrwpaper_1.pdf; Manley, "Cyberspace's Dynamic Duo: Forging a Cybersecurity Public-Private Partnership," 85.
79 Ponemon Institute, "Flipping the Economics of Attacks," January 26, 2016.

13 Training coalitions on cyber intelligence capability

Building capability through familiarity and relationships

Scott Bethel and John Whisenhunt

Lessons learned from experience

This chapter explores requirements for developing and enhancing international cooperation in cyberspace, and presents the obstacles faced on this pathway in the context of a recent military campaign. The starting point for this contribution is the experience of one of the co-authors in building a coalition's cyber teaming capabilities. Brigadier General Scott Bethel (Ret. US Air Force) was a military leader in the early stages of Operation Iraqi Freedom (OIF) who had theater-wide responsibility for intelligence, surveillance, and reconnaissance collection management, unmanned aerial vehicle allocation and targeting, plus conventional target identification, collateral damage estimations, and bomb damage assessments. Coalition cyber teaming capabilities can be improved based on the lessons learned from past experience. In the complex information management realm that characterized OIF, cyber operations struggled to find an effective advocate within the Multi-National Force Iraq (MNF-I) headquarters. Some coalition partners were adamant that cyber was a communications function, whilst US forces determined it was part of the targeting function, rightly placed in the Operations Directorate "Fires" section. Coalition members offered a number of interpretations on cyber activities, based on whether they were offensive and defensive operations, alongside artillery, surface-to-surface missiles, and helicopter gunships.[1] After much angst, all agreed cyber was best placed—for the entire coalition—in the Fires section.

As more networks were targeted in Iraq, and throughout the Southwest Asia region, synergy between the kinetic and non-kinetic methods grew in effectiveness. Furthermore, planning all attack operations as one aggregated plan worked well for this coalition operation. In particular, allies learned how to tailor operations and focus effort on effects (results), as opposed to the actual cyber tools. The MNF-I team was also able to conduct a great deal of on-the-spot training and education, which found its way into coalition partners' later operations. Relatively rapid process development was out of necessity in this scenario, yet effective partnering and preparation can benefit every coalition. More effective cyber coalitions must not only build and codify technical and procedural structures ahead of the battle, but they must also adhere to them in practice, and this requires good relationships.

Personal relationships among coalition teammates in this scenario were as important to rapid implementation as the procedures themselves. Based on this experience, this chapter argues that, to successfully develop combined cyber consortiums, the United States must become a successful partner and leader through sharing of information, best practices, and side-by-side experience with its allies. Sharing information and practices is essential to build understanding, and eventually trust between international partners. In the next decades, the effectiveness of the US cyber force will be inherently linked to its ability to build strong, durable, and reciprocal partnerships at an international level. Building robust coalitions based on trust will allow the US cyber force to harness cultural diversity and reinforce cyber defense.

Legacy trust

Decades ago, the developing cyber intelligence community was a relatively small group of highly skilled people, who built relationships based on circles of trust. Running a community numbering in the hundreds, and based in a few small, secured locations was relatively easy. Cyber crews, especially US government and military members, knew one another through the dynamics of tight teamwork, in very focused, limited information campaigns. Some commentators argue the United States is always too protective of its technically brilliant solutions, clever software coding, and its "wins" against equally resourceful adversaries. Others are quick to show the utility of cooperative cyber solutions in all levels of warfare, and to share the basic tenets of network-based tradecraft.[2] Throughout the past 20 years of cyber force evolution, political necessity and US government directives have placed increasing requirements on successful implementation of combined, international coalitions for nearly every global mission.[3] Through a balance of cultural development, information protection and sharing, and active exercises, the United States must develop successful coalitions that stand the test of time. The basis of coalition relationships is mandated, based on international directives, but it will grow and function based on strong familiarity, sustained through trust and relationship building.

Getting to know our partners

Critics hold that US forces never spend enough time getting to know their partners before they are pressed into action together.[4] Considering the compressed timeline given to most battlespace leaders, this is understandable. In recent decades, the cyber realm has evolved more quickly than any other capability, essentially forcing adoption of new techniques and doctrines by all coalition partners, both in the physical and the virtual world. The virtual side of cyberspace can allow coalition operations even if the partners remain in their own countries. Yet this distributed workforce can compound the socialization problem, where critics describe the nature of cyber operations as inherently impersonal, as well as vulnerable to unwanted sharing.[5] Though rapidly evolving, the overall coalition cyber force already has sufficient guidance, codified in combined and joint publications, to build strong *technical* cyber capabilities.[6] What is needed is a renewed commitment to growing and sustaining human relationships. As a self-identified community, the cybersecurity culture is sometimes described as overly protective, and too quick to classify its work, even by its own governing organization. Notably, the period 2001–2012 has seen significant growth in both classified material, as well as enhanced guidance on reasonable levels of protection.[7] Traditionalists, those possessing a Cold War-like mentality, offer a false dichotomy: more sharing always equals greater risk of losing sensitive data.[8] Fortunately, technical advances in multilevel security solutions can mitigate more of the assessed risks, whilst providing mandated sharing in a dynamic environment.[9] Cyber teams must balance the traditional need for confidentiality with the immediate need of building effective coalitions based on more direct human interaction.

Leaders and mentors are charged with providing the fiscal and structural systems required to organize, train and equip, plus build knowledge and allow learning. They seek out and hire talent from every possible institution, looking for a combination of solid performers, brilliant outliers, and insightful analysts who can build and execute well-reasoned cyber game plans. Every one of them has something to offer as a subject matter expert, but where does that "something," that expertise, actually live? Typically, it is inside the mind of that recently hired cyber performer; his or her tacit knowledge. For practitioners, one of the key challenges is to turn multi-step, complex series of linked thoughts and behaviors into teachable and repeatable actions. Trainers and educators must therefore attack the often Herculean problem of turning tacit knowledge into procedural knowledge, and finally into explicit, codified knowledge. For years, the default position has been characterized by the traditional checklist mentality of deconstructing complex actions into a series of steps, recording them, and "strapping them to your leg" or work platform. The modern implementation of such methods, through online resources, still serves the community well. The cyber force has some of the best traditional portal sharing implementations, extending codified products across regional detachments and training centers. Overall, the cyber education community should be more aware of its current toolsets and strengths, especially as it regards self-paced online learning.

Educational efforts should focus on the high-value realm of making cyber teaming a more personal experience. Every campaign is lived as a coalition effort. How can US forces build relationships when they do not understand or know their partners? The US military has spent considerable portions of formal military training building custom coursework, often as a final "top-off" prior to deployment, and has been reasonably successful in sending most service members to their expeditionary assignments with a basic level of cultural understanding. Often, however, cyberwarriors are not most service members. Many consider themselves elite, given their advanced technical training and expertise, and the potentially high-risk missions—such as offensive cyberattack—they perform. Like any low-density–high-demand force, sending people to multiple far-away locales is great for cultural immersion, but poses huge physical and psychological challenges for individuals. The value of cultural insight is essential to the conduct of warfare.[10] It is not enough to know what the allies and adversaries wrote, whether lines of code, paragraphs of words, or both, but warfighters need to understand what they meant.

Sharing cyber expertise

Cross-cultural scholars describe how finding commonalities is one of the best ways to start knowing and understanding others.[11] In the cyber realm, common languages and protocols, not often spoken aloud, already exist. They are constantly running on servers and devices, and in the brains of coders and analysts. If one considers, as some universities do, a major programming language as a foreign language equivalent, perhaps tech-socialization goals are reasonably within reach. Cyber experts may not speak Pashtu, Ndebele, or English, but they have their lingua franca of UNIX commands and C++. Fluent cyber operators who speak the same underlying network operating system language transcend differing alphabets and nation state boundaries. Groups of like-minded cyber culturists gather at venues across every global region to demonstrate and celebrate common skills.

In the current fiscal environment, using something as simple as attending a few conventions, or even creating a blog or community of practice with coalition partners could instill good cyber cultural values. In a time when chief executives and chief financial officers balk at adding travel dollars for such wasteful extravagance, addressing bridging and translation needs may be as straightforward as adding a few more opportunities for techie-to-techie rapport. Exposing cyber teammates to other aspects of their culture, in less restrictive and open environments outside comfort zones, offers ample exposure and immersion. Traditional intelligence analysts are sent to their assigned regions to gain and maintain expertise, and despite the utility of virtual environments, cyber teammates should be offered the same. Keeping networked warriors in secure workspaces is mandatory, but to keep with the hacker cliché: cyberwarriors need to get out of the basement.

In the past decade, the US government has made impressive and often surprising changes in policy and guidance regarding information sharing.[12] Part of this effort is driven by operational imperatives but also by the desire to continue developing relationships. Cyber intelligence professionals operate and protect some of the most sensitive surveillance and reconnaissance systems in existence, yet as coalition members, they must also share information and experiences. Whilst selected elements of cyber tradecraft should always be properly protected as national secrets, providing useful tools and methods to others is obligatory. The cyber force must deal with the complex process of getting the right products and materials officially recognized as shareable. This means tackling the typically lengthy, guidance-filled realm of foreign disclosure. The greatest traditional hurdle to rapid, appropriate sharing has been the slow transition from the traditional US government default setting of "No," to the new position of "Let me look at it." How can practitioners exchange or provide such information given a process that originally always leaned toward restriction rather than sharing? In the past five years, the Department of Defense has been pushing for reform in this domain, and supported high-profile release efforts.[13]

The Defense Technology Security Administration is in charge of US export control laws, regulations, and policies. By US law, cyber weapons must be considered under Department of State International Traffic in Arms Regulations. The cyber education community must acknowledge the lengthy interagency and intra-agency process of addressing detailed technical, scientific, and national security policy considerations. The Export Control Reform of 2010, signed by then US Secretary of Defense Robert Gates, aims to protect "crown jewel" technologies, whilst expediting transfers to allies and partners, and fulfilling international export control obligations. Though preventing exports to countries and entities of concern remains prominent, national security and export control efficiency are not mutually exclusive. Cyber community builders might state "The system is trying," but critics point out an ongoing attitude problem.[14] The cyber force must acknowledge that the United States often engages in what can be considered as "smart imperialism." Editorialists and bloggers describe US arrogance and associated poor international image, or at very least a tendency to be too paternal with partners.[15] Given the number of solutions, innovations, and new practices in Western cyber efforts, there is a tendency to become overconfident. Coalition partners' doctrinal publications may reinforce such views, given their attraction to the US model.[16] The US cyber force needs to consider how it treats its partners, technically and behaviorally, and better engage in open dialogue to understand them better. A good first step would be to learn about their approaches and doctrines.

Whether online or in print, professional development reading cannot always remain a nicety for which cyber professionals have no time. When has the line operator last examined what a coalition colleague really thought about the cyber business? Not long ago, many US leaders and analysts viewed open source information as having minimal value or insight; now it is a useful and relatively well-integrated tool.[17] Historians might be surprised if an editorialist from southern Asia provides a fresh perspective on the US Civil War, whilst a West African soldier may give a US information planner a unique and unexpected viewpoint. The previously noted aspect of substantive cross-cultural experience is key, and can allow US team members to leverage knowledge from coalition colleagues. A small variation in phrase, recognized as such by a careful and experienced reader, is the same whether a team is exploiting written essays or nested code modules. Experienced analysts can sense a distinctive signature, or a change in an identified entity's behavior. Analysts are at their best when they determine intent, or flag pending changes in a potential adversary. In short, useful analysis goes beyond description to address the "why" and the "what next." To appreciate such insight, analysts and the broader organizations in which they work have to look beyond their egos and the well-known tendency to mirror their behavior in others.[18]

Whoever can be trusted?

North America and Europe should not be the only places the US government looks for examples of how to act in cyberspace. Computer scientists and network security teams have researched various trust models, describing how combinations of perceived threat, safeguard effectiveness, costs, and self-efficacy affect security behaviors in computer users.[19] Arguably, the cybersecurity community does not have an accurate survey of existing trust models, nor does it have a good reading on those which need to be enhanced or revised. Better visibility into a variety of proposed cyber consortiums, even if the members are just beginning their efforts, is needed. Allies like the North Atlantic Treaty Organization (NATO) members have long-standing formal cyber centers of excellence, as could be expected from traditional and developed European partners.[20] Yet, a lot can be learned from the experiences in other regions and countries of the world.

In 2012, the African Union began developing the basic framework for *Confidence and Security in Cyberspace*, leading to a draft *Convention on the Establishment of a Credible Legal Framework for Cyber Security in Africa*.[21] In the sub-Saharan region, where many of the member states have been in protracted conflict—sometimes for decades—there is a clear and positive recognition of the interconnected importance of cyberspace. The African Union clearly acknowledges most of its members lack the necessary communication, adequate means, and human IT resources to achieve or guarantee a minimum level of security. Yet, this initial effort recognizes a need for joint efforts, guidelines, and shared resources. Sub-Saharan states may be able to overcome some of this friction, owing to the prevalence of skip-generation cyber infrastructure. Moving quickly from legacy colonial telecom infrastructure directly to wireless digital links pushes cyber guidelines out of sheer necessity. Similarly, the use of open license operating systems such as Linux and software under general public license has great appeal simply due to ease of access and the perceived resource savings of freeware and shareware.

Wary executives and chief information officers (CIOs) may want US experts to admire the work of young coders from distant developing nations, but recent DoD policy has already invited them in. In 2003, the DoD CIO issued a policy, popularly called the Stenbit Memo, outlining the basic concepts of using Free and Open Source Software (FOSS) under existing agreements such as the General Public License.[22] If the cyber education community wants a level of commonality between members, and build some sort of common cultural knowledge base, then the benefits of easier to obtain, more easily shareable open source versus proprietary solutions should be re-examined—and expanded. The Stenbit guidance directs that FOSS be treated the same as other commercial off-the-shelf government-purchased software, with the important provision that it meets existing information assurance standards. Current US government guidance supports the goal of a common cyber community culture, describing human-readable source code that is available for use, study, reuse, modification, enhancement, and redistribution by the users. The DoD CIO even quotes FOSS pundit and author David Wheeler, who calls it "freedom to tinker."[23] As a common cultural element, supportive of techie-to-techie relationship building, the cyber community must offer people and places to tinker freely.

The growing cyber culture

Cybersecurity has attracted a rapidly growing community of interest that augments both public- and executive-level awareness daily. DoD leaders are now in an ideal position to grow cyber-literate and culturally smart people, both within the United States and with coalition partners. Variances in coalition educational systems, learning objectives, and attempts to determine equivalent technical certifications may not always offer a clear indication of cyber talent. Coalition leaders need people with a range of aptitudes, good motivation, and the ability to interact within a variety of sociocultural groups. It is not always clear whether the current education and training efforts can achieve this cross-pollination. Despite the fact that it is fiscally constrained, the government–academic consortium must spend the time and resources to ensure current partnership programs thrive. Combined efforts by US civil and military communities, such as the current US Cyber Command's Cyber Guard series, show that government, public, private parties, and international participants can function as a consortium.[24] Russia's state-sponsored cyberattacks against NATO member Estonia in 2007 helped strengthen coalition cyber teaming among NATO members.[25] In a time when the federal government is considering new and increased public scholarship opportunities, a greater public and government cyber community must capitalize on this momentum, and ensure cyber disciplines are well represented at boards of regents and stakeholder meetings.[26] Ultimately, if it comes to hard budget calls, the cyber community should highlight—and demand—one particularly prominent need: practice.

Arguably, the best possible engagement—that which deeply involves and builds young cyber techs—is spending lots of time actively practicing tradecraft in a laboratory or other closed arena. Software developers call this "sandboxing," a testing and exercise environment or place to experiment. Alternatively, as a cliché among elementary school educators and sociologists, a sandbox is "a place to play nice." For cyber community purposes, building sandboxes is essential to nurture top talent. Learning government coalitions partnering with industry can offer substantive quality classroom instruction. Yet there is a need to build a cyber corps based on robust applied knowledge in an interactive environment, with opportunities for failure and success inside a realistic space. Virtual machines began as a way to provide efficient use of infrastructure, but not to construct high-fidelity cyber environments. Sandboxes are the perfect place to try out FOSS. When training security forces for convoy duty in Southwest Asia, the US military placed these forces in realistic, hostile physical spaces. Trainees were given working language skills, and allowed to repeat and learn. The cyber analogue is clear: if pressed to identify where to best spend money—build a lab.

Given the impressive research performed around the globe, the United States is fortunate to already be home to many of the world's best cyber labs. The Cyber Centers of Excellence in Education Program, begun by the DoD and academe in the late 1990s, has grown into a successful group of over 60 colleges and universities.[27] Those who recognized how rapidly information operations would become integral to both policy and warfighting also foresaw the need to build new kinds of experts. Long-standing military–academic relationships allowed the United States to grow some white hat hackers, perhaps best known as the CyberCorps. This expanded US government scholarship effort asks candidates to complete a cyber-related degree program successfully and on time, complete a summer internship with a participating US federal agency, and fulfill a one-for-one year-long commitment post-graduation.[28] As a trust-building exercise, real-life experience within the government system lets the US cyber community build not just skilled teammates, but potential leaders and ambassadors. Even if someone chooses to depart government service, he or she has the benefit and insights of knowing what it is really like on the inside. Such cross-sector pollination will, over the long term, help build further public–private collaboration. In an era when the government cyber community is under constant editorial scrutiny, a few under-30-year-old opinions could offer the strongest voices to shape tomorrow's cyber capabilities.

A question of oversight

In a community where the age range runs a broad spectrum of generations, technical areas, and talent pools, the US government requires oversight. Whilst letting the finest researchers and coders run freely in the carefully built lab environment, the executive level has an obligation to monitor and guide without being intrusive. The past few years, marked by a host of revelations about the National Security Agency's activities, have been filled with criticism of cyber surveillance policy, in the context of self-policing and perceived lack of oversight.[29] Combined with the previously identified issue of the United States having an overly assertive cyber hierarchy, where is the proper balance of guidance versus perceived intrusion?

Every cyber entity is part of a hierarchy, following protocols ranging from sub-netting of operational segments, to boardroom approval authority for major program actions. The US government clearly uses the concept of "trust but verify," coupling clearly stated consent to monitoring, with the inherent trust of possessing a security clearance. Alternatively, the concept of trust may be interwoven with an implied community standard of behavior. If any volunteer, based on their coding talent and interest, provides a source code submission, one must trust them to be self-policing among their own community.

This contrasts with the traditional US government tech establishment, which has embraced a more closed environment where software is crafted by clearly assigned, individual experts or specified expert teams. Yet, picking only one development team is like shopping at a single, expensive boutique store. As a community, cyber experts are generally accepting of small businesses entering into the defense contracting process, and the clichéd Silicon Valley lore of great things coming from yet undiscovered garage-based startups has merit. The optimal balance between traditional contract bidding by historically trusted single-source suppliers, and unrestricted open source community development by as yet untrusted talents, is currently underdeveloped. Even coalition trust relationships can be tried out in the lab. If the cyber community is bold, bringing talented foreign players into the mix offers additional opportunities for experimentation in the sandbox. The need for innovation needs to be balanced with traditional concerns over risk, exploitation, and industrial espionage, which are valid and mandatory. "Trust but verify" remains a valid boundary in coalition cyber operations.[30]

Conclusion

Former US European Command leader, Admiral James Stavridis, a notable coalition builder, observes: "although it is an incredibly complicated thing to do, internationalizing cybersecurity is absolutely possible."[31] Coalition team building is at once mandatory and vital, with daily cyber threats reminding all member countries of their shared vulnerabilities. Cultural understanding is the key to successful international teaming, and exploring the thoughts behind our adversaries' actions. The best effort cyber sponsors and educators can undertake is to make homes for cyber coalition members of all backgrounds, and allow them to build their talented teams.

A successful coalition effort must ensure both places and processes to accommodate diverse cyber cultures, through combinations of personnel exchanges, lab sessions, and tech rapport. Notably, cyber team leaders must fully energize executive boards, always emphasizing how relationships built in adequately funded developmental sandboxes pay great dividends on live networks. Achieving effective cyber awareness and primacy rests solely on the shoulders of motivated, trained human beings. Such results demand bending and perhaps breaking traditional trust models. This is why the cyber community should be willing to allow risky play in both training and active exercises. Successful coalition partnering is best served by offering shared knowledge, cultural immersion plus a willingness to put aside a modest portion of government tradition and protocol to let cyber teams extend their reach.

Notes

1 Department of Defense Joint Staff, *Joint Publication 3–12R, Cyberspace Operations*, (Washington, DC, 2013), IV-13-IV-15.
2 On cyber cooperation, see: Shavit Matias, "Combating Cyberattacks in The Age of Globalization," *The Briefing*, March 5, 2015, at www.hoover.org/research/combating-cyberattacks-age-globalization; Neil Robinson, "Cybersecurity Strategies Raise Hopes of International Cooperation," *RAND Review* (2013), at www.rand.org/pubs/periodicals/rand-review/issues/2013/summer/cybersecurity-strategies-raise-hopes-of-international-cooperation.html.

3 Elizabeth Young et al., "Enduring lessons from a decade of war," *Prism* 4/2 (2012): 132–135.
4 See, for example: Paul T. Mitchell, *Network Centric Warfare: Coalition Operations in the Age of US Military Primacy* (New York: Routledge, 2006).
5 Mike McGanon and David Hurley, "The dark side of social networking," *IO Sphere* (2009): 13–15.
6 Michael Warner, "Notes on Military Doctrine for Cyberspace Operations in the United States, 1992–2014," *Cyber Defense Review*, at www.cyberdefensereview. org/2015/08/27/notes-on-military-doctrine-for-cyberspace/.
7 Department of Defense Inspector General, "DoD Evaluation of Overclassification of National Security Information," September 30, 2013, at www.dodig.mil/pubs/ documents/DODIG-2013-142.pdf.
8 See, for example: Bowman H. Miller, "The Death of Secrecy: Need to Know ... with Whom to Share," *Studies in Intelligence* 55/3 (2011): 1–6; Richard A. Best, "Intelligence Information: Need-to-Know vs. Need-to-Share," *Congressional Research Service*, June 6, 2011.
9 Charles Phillips et al., "Information Security and Sharing in Dynamic Coalitions," in *Proceedings of the Seventh ACM Symposium on Access Control Models and Technologies* (New York: ACM, 2002), at http://dl.acm.org/citation.cfm?id=507726.
10 Colin Gray, *Another Bloody Century. Future Warfare* (London: Orion Books, 2005), 83–97.
11 Robert R. Greene-Sands, "Finding a common thread: Implications for the future of culture and language programs in support of international security," *The Journal of Culture, Language and International Security* 1/1 (2014): 3–17.
12 See, for example: US Congress, Intelligence Reform and Terrorism Prevention Act, December 17, 2004, Section 1016; Department of Defense, Department of Defense Information Sharing Strategy, May 4, 2007; Office of the Assistant Secretary of Defense for Networks and Information Integration, Department of Defense Information Sharing Implementation Plan, April 2009; Department of Defense, Mission Partner Environment (MPE) Information Sharing Capability Implementation for the DoD, Instruction 8110.01, November 25, 2014.
13 Nancy E. Soderburgh, *Transforming the Security Classification System: A Report to the President from the Public Interest Declassification Board*, November 2012, at www. archives.gov/declassification/pidb/recommendations/transforming-classification.pdf.
14 Timothy Wu, *The Master Switch: The Rise and Fall of Information Empires* (New York: Knopft, 2010).
15 Daniel Ventre, *Cyber Conflict: Competing National Perspectives* (New York: Wiley & Sons, 2013); David Sedowski, "The battle of narratives: A proposal," *IO Sphere* (2010): 4–8.
16 Jody Prescott, "War by analogy: US cyberspace strategy and international humanitarian law," *The RUSI Journal* 156/6 (2011): 32–39.
17 See: Hamilton Bean, *No More Secrets. Open Source Information and the Reshaping of US Intelligence* (Santa Barbara: Praeger, 2011).
18 Richards J. Heuer, *Psychology of Intelligence Analysis* (Center for the Study of Intelligence, 1999), 70–71; Timothy Walton, *Challenges in Intelligence Analysis: Lessons from 1300 BCE to the Present* (New York: Cambridge University Press, 2010), 123–129.
19 Huigang Liang and Yajiong Xue, "Understanding security behaviors in personal computer usage: A threat avoidance perspective," *Journal of the Association for Information Systems* 11/7 (2010): 394--413.
20 See, for example: "Cooperative Cyber Defence Centre of Excellence," at https:// ccdcoe.org/.
21 African Union Headquarters, "Draft Convention on the Establishment of a Credible Legal Framework for Cyber Security in Africa," *African Union*, at http://au.int/en/ cyberlegislation.

22 Department of Defense, MEMORANDRUM: Open Source Software (OSS) in the Department of Defense, May 28, 2003, at www.terrybollinger.com/stenbitmemo/sten-bitmemo_pdf.pdf.

23 David Wheeler, "Why Open Source Software/Free Software (OSS/FS, FLOSS, or FOSS)? Look at the Numbers!" July 18, 2015, at www.dwheeler.com/oss_fs_why.html.

24 Public Affairs Office, "Cyber Guard 15 Fact Sheet," at http://archive.defense.gov/home/features/2015/0415_cyber-strategy/cyber_guard_15_fact_sheet_010715_f.pdf.

25 Vincent Joubert, *Five Years After Estonia's Cyber Attacks: Lessons Learned for NATO?* (NATO Defense College—Research Division, 2012).

26 See, for example: The National Science Foundation CyberCorps Initiative: Editor, "CyberCorps (R) Scholarship for Service (SFS)," National Science Foundation, at www.nsf.gov/funding/pgm_summ.jsp?pims_id=504991.

27 Editor, "National Centers of Academic Excellence in Cyber Defense," May 4, 21016, at www.nsa.gov/ia/academic_outreach/nat_cae/.

28 Linda McLaughlin, "CyberCorps scholarships fund new generation of security gurus," *Software, IEEE* 22/1 (2005): 98–100.

29 Catherine Lotrionte et al., "International engagement on cyber IV: A post Snowden cyberspace," *Georgetown Journal of International Affairs*, at http://journal.georgetown.edu/international-engagement-on-cyber-iv-post-snowden-cyberspace-2014/.

30 Dennis K. Holstein and Keith Stouffer, "Trust but Verify Critical Infrastructure Cyber Security Solutions," in *43rd Hawaii International Conference on System Sciences (HICSS)*, 2010, 1–8.

31 James Stavridis et al., "Sailing the cyber sea," *Joint Forces Quarterly* 65/2 (2012): 66.

14 Conclusion

Aaron F. Brantly and Damien Van Puyvelde

Though cyberspace has been with us for over four decades, it is fair to say that humanity is still witnessing the dawn of the digital age. Cyberspace has expanded from a research network to a way of life, and as it keeps expanding, national cybersecurity will continue to undergo profound changes in the coming decades. The chapters in this volume have sought to advance the state of social scientific knowledge of cyberspace and its intimate relationship to national security. This conclusion synthesizes some of the main arguments made in this volume, and provides a path for future study of national cybersecurity for scholars and students alike.

The history of cyberspace and national security is far longer than most scholars, journalists, and politicians admit.[1] Yet the last decade has seen a profound increase in the velocity of change both within the domain itself, most notably with the growth of the Internet of Things, and outside of cyberspace as global society, economics, and politics became increasingly intertwined with cyber activities. The constant expansion of cyberspace and its current and future impact on humans around the world, makes its study important. Over two decades ago, William Gibson coined the phrase cyberspace as "a consensual hallucination experienced daily by billions of legitimate operators, in every nation, by children being taught mathematical concepts.... A graphic representation of data abstracted from banks of every computer in the human system."[2] This fictional vision of cyberspace has not become reality yet, but with the expansion of both the number of devices connected to cyberspace and their computing power, the value of cyberspace has largely become irreversible. Chris Demchak and Peter Dombrowski refer to cyberspace as a complex socio-technical-economic system, a substrate that underpins modern society.[3] Whilst the domains of land, sea, air, and space in many ways constitute discrete domains either physically or legally, cyberspace pervades each of them to enable new applications in all the domains of modern life, from economics to social interactions, and military command and control to space exploration. In sum, cyberspace has already become integral to both the physical and informational infrastructure of modern society.

The issues the United States will confront as it seeks to confirm its place and maintain its security in cyberspace in the years to come are extensive and cross intellectual and practical fields of study. It was our goal in putting together this volume to get our readers to learn about the complexities and nuance of cyberspace, but also to reconsider the meaning of a series of concepts and practices at the crossroads between international security and technology such as deterrence, norm building, innovation, intelligence, big data, cross-sector collaboration, and international cooperation. Whilst the focus of this volume has been artificially constrained to the United States, the issues raised in each chapter are not unique to the United States and much can be learned from its successes and failures in responding to security challenges in cyberspace.

Cyberspace is rife with complexity that spans civilian and military infrastructures in every country around the world. Complexity and newly evolving challenges to national security tend to result in hype that can lead policymakers and the general public away from the core issues at hand. Such discrepancies between objective security concerns and subjective representations of these concerns are dangerous, because they can lead to inefficient resource allocation, ineffective strategies and tactics. A more informed community of academics, practitioners, and policymakers is vital to charting the most appropriate course forward.

For the last several years, the study of cybersecurity within the context of international relations has been dominated by arguments on whether or not cyberwar will take place.[4] Whilst heuristically interesting, the study of cyber conflict within international relations need not be constrained by the writings of Clausewitz and other military strategists. The relevance of bits and bytes equating to bullets and bombs is less important than the information environment that is continually shaped by the theft and weaponization of information and computer systems for state objectives. The well-known attacks against Estonia in 2007, Georgia in 2008, Iran in 2010, Ukraine in 2015, and the United States in 2016 barely scratch the surface of the thousands of significant events occurring daily around the world. Attacks and intrusions, passive and invasive collection on US networks require a number of technical solutions to be implemented to foster more robust cybersecurity. Yet, social science offers an avenue for developing policies, strategies, and tactics that can harness technological solutions to effectively manage the problems being faced. From this perspective, social scientific contributions should not be limited to the study of cyberwar, but engage with a broader set of pre-existing policy and academic debates on deterrence, norms and law, innovation, intelligence, cross-sector collaboration, and international cooperation.

Filling the gap

The sections in this volume hone a diverse set of arguments and concepts associated with national security in cyberspace. Combined, they represent the continued development of novel thought on political, functional, and organizational aspects of cybersecurity. By developing and advancing novel and often contentious arguments they serve to fill the gap between what is occurring in cyberspace and what needs to be done to provide for national cybersecurity.

The first section examined a range of complex political issues. Jon Lindsay and Erik Gartzke examined the concept of cross-deterrence in Chapter 2, highlighting its complexity and the need for decision makers to think beyond a single domain as they consider cyber policy options. Lindsay and Gartzke draw fascinating parallels that begin to tease out the interconnected nature of conflict in cyberspace and other domains. Their analysis sets the stage for a robust discussion about the international security in cyberspace that requires understanding the nuance and interconnected complexities of the domain. Taking a further step into understanding the nuance and complexity of the domain to meaningfully engage in deterrence of any sort requires a robust understanding of what constitutes cyberattack, and how developing national and international norms and laws might shape policy options for dealing with such attacks. Chapters 3 and 4 by Nerea Cal and Brian Mazanec contribute to contemporary discussions about the development of laws and norms that can alter behaviors in and outside of cyberspace. Both chapters provided detailed analyses that tug at some of the underlying issues brought forward in the first chapter. By examining the legal and normative aspects of the domain, policymakers and practitioners are better able to assess what is and is not appropriate behavior in cyberspace, and how and where new laws and norms need to be established. The final chapter of the first section, by Tim Ridout, reveals the sheer complexity of defining an international governance framework for a new domain, be it outer space or cyberspace. The parallels drawn by Ridout link the discussions on cross-domain deterrence and international laws and norms by providing a relevant framework within which to analyze state actions and intent in cyberspace. Absent rules of the road and strategies to induce cyber actors to follow new rules, problems multiply and conflict becomes more likely. Both Mazanec and Ridout agree that the road toward binding norms in cyberspace is long and tortuous.

The second section examined a variety of concepts for engaging and improving national security practices in cyberspace. In Chapter 6, Jan Kallberg reminds us that the future of military interactions in cyberspace are likely going to differ dramatically from the present, in both speed and complexity. Kallberg's chapter highlights the unique character of cyberspace: a man-made and near instantaneous domain where actors can use digital means to hide their identity. Strategists might need to develop new theories that are more tailored to the relatively unique conditions of cyberspace. In Chapter 7, Aaron Brantly provides insights into cybersecurity through leveraging an analogy to epidemiology, another field known for rapid responses to invasive and damaging pathogens. Brantly highlights an alternative framework to approach and develop national cybersecurity policies, one that is increasingly being addressed within the cybersecurity community. In Chapter 8, Ernest Wong et al. argued that a defender's mentality leaves cyber operators at a disadvantage. Cyber strategies need to emphasize disruptive innovation to be successful. Chapters 9 and 10, by Stephen Gary, Randy Borum, and Aaron Brantly examined the evolving nature of intelligence in cyberspace. The present age is sometimes referred to as the new golden age of intelligence. New sources and methods of analyzing data and developing intelligence are benefiting and challenging the intelligence community. These benefits and challenges of cyber intelligence and big data analytics are directly relevant to the issues raised by Kallberg and Wong et al., as they influence the government's ability to act and react within cyberspace.

The third section examined some fundamental organizational aspects of cybersecurity both between nations—Chapters 11 and 13 by Kris Stoddart and Scott Bethel and John Whisenhunt respectively—and within the United States in Chapter 12 by Damien Van Puyvelde. Each of these chapters examined how organizational structures can foster trust and cooperation, both between states and within states. Combined, they established the mutually recognized complexity of aligning the incentives of complex organizations and partners who seek to make sense of an evolving domain. All authors in this last section agree that fostering collaboration between the multiple actors who evolve in cyberspace is the key to improving national cybersecurity.

The combined analytic rigor of the chapters establishes a robust framework in which to assess the continuing development and importance of cyberspace. By providing a diversity of analyses on a range of interrelated topics, this volume advances the field and challenges scholars, practitioners, and students to develop more robust and nuanced assessments of interactions within cyberspace.

Moving forward

The study of cyber conflict and espionage requires nuance and a willingness to engage with multiple disciplines. National cybersecurity is not and cannot be pursued by the US government alone. In cyberspace, national security decision makers are confronted with a series of overlapping problems that span the public and private sectors, both domestically and internationally. Given the global character of cyberspace, the challenge they confront, when seeking to enhance national cybersecurity is immense. Where should we, students of cybersecurity, go from here?

First, social scientific inquiry into phenomena occurring within and through cyberspace must continue to rise in prominence within the field. Whilst cyber phenomena do not obviate the need to study other traditional focal areas of international politics, they can help refine existing models to make them more comprehensive. The growing number of cybersecurity researchers in the social sciences also have a duty to challenge the assumptions of operators, policymakers, and other cyber experts to advance the field and refine cybersecurity practices.

Second, the study of national cybersecurity should not occur in the absence of a rigorous understanding of theories that explain both social and technical phenomena that predate it. Just because cyberspace is a relatively new, and possibly unique, domain does not eliminate the need to understand it in the context of established theories. These theories might not all be directly applicable, but they can help in examining cyber phenomena from divergent viewpoints and foster a vibrant debate that can reduce uncertainty and mitigate risks to national and international security.

Third, scholarship absent policy relevance in a domain changing as rapidly as cyberspace will grow stale quickly. Each of the works in this volume has direct policy relevance to different sets of actors. Whilst not all the chapters are relevant to every policymaker, they challenge them to examine cyber issues from novel and diverse perspectives. The policy relevance of research in the social sciences related to cyberspace is critical. The development and deployment of systems without regard to social, political, and economic consequences occurs frequently and creates large disruptions that need to be understood. If it is possible to understand disruption preemptively, it might be possible to minimize the likelihood of conflict.

The number of Internet-enabled devices is set to grow voluminously in the coming decades. The embeddedness of cyberspace into every aspect of our daily lives, and by extension in national security, will continue to alter how governments defend their homeland and win wars. Beyond traditional national security concerns, the ubiquity of cyberspace will continue to affect the social, economic, and political structures of the United States and nations around the world. We reiterate that we are at the dawn of the digital age. Whilst the boundaries of land, air, and sea are fixed, the boundaries of cyberspace, much like the boundaries of space itself, are nearly limitless. So too are the opportunities to shape cyberspace as a field of study and a field of practice.

Notes

1 Michael Warner, "Cybersecurity: A pre-history," *Intelligence and National Security* 27/5 (2014): 781–799.
2 William Gibson, *Neuromancer* (New York: Ace Books, 1984), 51.
3 Chris C. Demchak and Peter Dombrowski, "Rise of a cybered Westphalian age," *Strategic Studies Quarterly* 5/1 (2011): 32–61.
4 Thomas Rid, "Cyber war will not take place," *Journal of Strategic Studies* 35/1 (2012): 37–41.

Index

Page numbers in *italics* denote tables, those in **bold** denote figures.

Taylor & Francis eBooks

Helping you to choose the right eBooks for your Library

Add Routledge titles to your library's digital collection today. Taylor and Francis ebooks contains over 50,000 titles in the Humanities, Social Sciences, Behavioural Sciences, Built Environment and Law.

Choose from a range of subject packages or create your own!

Benefits for you
- » Free MARC records
- » COUNTER-compliant usage statistics
- » Flexible purchase and pricing options
- » All titles DRM-free.

Benefits for your user
- » Off-site, anytime access via Athens or referring URL
- » Print or copy pages or chapters
- » Full content search
- » Bookmark, highlight and annotate text
- » Access to thousands of pages of quality research at the click of a button.

REQUEST YOUR **FREE** INSTITUTIONAL TRIAL TODAY

Free Trials Available
We offer free trials to qualifying academic, corporate and government customers.

eCollections – Choose from over 30 subject eCollections, including:

Archaeology	Language Learning
Architecture	Law
Asian Studies	Literature
Business & Management	Media & Communication
Classical Studies	Middle East Studies
Construction	Music
Creative & Media Arts	Philosophy
Criminology & Criminal Justice	Planning
Economics	Politics
Education	Psychology & Mental Health
Energy	Religion
Engineering	Security
English Language & Linguistics	Social Work
Environment & Sustainability	Sociology
Geography	Sport
Health Studies	Theatre & Performance
History	Tourism, Hospitality & Events

For more information, pricing enquiries or to order a free trial, please contact your local sales team: www.tandfebooks.com/page/sales

Routledge
Taylor & Francis Group

The home of
Routledge books

www.tandfebooks.com

For Product Safety Concerns and Information please contact our EU
representative GPSR@taylorandfrancis.com
Taylor & Francis Verlag GmbH, Kaufingerstraße 24, 80331 München, Germany

www.ingramcontent.com/pod-product-compliance
Lightning Source LLC
Chambersburg PA
CBHW071421050326
40689CB00010B/1923